Art Law

Art Law

A Concise Guide for Artists, Curators, and Art Educators

Michael E. Jones

ROWMAN & LITTLEFIELD
Lanham • Boulder • New York • London

Published by Rowman & Littlefield
A wholly owned subsidiary of The Rowman & Littlefield Publishing Group, Inc.
4501 Forbes Boulevard, Suite 200, Lanham, Maryland 20706
www.rowman.com

Unit A, Whitacre Mews, 26-34 Stannary Street, London SE11 4AB

British Library Cataloguing in Publication Information Available

Library of Congress Cataloging-in-Publication Data

Names: Jones, Michael E., author.
Title: Art law : a concise guide for artists, curators, and art educators / Michael E. Jones.
Description: Lanham, Maryland : Rowman & Littlefield, 2016. | Includes bibliographical references and index.
Identifiers: LCCN 2016003840 (print) | LCCN 2016004985 (ebook) | ISBN 9781442263147 (cloth : alk. paper) | ISBN 9781442263154 (pbk. : alk. paper) | ISBN 9781442263161 (electronic)
Subjects: LCSH: Law and art—United States. | Artists—Legal status, laws, etc.—United States.
Classification: LCC KF4288 .J66 2016 (print) | LCC KF4288 (ebook) | DDC 344.73/097—dc23
LC record available at http://lccn.loc.gov/2016003840

∞™ The paper used in this publication meets the minimum requirements of American National Standard for Information Sciences—Permanence of Paper for Printed Library Materials, ANSI/NISO Z39.48-1992.

Printed in the United States of America

Contents

Figures

Preface

After many years of teaching and lecturing on the rich subject of art law, I realized it was time to share a lifetime of observations and perspectives on this broad subject with a larger audience. I come to the field from a multitude of experiences: visual fine artist, art collector, consultant to museums, advisor to artists rights societies and individual artists, board trustee for an art college, author on an intellectual property rights book for artists, judge, university professor, and someone trained in museum studies from Harvard University. My goal in writing this book, *Art Law*, is to introduce in clear and uncluttered language the key art law concepts and issues facing art educators, students, gallery owners, curators, museum trustees, dealers, museum professional staff, collectors, docents, investors, and artists.

The textual flow of the chapter material is designed sequentially starting from the challenges facing professional fine artists in their commercial dealings with galleries, collectors, museums, and even landlords. The explanatory material includes sample business contracts and licensing agreements. A special focus on copyrights and moral rights of fine artists, and the challenges of protecting these rights from appropriation in a digital world are addressed. In an increasingly global economy, museums, auctioneers, and galleries are subject to changing rules in dealing with cultural property, stolen art, Nazi-era art claims, and even historically underrepresented artists of gender and race. Succinct analyses of the ethical and legal obligation of these significant challenges are presented. This book tackles the special requirements of museums, and the fiduciary role of trustees, in acquiring, collecting, exhibiting, lending, and deaccessioning objects of art in light of current practices and policies. Constitutional and other legal restraints on creating, exhibiting, and funding fine art projects via private foundation and government grants are covered in the final chapter.

The field of art law draws from many different interdisciplinary subject areas: art history, contracts, constitutional law, intellectual property, torts, estate and tax law, administrative law, economics, criminal law, international rules, and ethical codes. The evolution of new technologies that alter the way visual fine art is created, distributed, collected, exhibited, and sold presents new questions and opportunities for the art community. *Art Law* intends to provide the reader with a thorough understanding of the vibrant and engaging issues that confront those who live, practice, enjoy, and seek to thrive in the fascinating world of art. Finally, my hope is that from reading and thoughtfully considering the topics that you will discover, in the words of Picasso, that "(a)rt washes away from the soul the dust of everyday life."

Acknowledgments

My initial appreciation for the visual fine arts began as a ten-year-old model for my mom, Marlen Naumann Jones, and her studio art cohorts. She had received early drawing and painting instruction in Dusseldorf at a time when German expressionists were playing a vital role in the development of modern art. After emigrating from Germany to the United States, she attended college on an art and music scholarship. Later on, during my formative years, under her tutelage and that of Pennsylvania artist Mary Shawmaronic, I was encouraged to learn to observe the world by sketching nature. Eventually, my life extended beyond the walls of an art studio to galleries, museums, and academia.

Besides the talented artists that have shared their instructional gifts, I am indebted to numerous museum curators, executive directors of cultural institutions, auction house dealers, gallery owners, and academic colleagues that have contributed to my growth as an insightful student and scholar of art law. Over the years, I have enjoyed the enormous privilege of guest lecturing at art colleges, professional conferences, and museum schools on subjects ranging from licensing of art to the limits of copying works of art. A special thank you is due the University of Massachusetts Lowell, which afforded me a professional lifetime of teaching art law to hundreds of students.

Finally, I wish to acknowledge and thank my spouse, Christine M. Jones, for her love, enthusiasm, and creative energy in support of this book. My children, Elka and Katarina, offered periodic insightful comments that improved the final manuscript. A special appreciation is due to Charles Harmon, editor, for his guiding hand and professional contribution to the realization of this project.

Introduction to Art Law

"What Genesis is to the biblical account of the fall and the redemption of man, early cave art is to the history of his intelligence, imagination and creative power."

—Helen Gardner (*Art Through the Ages*)

"Art is making something out of nothing and selling it."

—Frank Zappa (*Zen Masters: The Wisdom of Frank Zappa*)

This book explores the key legal and ethical aspects of the world of visual fine arts. It is written for art and museum studies students, art educators, museum curators, collectors, patrons, gallery directors, museum trustees, and of course, artists. This book is unique in its field because it covers a broad scope of law in relation to the world of art and artists and persons who support, preserve, govern, display, and even sell art. Those who are interns, volunteers, or work for nonprofit museums, art foundations, academic institutions, libraries, or for profit-making commercial art enterprises such as galleries and auction houses will find clear and readable descriptions and answers to the common legal challenges facing members of the art community.

The subject of art law encompasses a variety of different legal disciplines and principles that are fact specific to the subject of visual fine art. Taken as a whole the body of law related to creating, acquiring, collecting, lending, installing, exhibiting, marketing, dismantling, and disposing of art includes subjects such as the Constitution, international treaties, intellectual property, contracts, commercial transactions, torts, taxes, and statutes. The inventive process of skillfully creating art to express an idea or communicate an emotion could create conflicts with those who may not share the same viewpoint or opinion. Visual art that is displayed as graffiti on a street wall may raise issues of freedom of political expression or unlawful trespass on a privately or publicly owned building. An installation artist who contractually promises to construct an exhibition for a museum and then fails to complete the work might lead the museum to inquire about remedies for breach of contract or addressing accusations of violating the artist's "moral rights" in the works of art when the partially built installation is removed. A duped art buyer upset that an art gallery unintentionally sold a "fake" masterpiece after relying upon an expert's authenticity opinion could seek restitution. Meanwhile, the dealer is distraught over the reputation damage from news accounts and is troubled by the expert's inability to distinguish a "fake" from a real work of art. In many cases it is the business of the law, including judges who are frequently called upon to hear these disputes, to resolve these controversies.

WHAT IS ART?

Art, as we view it today, is an invention of the last two hundred and twenty years. Fragments of ancient clay pots, Sistine Chapel frescoes, the cave drawings of hands at Les Eyzies and Lascaux, and a five-inch-high female fertility figurine created 15,000 years ago known today as the Venus of Willendorf, at the time of their creation were not art. The objects we now call art were embedded in the social, spiritual, and political fabric of the cultural lives of distant people. Religious frescoes were instruments of the church and political rule. Leonardo da Vinci's paintings and drawings were a means to observe and record knowledge as a way to better understand humanism and the divine state. The Venus of Willendorf, as seen in figure 0.1, is admired for its eloquence. Yet, historians have no idea of how the object functioned or what it represented to the people who made or used it. In each case, the purposes were different from the objects we now call art.

To consider these examples of objects or drawings as art requires disregarding or putting aside the differences between the historical moment and context of their formation and our own perceptions. One of the great inventions of the modern era was the appropriation of these stately objects, artifacts, and relics into our culture and the transformation of them into art. This phenomenon occurred fairly recently when society—art historians, museums, galleries, art critics, collectors, patrons, academicians, gift shops, bookstores, and artists—imbued these things with meaning, currency, and ultimately value. Art began to circulate by traveling to and from museums, and by being treasured and consumed by a culture eager to discover, engage, and respond to the good and bad of art. By the middle of the twentieth century reproductions of what we now refer to as art were mass-

Figure 0.1. Venus of Willendorf, c. 15,000–10,000
B.C. *Photo courtesy of Wikimedia Commons.*

produced and shared with a wider public than ever before. In some cases the
reproductions through new mediums, such as Andy Warhol's iconic silkscreen
Pop Art images, as represented in figure 0.2, became art embedded with unique
cultural codes and symbols that were used by other artists.

DOES LAW PROTECT ART?

The ancient Greeks referred to art in the broadest sense to include all types
of human activity. There were rules and forms to be followed by crafts persons and artisans. During the Renaissance period the meaning of art began to

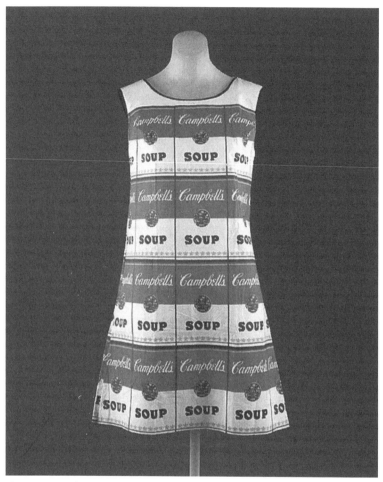

Figure 0.2. *The Souper Dress.* Purchase, Isabel Schults Fund and Martin and Caryl Horwitz and Hearst Corporation Gifts, 1995. *Photo image courtesy of the Metropolitan Museum of Art.*

change, and started to resemble something closer to the present understanding of fine art. It encompassed a range of aesthetic human pursuits that lead to the creation of something tangible, which may or may not be utilitarian. The list included performance arts such as theater, dance, song, and poetry together with traditional forms of expression found in literature, pottery, tools, textiles, decorative works, stage design, and architecture.

For the purposes of this book, "art" refers to the visual fine arts, which consist of paintings, drawings, sculpture, prints, photography, and installations, regardless of the medium. The definition of visual fine art is not always precise and this list isn't necessarily complete. The range of two- and three-dimensional images or objects covered is expansive. The array of qualifying images and objects are diverse. It now comprises works such as the fifteenth-century mural painting *The Last Supper* by Leonardo da Vinci, the incorporation of mass-produced articles and paint on canvas by Georges Braque, the provocative photographs exploring the contemporary construction of identity by Cindy Sherman, and the examination of the library as a physical space in the installation exhibition "Bibliothecaphilia," the brainchild of a Williams College curatorial internship student.

In some ways it is the "originality" aspect of an artist's tangible work that separates the visual art form from craft or mechanical art. The nature of the materials employed or the process is irrelevant. A 1954 US Supreme Court decision made clear that the type of art protected under copyright law, for instance, must incorporate design elements separate and independent of the utilitarian or useful aspects of the object (*Mazer v. Stein*, 347 US 201 [1954]).

The noted art historian and author of the *History of Art*, H. W. Janson, was correct in his observations that deciding what is art and evaluating a work of art as good art or bad art are separate puzzles to solve. It is not the role of the court, though, to decide whether a visual fine artist that shapes "good" or "beautiful" art receives recognition, rights, and protection under various federal and international rules, while "bad" art does not. To be considered as visual fine art there must be some creative expression, image, or message infused or embodied in the work.

For example, consider Pablo Picasso's *Bull's Head*, created in the 1940s using found objects: bicycle seat and handlebars in a junk pile as shown in figure 0.3.

The rights of artists frequently turn on the legal definition of whether the object or image designed and built is a form of visual fine art or even art as speech. Pictorial, graphic, and sculptural works are subject to copyright protection. The independence to create visual fine art is acknowledged as a form of speech free from government censorship. Does Picasso's *Bull's Head*, created during the horrors of World War II, fall within these specifications? Standing alone the bicycle seat and handlebars are not art. Art critic Eric Gibson described Picasso's unusual welded construction "as an assertion of the transforming power of human imagination at a time when human values were under siege." Visitors so disliked this sculpture when it was first displayed that curators removed it from the wall of the exhibition. Today, *Bull's Head* is part of the permanent collection of Musée Picasso in Paris. Picasso's fixed tangible medium of expression is original and creative. Yes, it is a work of visual fine art recognized and protected by the law of copyright. The libertarian goals of the French granted Picasso wide latitude in expressing his imaginative ideas in an object free from government constraints.

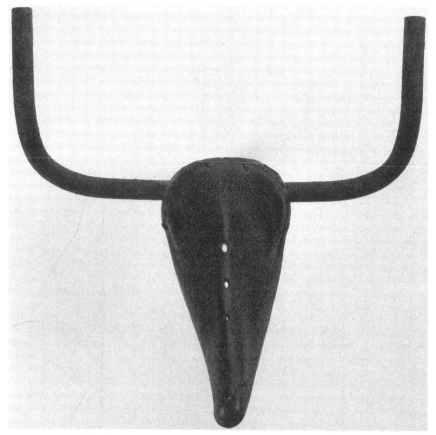

Figure 0.3.   Pablo Picasso, *Bull's Head.* © *RMN-Grand Palais/ Art Resource, NY,* ©
Estate of Pablo Picasso/ Artists Rights Society (ARS), NY.

SUMMARY

In the postmodern technologically driven art world, the artists and art institutions devoted to producing, collecting, appreciating, patronizing, displaying,
marketing, visiting, selling, and reproducing visual fine art face new challenges in the way society views and protects old and new original and creative works. This book is written to aid the reader to look beyond the frame
to see and understand the array of legal issues that arise in the everyday world
of art and artists.

1

The Professional Artist's Life

"In this world, I have given up sleep for dreaming and art is still our only flying car."

—Erin Belieu ("Ars Poetica for the Future," *Slant Six*)

Each spring thousands of aspiring Cindy Shermans, Gerhardt Richters, and Banksys receive Master of Fine Arts degrees. According to the latest statistics from the US Department of Education, there are more master's degrees conferred in the visual arts than chemistry degrees. Despite the growth in formal art education, the last great galvanizing visual fine arts movement occurred more than fifty years ago, orchestrated by the Pop Artists who broke from the notion of art as abstract form. This movement happened around the same time that art history and critical thinking about art, rather than the creative skill of art, became lodged in universities. Meanwhile, by the turn of the twenty-first century the genre of drawing and painting started to lose its dominance, its persuasive culture, and its aesthetic power. Nowadays, the term visual arts as introduced in the preamble consists of the kind of art that speaks to the sense of seeing: drawing, painting, sculpture, photography, print making, mixed media, installations, and even the more practical design and graphic arts fields along with cutting-edge videos and performances.

The visual elements of an artist's work still matter today—that is, the expressive use of color, two-dimensional or three-dimensional shape, line, texture, space, and composition, regardless of the medium, technical skill of the artist, or obsession with the belief that critical theory is the path to enlightenment.

In the eighteenth century, the French Neoclassical guardian of academic orthodoxy, Ingres, remarked to his life drawing students that "We will begin by drawing, we will go on to drawing and then we will continue to draw," as the ideal way to develop observational skills. It is less likely in today's learning environment that art students gain a solid grounding in the visual arts strictly from working with a live nude model or plaster casts. Even the non-degreed art schools that flourished during the 1950s and 1960s, such as the Art Students League in New York City, the Black Mountain College in North Carolina, and Hans Hoffman's summer School of Art in Provincetown, where all works of art began and ended in the studio, lost their popularity. A generation of artists discovered strategies for creating fine art without constantly laboring in studios, while earning academic credits and certification in the form of a market driven BFA or MFA degree. The current teaching of visual art model is rooted in art and design colleges and universities that permit on-campus and online learning, professional mentorship and internship, and real-world projects that lead to enhancing skills, social networking, and building a portfolio. Although the materials, instructional methods, techniques, economics, and philosophy behind fashioning art are ever-evolving, an artist's life nevertheless requires a place to make art or what the French refer to as an *atelier*. It is in that place where art is designed and produced, firmly linked with the business and law of art, that the remainder of this chapter is devoted.

ARTIST'S WORKPLACE

Almost any visual artist regardless of age, gender, race, sexual preference, or ethnicity could share stories about how difficult it can be to achieve both artistic and financial success. Andy Warhol, in his book *The Philosophy of Andy Warhol: From A to B and Back Again*, recalled during the 1960s and 1970s that earning money from art was deemed a bad idea. Warhol, though, was never shy about acknowledging that "making money is art and working is art and good business is the best art." Even for those artists that do not seek to earn a living wage from a career in art, but want to exhibit their works at a gallery, community fair, library, or museum, they need a location to paint, draw, or construct, and some form of public exposure or marketing. On the flip side, the place where art is exhibited or sold often is in the business of making money from the sale of art, admission tickets, or images reproduced on posters, calendars, and coffee mugs. In any event, beginning from the point of sitting in front of an easel with brush in hand or by mixing clay by hand to remove air bubbles, an artist must gain a comfortable level of familiarity with art law to identify and avoid unnecessary risks, hazards, and victimization.

The practice of an artist living and working in the same space originated decades ago in places like the SoHo district of New York City. In time, zoning laws changed and the market demand to convert old warehouse-like buildings into custom residential spaces increased dramatically in cities like Boston, Chicago, and New York, pushing the working artist out the door. In response, the city of New York, for instance, enacted a statute in the 1970s that permits visual fine artists, defined as persons who are "regularly engaged in the fine arts, such as painting and sculpture," to share the same living and working space in designated commercial areas upon certification (**N.Y. Multiple Dwelling Law, Section 276**). The government body charged with certifying that only visual fine artists, and not commercial artists, inhabit these specific living and working quarters is New York City's Department of Cultural Affairs. The city of Chicago has a nearly identical statute. In 2012, it was expanded to allow a commercial artist working as a small business to live in low-intensity zoned business districts. Similarly, Los Angeles enacted an ordinance that legalized "lofts" for "bona fide artists" in districts zoned for manufacturing. Cities like Baltimore, Providence, Minneapolis, and Long Beach reacted to the skyrocketing rent crisis by offering tax incentives to developers to provide affordable living/studio spaces for working artists. While many communities have eased zoning laws to benefit artists and foster a creative community milieu, the definition of the category of artists that qualify for shared living and working space varies from city to city.

Not all conversions from work area to residential loft/studio have gone smoothly or lawfully. In the SoHo district, some artists rented commercial property under a written lease agreement. The landlord convinced the artists, at no small expense, to transform the space into a habitable loft. After making substantial improvements to the property, the landlord then sought to evict the artists for violating the building's Certificate of Occupancy.

Earlier, New York had enacted a statute, referred to as the "Loft Law," to prevent the kind of "plundering as booty" tactic that was occurring throughout SoHo, as illustrated by the efforts of the corporate landlord in this case. The court found that the landlord's attempt to evict the tenants after permitting them to change the work area to desirable habitable quarters was unacceptable, especially after the tenants' conversion markedly increased the value of the building (*Stolzfus v. 315 Berry Street Corp.*, 504 N.Y.S.2d 349 [Sup. Ct. 1986]).

The 1968 landmark civil rights **Federal Housing Act**, adopted after the killing of Martin Luther King Jr., made it illegal to refuse to sell or rent housing on the basis of race. A 2015 US Supreme Court decision held that prospective occupiers of a home or an apartment, including artists of color, can use statistics and corollary evidence to demonstrate discriminatory effect, as opposed to proving discriminatory racial intent (*Texas Department of Housing and Community Affairs v. The Inclusive Communities Project, Inc.*, 576 U.S. [2015]).

Federal, state, and local laws in the form of zoning rules, anti-discrimination housing orders, licensure or permit requirements, building and safety codes, and restrictions on outdoor signage are not the only forms of regulation that may impact the ability of artists to work at home. For example, for many years the US Department of Labor prohibited persons from producing certain kinds of crafts at home for a profit. In 1990, these regulations were largely lifted; however, crafting homemade jewelry when it entails working with metals and alloys is still barred because of their toxicity. In the event an artist hires an apprentice or assistant, then compliance with state and federal wage labor laws is required. The US Small Business Administration has produced a helpful pamphlet available online at www.empowermentzone.com/from home.txt for artists interested in learning more about the basic considerations for starting and managing a business from home.

A fascinating case arose in South Carolina that did not turn on the studio/ living space issue; rather it addressed the legal question of who qualifies for protection under the law as an artist. In South Carolina, a person that was engaged in the "art" of tattooing at his personal residence was arrested. At the time the state prohibited tattooing by anyone other than a licensed physician for cosmetic or reconstructive purposes. The basis for the statute was to protect the public's health. Shockingly, the Supreme Court of South Carolina upheld his criminal conviction notwithstanding a strenuous dissent that "creating a tattoo is a form of art which is entitled to the same protection as any other form of art." The dissenting judge argued that the person tattooing ink on skin is no different from a painter that creates an image on a piece of canvas, thereby, entitling him to "speech" protection under the **First Amendment** (*State v. Ronald P. White*, 348 S.C. 532 [2002]). Two years later, in 2004, the legislature of South Carolina passed a new statute that acknowledged the right of properly licensed non-physicians to perform tattoos in their place of business, including studio/ residences, so long as they comply with health safety standards.

ARTISTS' HEALTH AND SAFETY

The odds do not always favor visual artists in regard to being able to support themselves directly out of art school. The growth of postgraduate artists interning or working as assistants to well-established artists such as Jeffrey Koons or Richard Prince, or design firms such as Johannes Leonardo or Pentagram, is becoming the norm. The young artist eager to make her mark in an existing studio setting more than likely does not have much control over the studio work environment. Yet, it is important for all visual artists to appreciate that the materials that artists employ may cause adverse health effects.

An initial basic preventive practice is to limit the concentration and exposure times to known acute (immediate) and chronic (long term) hazardous
art materials. In particular, exposure to chemicals, such as paint solvents and
cadmium-based oil paints, through inhalation, skin absorption, and accidental ingestion are particularly worrisome dangers. The US Consumer Product
Safety Commission (CPSC) requires the labeling of art materials that could
cause adverse chronic health effects under the definition standards of the
Federal Hazardous Substance Act (FHSA). The **Labeling of Hazardous
Material Act (LHMA)** amended the FHSA. It requires the *suppliers* of art
materials to label products that have the potential to cause chronic adverse
health effects based on international standards. Separate compliance labeling
standards are in place for art materials for children under twelve years of age.
Commonly found compounds in paints, ceramic glazes, and photo chemicals
and their possible health effects are charted in table 1.1.

The state of California expanded the federal labeling requirement for
manufacturers of art materials that contain chemicals that have been shown to
cause cancer, birth defects, or other reproductive harm. The California Proposition 65 icon as seen in figure 1.1 is an indicator that harmful chemicals,
even trace levels, are found in the manufactured art product.

Besides government oversight of labeling, the nonprofit industry trade
association, the Arts and Creative Materials Institute (ACMI), analyzes and
certifies art materials to ensure compliance with state and federal labeling
requirements. The ACMI breaks down its product seal description into two
categories: the Approved Seal (AP) certified nontoxic and Cautionary Labeling (CL) certified toxic or hazardous, although safe to use with caution. The
ASTM D 4236 on the icons in figure 1.2 refers to those art materials offered
for sale that have undergone a toxicology review for the potential of adverse
chronic health effects. For an art product to be sold to consumers in the
United States it must comply with these minimal labeling standards.

An artist should not be so naïve to believe that by reading the notice of potentially toxic or hazardous chemicals on paint tubes or toners and hardeners
used in photographic processing that her studio is safe. According to a study
conducted by the National Cancer Institute, artists have two to three times the
average rate for cancer. In many ways this statistic is understandable. There
are more hazardous art materials, ranging from solvents in graphic arts to
metal fumes from welding to airborne heavy metals inhaled while airbrushing
paint, that are used in more inventive ways than ever before. The product labeling information is based on artists using the material as intended following
best practices, which does not always happen. The safest bet to avoid potential
harmful exposure is to use ACMI nontoxic certified products, for instance,
linseed and poppy seed oils to clean brushes when painting with oil colors.

Table 1.1. Chart of Common Compounds in Art Materials and Possible Health Effects. *Toxic Link Factsheet No. 25.*

Art Material	Ingredients/Function	Health Concerns
Paint	Oil-based, acrylic, and watercolor paints	• Volatile Organic Compounds (VOC) to control paint fluidity. • Pigments to impart color. • Additives such as fungicides, inhibitors, and preservatives. • Binders (oils, resins, plasticisers) to hold pigment together.	• Damage to the nervous system, blood, and kidneys. Lung damage. • Exposure to heavy metals (cadmium, chromium, lead, and mercury) can impact respiratory function, memory, muscular function. Irritants. • Carcinogenesis.
Ceramic glazes	Used on pottery and sculptures	• Cadmium, lead, chromium, nickel, and other heavy metals. • Lustre glazes have solvents.	• Exposure to heavy metals can impact respiratory function, memory, muscular function, central nervous system, kidney, and blood cells. Can be an irritant of the skin. • Can affect all systems in the body.
Photo-chemicals	Used in photoprinting	• Chromic acid bleaches, lead toners, mercury intensifiers, preservatives and intensifiers, uranium nitrate toners, cyanide reducers, and intensifiers.	• Respiratory ailments, acute bronchitis, chemical pneumonia, emphysema, allergies, asthma, acute anemia, reproductive system harm.

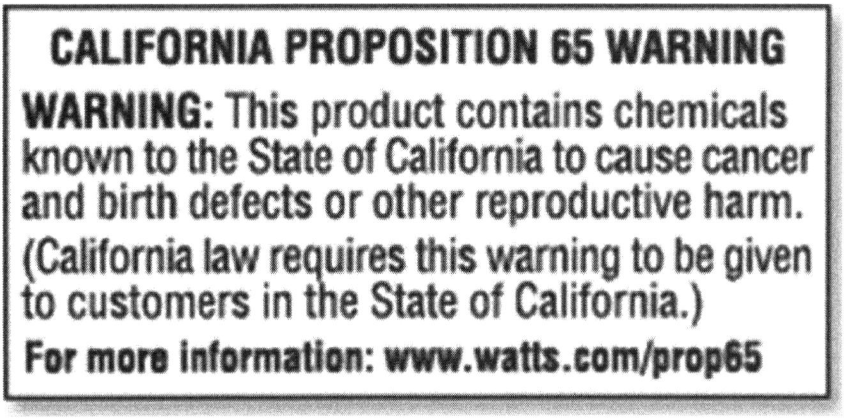

CALIFORNIA PROPOSITION 65 WARNING
WARNING: This product contains chemicals known to the State of California to cause cancer and birth defects or other reproductive harm.
(California law requires this warning to be given to customers in the State of California.)
For more information: www.watts.com/prop65

Figure 1.1. California Prop 65 Warning. ***watts.com/prop65.***

Proper ventilation to minimize exposure to VOCs (volatile organic chemicals), which are emitted as gases from a variety of chemicals used as an additive in paints, is equally important. The long-term presence of VOCs in an indoor studio can lead to damage to the nervous system, kidneys, and blood.

Historically, artists have been blasé regarding taking appropriate steps to protect themselves from materials and fumes that could harm their bodies and contaminate their studio environments. As early as 1713, the Italian physician Bernardino Ramazzini described mysterious symptoms he observed among art-

ACMI
AP
ART & CREATIVE MATERIALS INSTITUTE CERTIFIED
Conforms to ASTM D 4236
ACMI
CL
ART & CREATIVE MATERIALS INSTITUTE CERTIFIED
Conforms to ASTM D 4236

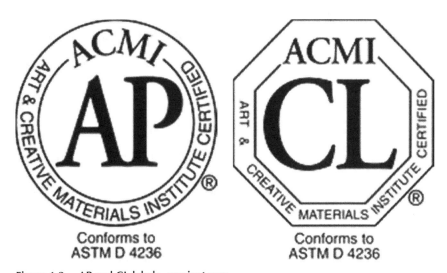

Figure 1.2. AP and CL labels. ***acminet.com.***

ists: "Of the many painters I have known, almost all I found unhealthy. . . . If we search for the cause of the cachectic and colorless appearance of the painters, as well as the melancholy feelings that they are so often victims of, we should look no further than the harmful nature of the pigments." (www.theatlantic.com/health/archive/2013/ll/how-important-is-lead-poisoning-to-becoming-a-legend ary-artist?). Not all artists might have known about the connection between their materials and their health. On occasion Goya used his fingers to apply paint to his canvas, which some experts believe was the direct cause of his trembling hands, blindness, and weakened limbs. Van Gogh is thought to have had an array of medical maladies related to exposure to lead from his paints. Recently, the *Santa Fe New Mexican* newspaper reported the story of an artist who suffered lead poisoning from spreading paint on canvas with her bare hands.

In addition to these legislative and industry attempts to educate artists, many states have Right to Know laws that entail public warning of the presence of toxic materials in the work place. For instance, the Bow and Arrow Press was temporarily designated a machine shop instead of a letterpress print shop for students affiliated with Harvard University. The machine shop description would have required the press to post more detailed work place warnings in the form of Material Safety Data Sheets, including identifying the allergy risks associated with wearing disposable latex gloves.

Another health concern that artists in the studio should guard against is the presence of bacteria and mold in paint products, such as oils, acrylics, temperas, and poster paints. All paints are subject to eventual spoilage once they are opened. Storing once-open containers in a properly ventilated and cool, dry location reduces the potential sources of contamination.

Nearly every state restricts the disposal of even small amounts of waste oil paint, solvents, or photographic chemicals down the drain. In many communities, noncommercial fine artists can drop off spent solvents, aerosol paint cans, paint wastes, cleanup wipes, and other wastes generated in an art studio free of charge at municipal trash spots. In general, commercial artists are considered a small business and must abide by different disposal regulations than hobby artists. In the state of Rhode Island, for example, commercial artists are required to register with the state as a hazardous waste generator, and must hire a licensed hazardous waste transporter to remove waste for proper recycling (see "Narragansett Bay Commission: Environmental, Health and Safety Best Management Practices for Fine Art Painting Studios," found at http://www.brandeis.edu/ehs/docs/ArtistBMP.pdf). The state of California bars commercial artists from even transporting hazardous materials. Violators of these regulations are subject to civil penalties and potentially criminal charges under both state and federal law. However, no prosecutions against artists for environmental offenses have been publicly reported.

Many of the leading art schools, including the painting departments at the New Hampshire Institute of Art, Rhode Island School of Design, San Francisco Art Institute, and the print department of the College of Santa Fe, have "du-turped" their schools. They now rely upon substances like vegetable oil to clean brushes and printing presses. The Gamblin Artists Colors Company advertises that it manufactures oil paints, mediums, and solvents that greatly reduce the toxic levels in studios. The products are sold under the "Gamsol" label, and are purportedly used by leading contemporary artists David Hockney, Chuck Close, and Wolf Kahn.

ARTISTS' INCOME, EXPENSES, TAXES, AND ESTATE

A research study conducted by the Center for Postsecondary Research, School of Education, Indiana University (Strategic National Arts Alumni Project), dispelled the cynical notion that a degree in the visual arts is a ticket to the unemployment line. In fact, the vast majority of artists that graduated from art schools between 1999 and 2009 are "finding ways to put together careers and be employed." On the flip side, a little less than half of the fine arts and studio art graduates reported that they are working as professional artists. The vast majority of the surveyed artists indicated that they were working as self-employed visual artists, although most were unhappy with their income.

Women professional artists earn substantially less than men artists. The poster shown in figure 1.3 arose out of the mid-1980s protest by an organized group of women, the Guerrilla Girls, against the Museum of Modern Art (MoMA) for the inequality in exhibiting works of art by women. Statistically, earnings have improved for women; however, the poster illustrates an ongoing economic disparity and cultural concern.

Bona Fide Business or Hobby

Unfortunately, all too few women and men visual artist students receive any formal academic training at art schools in the business of being an artist. This book helps to fill that gap. The law, though, especially tax law, treats the professional artist as a businessperson subject to a variety of local, state, and federal tax provisions. The initial hurdle for visual artists is to determine whether their "art" qualifies as a business, under the guidelines of the **Internal Revenue Service (IRS)**. Visual artists that conduct themselves in a manner consistent with *a trade or business* activity, and not merely a personal *hobby*, are able to deduct various business expenses. An artist who creates art

Figure 1.3.   Guerrilla Girls' *Women in America* poster. © *Guerrilla Girls, photo image courtesy of guerrillagirls.com.*

as a hobby or for recreational purposes, is limited in deducting expenses only to the extent the hobby generates reportable income. It is always possible to convert a hobby into a genuine business.

The legal test to distinguish between a hobby and bona fide business is codified into nine criteria that can be found in various publications distributed by the IRS (see http://www.irs.gov/Businesses/Small-Businesses-&-Self-Employed/Publications-and-Forms-for-the-Self-Employed):

1. Whether you carry on the activity in a businesslike manner.
2. Whether the time and effort you put into the activity indicate you intend to make it profitable.
3. Whether you are depending on income from the activity for your livelihood.
4. Whether your losses from the activity are due to circumstances beyond your control (or are normal in the start-up phase of your type of business).
5. Whether you change your methods of operation in an attempt to improve the profitability.

6. Whether you have the knowledge needed to carry on the activity as a successful business.
7. Whether you were successful in making a profit in similar activities in the past.
8. Whether the activity makes a profit in some years, and how much profit it makes.
9. Whether you can expect to make a future profit from the appreciation of the assets used in the activity.

The IRS presumes that if you make money three out of five consecutive years then your art endeavors are considered a business for federal tax purposes. Failing to meet this legal standard does not disqualify the activity from being deemed a business; however, the artist must demonstrate a genuine intent and effort to conduct his or her affairs as a business. At a minimum, to meet this test the artist must prove that she has developed a business plan, was attempting to earn money, and maintains records of all income sources and expenses. This is not an easy burden to overcome.

A 2014 Tax Court opinion is proof, however, that it is possible for an artist who also has a full-time job, and never earned a profit from her art, still to have her art activity be considered a business. Professor Susan Crile taught studio art at Hunter College in New York City. Her art was created over a forty-year professional span that was highly exhibited and collected. Crile's failure to earn a profit in any year meant that she had to prove under a behavior-based test that her activities constituted a business, not a hobby loss, as the IRS had determined.

Crile appealed the IRS's adverse finding to the US Tax Court. The court reviewed Crile's activities and motivation for creating art under the nine factors outlined above. On the whole, it was found that she kept fairly good although not perfect business records; employed a bookkeeper; actively marketed her art by creating slides and sending them to interested parties; spent about thirty hours per week during the college term on her art and kept at it full-time during the summer; was skilled and knowledgeable about her art; expected the value of her art would increase over time; did not become an artist to shield other income; and was serious about her art even though she derived personal pleasure. After weighing all the factors the court held that her art activity was primarily engaged to earn money and therefore qualified as a business (*Crile v. Commissioner* [T.C. Memo 2014–202]). As such, expenses related to the research, production, marketing, exhibiting, and selling her art, including premiums to insure the art, commissions to agents, cost of art materials, art books and periodicals, office equipment, repairs, travel for business purposes, office expenses, phone for business use, and legal and accounting fees were fully deductible against all her sources of income.

Sources of Income and Reporting

Visual artists receive compensation in a variety of ways, such as from the sale of works of art, prizes that have a monetary value, foundation grants, scholarships, earnings from commissions, copyright and trademark royalties, fellowships, and wages. In nearly every instance, except fellowship and scholarship grants for artists studying for a degree at an educational institution unless it involves teaching, the compensation received is taxed as ordinary income for federal, state, and local reporting purposes.

The failure to properly report earned income could have severe consequences as a famed Pop Artist learned. The artist Peter Max, best known for his psychedelic rainbow poster design of Bob Dylan and the Yellow Submarine Beatles image, pled guilty in federal court to tax evasion. Max admitted that he bartered paintings for property in the Virgin Islands and New York without disclosure, received undeclared cash, structured the receipt of payments in amounts under $10,000 to avoid detection, and created fake documents to conceal his illegal activities. Max hid more than $1 million in income connected to the sale of his art works (see http://www.nytimes .com/1997/11/11/nyregion/pop-artist-peter-max).

Besides the triggering of ordinary taxes on earned income, the sale of an artist's works might require the collection of a sales tax depending on the jurisdiction where the art is sold. A visual artist that sells works online at websites like Etsy, eBay, or Amazon has an obligation to collect the appropriate sales tax from an out-of-state customer only when the artist has established a "nexus" or physical presence in that state. Online or in-person sales to customers that live in the artist's home or nexus state require that the artist collect a sales tax on all sales, assuming the state charges a sales tax on these transactions. In many states, the local departments of revenue compel artists that sell works retail or wholesale to apply for a resale tax number. An artist with a resale tax number is entitled to purchase materials and supplies used in the process of creating art without having to pay any sales tax. The rules on sales taxes are specific to each artist's jurisdiction so it is difficult to recite any general rules that cover all or most situations. Some states, such as Rhode Island, exempt artists from collecting a sales tax when they live and work within a designated cultural arts district. The policy reason behind this exclusion is to encourage economic development, tourism, and employment opportunities along with supporting the local arts community.

All working visual artists, whether they are self-employed or employed, are covered by the **US Social Security** system based on their financial contributions from their earned incomes. Payments into the system are automatic for employed artists. A self-employed artist is obligated to independently compute the social security tax owed and pay the tax. Federal tax law permits self-employed visual artists to establish a **Keogh** retirement plan, and make deductible contributions based on gross income. In the alternative, a self-employed artist might establish a **Simplified-Employee Pension** (**SEP**) plan. In addition, under certain conditions, an artist may qualify to contribute to an **Individual Retirement Account** (**IRA**) plan. Zero-cost financial planners are readily available to assist the self-employed artist establish an appropriate retirement plan.

The Home Studio Tax Dilemma

Returning to the deduction of expenses for an artist, a typical deduction is the cost of renting a studio. An artist that leases space apart from where the artist resides is permitted to deduct all of the rent and expenses connected with the work studio, such as utilities, heat, and maintenance. The IRS restricts the deductibility of business expenses when the studio is part of the artist's personal residence like the "loft" example from the earlier chapter material. A business deduction is permitted for an in-home studio so long as the area is maintained exclusively, and on a regular basis, with the trade or business of creating art. The term "exclusive" means that an artist may not combine personal and business use with the studio. In the case of a loft this might require the artist to place a partition between working and living spaces. The IRS tax code places a limit on the amount of the deduction that is allowed in these studio/home cases. According to the March 2015 issue of *Kiplinger Magazine*, a person who takes a home deduction escalates the likelihood of the IRS auditing the tax return. There are also capital gains consequences when an artist deducts expenses related to maintaining a studio at home and later sells the personal residence. A visual artist that is contemplating the home office-studio/home deduction is advised to consult a tax professional because of the complications and consequences related to this judicious business decision.

Donations of Art

Since 1917, the public-good benefits of private contributions to not-for-profit charitable organizations, such as museums, colleges and universities, and libraries, have been recognized in the federal tax code. The IRS refers to these nonprofit groups as **501(c)(3)** organs. A cash contribution by an individual taxpayer including art dealers and collectors to an IRS-recognized 501(c)(3) usually results in an income tax deduction of the cash gift.

Before 1969, an artist who donated her work of art to a 501(c)(3) organization was permitted to take a tax deduction based on the art's fair market value. After 1969, when Congress amended the tax code, an artist could only deduct the cost of materials and supplies used to create the work. This abrupt break with previous tax law has led to a dramatic reduction in charitable gift giving by artists to museums, libraries, and higher education institutions. For instance, according to a report by the Americans for the Arts, MoMA reported a decrease in art donations of more than 90 percent in the period shortly after the change in law compared to a period before the law was altered (see http://www.americansforthearts.org/by-program/reports-and-data/legislation-policy/legislative-issue-center/charitable-giving-tax-reform).

Estate Planning

The final business law issue to consider is the impact of tax laws on an artist's estate planning. Arranging the disposal of an artist's assets that might include unique and valuable works of art is a complex process that should incorporate the advice of a seasoned tax attorney, accountant, and in some cases, insurance agent. The goal of an estate plan is to address both the gift-giving desires of the artist, while recognizing the financial and tax consequences in distributing art after death. Minimizing the payment of taxes and expenses of probate, while maximizing the testamentary wishes of the artist should be the objective of every effective estate plan.

Unfortunately, most visual artists do not like to think about the possibility of dying. A trip to a lawyer's office to draft a will is easily postponed. The failure to execute a legally binding will might have unintended consequences. The general rule for a person that dies without a will is for the state to appoint someone to oversee the disposal of the assets of the estate according to the laws of descent and distribution of the deceased's place of residence. Without any instructions, and maybe even money, to guide the estate, the heirs are left with the daunting task of deciding what to do about the works of art left behind. Fortunately, a simple and inexpensive will for small to medium-sized estates usually suffices especially when the total value of an artist's estate does not exceed the current $5.43 million estate tax threshold. This is the amount that an individual artist may gift during her lifetime or bequeath at death without incurring gift or estate taxes. In addition, each year a visual artist may gift art, cash, or any other asset, such as stocks or bonds, in the amount of $14,000 per organization, such as a charity, or individual without paying taxes on the gift or reducing lifetime gift/estate tax benefits.

The basic estate plan of drafting a will that declares the dispositional preferences of the artist's property, and names a spouse, partner, or family friend to serve as executor or executrix to gather and donate, sell, or bequeath assets as specified, might not always transpire as intended depending on the contours of the artist's postmortem wishes, the size of the estate, and family dynamics. As part of the legacy planning process, regardless of the size of the estate, it is important to create an inventory of works of art, set aside money or assets to help cover the expense of storage and insurance, and unless the art is worth a substantial amount of money consider gifting or selling as much art as possible during the artist's lifetime.

The complications of not strictly following the formalities of drafting, signing, and witnessing a will were played out in an open feud between the estranged spouse of Thomas Kinkade, the renowned "Painter of Light," and his live-in girlfriend. Kinkade and his wife had separated, but their divorce was not finalized, at the time of his unexpected death at the age of 54, in 2012. Apparently, a few months before Kinkade's death he handwrote two notes that allegedly granted his girlfriend title to his 7,000-square-foot home in California, and $10 million to establish a museum of his paintings. His girlfriend interpreted the handwritten notes to mean that she was entitled to some of his paintings, all of which were valued at in excess of $65 million; otherwise she would not have any paintings to display in the museum. An added twist to this convoluted affair were reports that Kinkade was an alcoholic, which raised an issue of whether he was of sound mind when he executed the handwritten notes. Ultimately, Kinkade's wife and girlfriend settled their dispute privately. The lessons learned are to continually update estate-planning documents as family circumstances change, and write the will and any changes (codicils) in a clear, concise, and unambiguous fashion.

David Smith was a pioneer of welded abstract sculpture. It was not until his death that his works gained international prominence. He died leaving an inventory of 425 works of metal sculpture. In Smith's will he named three executors to exercise control over these works after his death: the celebrated art critic Clement Greenberg, the abstract painter Robert Motherwell, and an attorney. During Smith's lifetime he granted the Marlborough Gallery in New York City the right to sell his work, subject to a one-third commission on the sales price. In valuing or appraising the works of art in the estate for tax purposes the executors successfully claimed that if all the sculptures were offered for sale by the gallery at the same time, then it would drastically lower the sales price of the works. The executors and the gallery wanted to sell the sculptures over a ten-year period, as the estate plan intended, to sustain interest and higher prices. The tax court agreed and applied a 37 percent blockage discount to the overall value of the estate's art assets for tax purposes (*Smith Estate v. Commissioner*, 57 TC 65, [1972]).

Even in Smith's carefully planned will, a challenge arose regarding the executors' failure to fully support postmortem the integrity of Smith's works of art. They allowed some of his most prized sculptures to be altered from their original state. For instance, *Circle and BoX* was stripped of its original white paint and varnished, and *Primo Piano III* was repainted from a white color to brown. The actions of these three executors paled in comparison to the litigation that occurred over the handling of the 798 paintings in the estate of Mark Rothko. A few months after Rothko's death, his carefully chosen executors entered into unusually lucrative contracts with the Marlborough Gallery. The deal gave the gallery a 50 percent commission on the sale of 698 of his paintings and an outright sale of the other 100 for a set price to be paid over twelve years. Rothko's heirs and the Attorney General (AG) of New York filed suit against the executors for breaching their fiduciary duty to the estate. The AG became involved because some of the proceeds from the sales were to benefit the charitable Mark Rothko Foundation, and the AG's office oversees charitable organizations in the state of New York. Ultimately, the contracts were rescinded and substantial damages were awarded against the executors and the gallery by the court.

The greed and deceit that was publicly revealed in the "genteel" art world by the sordid Rothko case was unprecedented. In a follow-up article to this twelve-year-long estate fight, Judith Dobrzynski for the *New York Times* wrote: "Over the years, artists, dealers, and museums have seen their share of scandals, but few if any have approached the level of the Rothko affair in size or notoriety" ("A Betrayal the Art World Can't Forget; The Battle for Rothko's Estate Altered Lives and Reputations," the *New York Times*, November 2, 1998).

It is not uncommon for visual artists or collectors of fine art to donate their works of art to charitable institutions, such as museums, hospitals, libraries, and schools, that are thus subject to *gift restrictions*. The leading art-museum law case that highlights the difficulty of always being able to abide by the intent of a well-meaning donor occurred in the infamous Barnes case. In 1922, Dr. Barnes established the Barnes Foundation for the purpose of educating the public about art and sharing his extensive art collection in an unconventional fashion at a site within a suburban neighborhood. The gift restrictions to the foundation prevented the sale or loan of Barnes's vast collection of impressionistic, postimpressionistic, and modern art. After his death, by judicial decree, and against Barnes's express gift restrictions, the trustees of the foundation were allowed to lend art from the collection to raise funds to renovate the building that housed the art. Later, in direct contradiction to the foundation's charter, a court permitted the financially strained trustees to actually move the collection into downtown Philadelphia near the Philadelphia Museum of Art, an institution loathed by Dr. Barnes. The new Barnes building with its holding of more than 2,500 objects of art including 900 paintings opened to the public in 2012. The 2009 documentary film, *Art of the Steal*, chronicles the controversy surrounding these court decisions that were initiated by the foundation's trustees.

Not all gift restrictions result in messy litigation. For instance, by a quirk of fate nearly thirty works of art by one of the progenitors of American Abstract Expression, Arshille Gorky, landed at the Whistler House Museum of Art in Lowell, Massachusetts. The heirs of Mina Boehm Metzger, whose estate owned the art, were looking for a museum that would agree to continuously exhibit these sketches, paintings, prints, and the only known Gorky bronze sculpture still in existence in a special room. Initially, the family was drawn to the Whistler because it owns and displays the only known impressionistic style painting by Gorky, *Park Street Church, Boston* (1924). Under the terms of the gift-permanent loan agreement, the museum agreed to the family's request that the works were to be properly restored at a collection conservatory at the museum's expense prior to perpetual display. The terms of the gift restriction, however, do not include the commercial right to exploit the copyrights in the works.

There are many outstanding booklets for artists that are interested in learning more about preserving their art for future generations. The Joan Mitchell Foundation has produced a pamphlet titled "Creating a Living Legacy Program for Visual Artists" that outlines helpful steps to follow to document and archive works of art. The Committee on Art Law of the Association of the Bar of New York City in conjunction with the Marie Sharpe Walsh Art Foundation has developed a beneficial guidebook on estate planning for visual artists.

MARKETING

The romantic idea of a dedicated fine artist working alone or as an apprentice devoted to mastering the "art" of drawing, painting, or sculpturing in a studio is changing. In what William Deresiewicz of the *Atlantic* magazine refers to as "the Birth of the Creative Entrepreneur," a new breed of savvy collaborative interactive visual artists versed in the skills of making art, the business of art, drawn to the connections among different disciplines, and networking are the latest modernists. This paradigm transformation coincided, and was reinforced, by the push and pull of new technology on old-school artistic tendencies. As later chapters in this book will illustrate, works of art increasingly are becoming *commodities* sought after by dealers, collectors, museums, and other consumers of art.

The vehicles to market, exhibit, curate, and sell not merely art, but the backstory and life story of the producers of art, can now be told in real time on the web via Facebook, Snapchat, Instagram, YouTube, Vibe, and countless other sites. Today, an artist possessing a laptop and access to relatively inexpensive software can discover a global audience by creating a blog or web site and develop into a potent cultural force.

SUMMARY

The manner in which visual fine artists are trained has changed over time. In recent years, professional academic institutions have begun bestowing academic credentials as currency for artistic achievement in the form of MFA and BFA degrees. Not all artists seek financial glory, but the business of creating art and the notion of art as a commodity are integral components of the lives of many artists, especially professional working artists. It is in this area of an artist's life that understanding the business law and tax law implications is a necessity.

The range of legal issues that an artist frequently confronts include complying with zoning regulations, following health and safety codes, limiting exposure and proper disposal of hazardous chemicals, and preparing and submitting sales and income tax forms. Donating art during an artist's lifetime or after death to implement an artist's intent and minimize the payment of taxes often requires sophisticated planning and professional advice. At a minimum all artists are advised to execute a will to carry out testamentary wishes and avoid future disputes.

WORKS REFERENCED

Alan Bamberger, "Income Tax, Gift & Estate Tax Issues: Tips for Art Collectors & Artists," 2011, http://www.artbusiness.com/estax.html.

Bill Chappell, "In Fair Housing Act Case, Supreme Court Backs 'Disparate Impact' Claims," *NPR*, June 25, 2015.

Tad Crawford, *Legal Guide for Visual Artists*, 5th ed., New York: Allworth Press, 2010.

Leonard DuBoff and Christy King, *Art Law*, 3rd ed., St. Paul, MN: Thomson, 2000.

William Deresiewicz, "The Death of the Artist—and the Birth of the Creative Entrepreneur," in *The Atlantic*, January/February 2015.

Factsheet 25 on Paints, *Toxic Link*, July 2005.

Fine Arts and Art Studies, Other, National Center for Education Studies, U.S. Department of Education, Washington, DC. https://nces.ed.gov/ipeds/cipcode/cipdetail.aspx?y=55&cip=50.0799.

Hal Foster (ed.), *The Anti-Aesthetic: Essays on Postmodern Culture*, Port Townsend, WA: Bay Press, 1983.

Marie Malaro and Ildiko Pogany DeAngelis, *A Legal Primer on Managing Museum Collections*, 3rd ed., Washington, DC: Smithsonian Books, 2012.

John Henry Merryman, Albert Elsen, and Stephen Urice, *Law, Ethics and the Visual Artist*, 5th ed., The Netherlands: Kluwer Law, 2005.

Robinson Meyer, "The Artist Endures," in *The Atlantic*, December 30, 2014.

Narragansett Bay Commission, Environmental, Health and Safety Best Management Practices for Fine Art Painting Studios, December 31, 2013.

Camille Paglia, *Glittering Images*, New York: Pantheon Books, 2012.

Monona Rossol, *The Artist's Complete Health and Safety Guide*, 3rd ed., New York: Allworth Press, 2001.

Stephen Saitzy, *Art Hardware: The Definitive Guide to Artists' Materials*, New York: Watson-Guptill, 1987.

Julia Prodis Sulek, "Secret Deal Ends Girlfriend-Wife Feud over Painter Thomas Kinkade's Estate," in *Mercury News*, December 19, 2012.

Roger White, *The Contemporaries: Travels in the 21ˢᵗ Century Art World*, New York: Bloomsbury, 2015.

2

Navigating the Art World

Movements, Critics, and Merchants

"The goal of the artist must be aesthetic development, and in a universal
sense, to make in his own way some contribution to culture."

—Norman Lewis (*From the Harlem Renaissance to Abstraction*)

The Harlem-born African American painter Norman Lewis epitomized the
complicated relationship between an artist who was concerned with race
and racism during the 1940s era of Jim Crow laws through the civil rights
advances of the 1960s and the desire to sell his art in blue-chip galleries.
Observers of Lewis's works saw the duality of abstraction transposed over
realism that began during an art movement referred to as *Social Realism*. In
later years, he shifted styles to Abstract Expressionism, leaving behind earlier
references to bread lines for poor black folk and depictions of police brutal-
ity. The color *black* frequented his work throughout his career, yet his atmospheric paintings revealed expressive palettes. After his death, as happens all
too often for visual artists, his gestural works gained greater recognition and
became more collectible.

Lewis's works never reached the commercial heights of his Harlem col-
league, Jacob Lawrence, best known for his *Migration Series* paintings. Recently, the Jewish Museum in New York City joined the works of Lewis with
a collection of small paintings by Lee Krasner, spouse of Jackson Pollock.
One critic labeled the two artists, who shared a visual language, but sprung
from different cultural and ethnic roots, as "hidden in plain sight" (Karen
Rosenberg, "Lee Krasner and Norman Lewis at the Jewish Museum," in the
New York Times, September 11, 2014).

A little more than twenty-five years ago, the art historian Michael Rosenfeld opened an art gallery and art advisory business focusing on lesser-known

artists that contributed to the establishment of Surrealism, Social Realism, and Abstract Expressionism. Today, his gallery represents the estate of Norman Lewis. It assists the estate by loaning his works to museums, engaging in scholarly research, and selling his drawings and paintings both online and at the physical gallery space in New York City. Figure 2.1 is a sample of one of the works by Lewis currently for sale.

Lewis's interest in art progressed from pictorial immersion in the turmoil of social causes to focusing on the modern Abstract movement of the 1950s. As Lewis's art began to appeal more directly to the wishes of large city galleries and leading museums, his works simultaneously gained recognition in the eyes of the press and critics. This is a familiar arc for many visual fine artists throughout the modern and contemporary art movements.

This evolution favors certain visual artists that are a part of the nexus of the gallery-auction-house-collector-major-museum-complex, but not all artists. The "art" of selling and buying fine art is changing in two significant ways. In what the *Wall Street Journal* refers to as the "New Masters of the Art Universe," a small subset of wealthy international buyers acquire high-end paintings, sculptures, photographs, and mixed media works from famous artists at auctions or art fairs, such as the London Art Fair, LA Art Show, and Art Basel, with the help of art advisors. At the opposite extreme, are those artists that lack the hedge-fund appeal of Chuck Close or Gerhardt Richter. For these fine artists, social media platforms, such as Instagram and Gertrude.

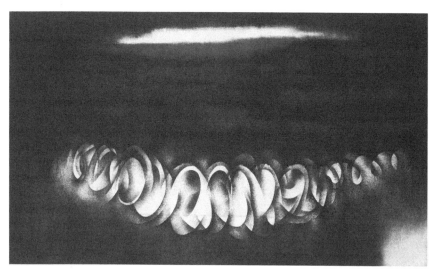

Figure 2.1.   *Ebb Tide*, 1975, Norman Lewis. © *Estate of Norman W. Lewis, photo image courtesy of Michael Rosenfeld Gallery LLC, New York, NY.*

com, and online auction houses, such as Arsty.net and Lofty.com, serve as vehicles to launch careers to a different tiered consumer market. For example, Kate Zimmerman, a hip, young recent graduate of the College of Fine Arts, University of Texas at Austin, personifies this new breed of visual fine artists who leverages social media to display and sell art. Zimmerman, a visual storyteller, has over 70,000 followers of her postings of photographs on her Instagram site. They have led to licensing of her images for commercial interests and magazines that might never have occurred otherwise.

This chapter looks at the history of the relationship among the various modern artistic movements and the merchants of art, while also considering how artists have been both vilified and supported by the critics who have helped to shape the public's opinion of their works.

MODERN ART MOVEMENTS AND MERCHANTS

Art historians would dispute any attempt to classify a distinctive style of art with a specific time period, where the artists of that era all created art in a similar manner. Yet, the history of art movements looking back visually makes sense when it is viewed as a stack of chronological periods attached to a series of dates. As a starting point, the *Gothic* art period occurred during the late Middle Ages. It is associated most closely with vaulted ceilings in churches, sculptured monuments to the apostles, illuminating manuscripts, frescoes, and biblical-referenced stained glass windows. In the larger cities of Europe, artists were required to join *guilds*. The names of some of the artists from this period are known because of the records kept by the guilds. Occasionally, brave painters signed their names to their works. Around 1400, Europe experienced a revival in the classic arts, centered in Italy. The French word for "rebirth" is "renaissance." For the next three hundred years a process began that embraced the Classical Greek principles of art and sculpture fueled by a new sense of individual self-awareness and self-determination. The "Age of Faith" was replaced by the "Age of Reason."

Visual artists of the *Renaissance* period learned their "crafts" working as apprentices for master artists. A master artist was reliant upon a wealthy patron to earn a living. The Medici family from Florence, Italy, serves as an example of successful bankers and traders who were educated on humanistic principles, became active in government affairs, and commissioned architects to design mansions and painters to portray family members.

Domestic themes, such as birth of a child, marriage, and family gatherings, were commonly portrayed in commissioned paintings. Advances in the sciences led to the creation of new painting pigments. In Venice, Titan and other prominent painters developed a technique of applying oil paint directly on canvas. This process allowed a fine artist to paint over or repaint a used canvas. A master artist was not limited solely to oil painting on canvas or fresco painting sacred images for religious leaders. The renowned Renaissance artist Leonardo da Vinci, famous for his enduring works the *Mona Lisa* and *The Last Supper*, reportedly listed thirty-six different commissionable art skills for patrons.

Apprentice artists that received formal training from a master artist could join a guild. The guilds, which continued from the Middle Age era, were formed on the basis of the artist's medium, and were the province only of men. In the later Renaissance period, there were guilds for sculptors, painters, printers, bookbinders, glassmakers, and art dealers. The guilds served as economic cartels to control the training of artists and regulate the purchase and sale of works of art. Apprentice artists were forbidden to sell their art under their own names. Membership in a guild was a requirement to market art locally. A famous master artist like the Dutch painter Rembrandt was highly sought as a teacher. Another celebrated Renaissance artist, Vermeer, secured numerous commissions from a wealthy patron, yet is known to have earned extra money by representing other artists in trade dealings.

The traditional painting themes during the Renaissance were history, religious, seascapes, portraits, landscapes, still-lifes, and genre or ordinary life. By the end of the Renaissance, landscape paintings began to overtake history and religious subjects in popularity. Figure 2.2 is an example of a Renaissance period landscape painting by Rembrandt.

The century that followed the Renaissance art movement, 1750–1850, was marked by cataclysmic political and civil changes that directly impacted the next great art movement: *Neoclassicism*. In response to the flurry of lofty democratic ideas that arose from the American and French Revolutions, a new socioeconomic order was born that led to the creation of a middle class in the United States, France, and other parts of Europe. The growth of a prosperous middle class helped propel a remarkable interest in the fine arts.

The Neoclassical artistic style was an extension of the Renaissance movement insofar as it drew inspiration from classical notions of balance and restraint from ancient Roman and Greek art and architecture. This form of art reflecting principles of order and reason was consistent with the intellectual movement by academics, scientists, and writers during this Age of Enlightenment.

Two professional art societies in Europe established schools of art instruction that significantly influenced the public's opinion of fine art and provided venues for artists to exhibit sculpture, paintings, prints, and drawings to patrons. These schools or academies, the Royal Academy of Art in England and the Académie des Beaux-Arts in France, became models for similar art

Figure 2.2. *The Stone Bridge*, Rembrandt van Rijn. *Courtesy of rembrandtpainting.net.*

academies throughout Europe. The French Academy is considered the birthplace of the Neoclassical movement.

The art academies embarked on a disciplined and competitive form of instruction that ultimately was undermined years later by avant-garde movements. According to Allison Lee Palmer, author of *Historical Dictionary of Neoclassical Art and Architecture*, design was preferred over color, and students were "classified" in a hierarchical fashion. The painting of historical and religious figures was viewed more favorably than those that painted portraitures, still-lifes, or landscapes. The academy students' works were critically judged and their works approved, not unlike the senior seminar reviews before faculty that occur in today's art colleges, as a condition to graduation. Artists that passed through this rite of academic passage were eligible for membership in the academy in the categories of architecture, sculpture, engraving, and painting or at a different level as art critics, dealers, and collectors.

The academies hosted frequent exhibitions or *salons* of their members' works of art. It was in this manner that visual artists could gain notoriety and critical acclaim, and develop a following from dealers and collectors. Members of the public, including the flourishing middle class along with wealthy patrons, were invited to attend the salon exhibitions. The amount of money artists received from the sale of their paintings reflected the canvas size, amount of materials, and subject matter. A large religious oil painting would sell for more money than a small domestic-scene etching. Commissions by patrons endured as a source of income for established academy artists. Artists who were not trained at an academy or were not academic artists were ineligible to exhibit at the salons.

The art academies' and salons' control over training and display practices initially resulted in limited artistic deviations in style and painting techniques. However, during the later stages of the Neoclassical movement, artists like J. M. W. Turner of England began to create luminous landscapes and seascapes, capturing mystic visions of nature that forecast the works of the next major art movement, the *Impressionists*. The art critic John Ruskin acclaimed the English painter Turner "the greatest in every branch of scenic knowledge" (Walker, 1983).

A sample of one of Turner's paintings that was exhibited at the Royal Academy and later acquired by the Tate Museum is shown in figure 2.3.

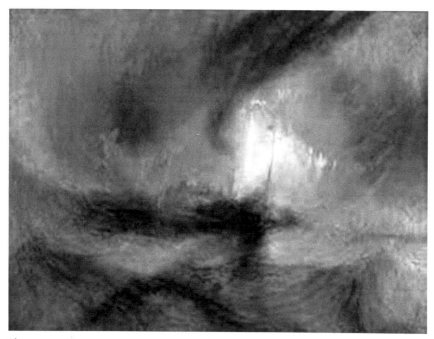

Figure 2.3.   *Snow Storm—Steam-Boat off a Harbour's Mouth,* JMW Turner. *Photo image courtesy of turnerpainting.org.*

The genre artists of this period had a profound influence on the development of two of the most notable American painters of the late nineteenth and early twentieth centuries. James Whistler, a native of the industrial city Lowell, Massachusetts, began his formal studies at the Imperial Academy of Fine Arts in Scotland after a genre artist, Sir William Allen, recommended him for classical training in art. Whistler received further education at other art academies before joining a group of bohemian artists in Paris that rejected the formalities of conventional drawing and painting. In 1859, the leading French Salon scorned his nontraditional painting, *At the Piano*, which in style and setting portends his most celebrated painting: *Arrangement in Grey and Black: Portrait of Whistler's Mother* (see Francis Spalding, *Whistler*, 1979). John Singer Sargent, considered by many to be America's greatest portrait artist, earned a silver prize for painting as part of the competitive education practice of the acclaimed École des Beaux-Arts. (In 1863, the Académie des Beaux-Arts became a private institution when it was granted independence by the French government. In 1897, for the first time, women were admitted into the newly named École des Beaux-Arts.) In 1887, Sargent's painting of young girls in an English garden drew praise and profit when exhibited at the Royal Academy. The Tate Museum purchased the painting after the exhibition closed. Sargent's achievement encouraged him to travel to Boston and New York. There he produced dozens of commissioned portraits. None was more famous than that of his renowned patron, Isabella Stuart Gardner. Sargent had his detractors, though. The English critic Roger Frey of the Bloomsbury Group, in commenting on a retrospective exhibit stated, "Wonderful indeed, but most wonderful that this wonderful performance should ever have been confused with that of an artist" (see Prettejohn, *Interpreting Sargent*, 1998).

The creative class began to reject the rigid rules of compositional balance and restraint of the Neoclassical period. Instead, writers and artists searched for meaning and inspiration in nature and the spiritual world. The works of painters during the *Romantic* movement were characterized by brighter use of color and expressive brushstrokes in what critics called "action paintings." In this era, exotic images and subjects from non-Western cultures replaced the stable compositions of the Neoclassical era.

While painting, etching, engraving, and drawing in the context of this book have been considered "art," the reality is that works prepared by artists provide a dual function. An artist's depiction of a subject or theme, such as a family portrait, a church wedding, water falling off a ledge, a building on fire, musicians playing at a dance club, or a tranquil farm scene, functioned as a way of visually memorializing and commemorating topical events and sharing information. However, in 1839, a French commercial painter and theater promoter invented a device that altered the standard of representational accuracy in a manner that no other artist could hope to duplicate. From that moment of his miracle invention, the way the public and artists saw the world was changed forever.

Louis-Jacques-Mandé Daguerre devised a technique to permanently fix an image thrown by a lens on an object. Drawing by light, now called photography, was originally named for its inventor or daguerreotype. Despite inevitable initial accusations that photography was a "smear" against fine artists that painted in a realistic fashion, established salons and museums eventually accepted this new medium as visual fine art.

In the words of H. W. Janson, "(p)ainting needed to be rescued from competition with the camera" (Janson, *History of Art*, 1969). Conceptually, two French artists were primarily responsible for laying the groundwork to the response of this new medium that negatively impacted the livelihood of portrait artists: Edouard Manet and Claude Monet. According to Janson's seminal work on this subject, Manet thought a painted canvas as something that is looked "at" and not "through." Monet adapted Manet's theories, by applying multiple light-fueled pigments of color patches on landscapes, while painting "plein air" or out-of-doors on the banks of the river Seine in France. The desire of Monet was not to render a simple landscape, but rather to take leave of any realism and depict the sensation produced by observing the fully lighted landscape.

The name for this radical intellectual and artistic shift that developed in the late 1870s was *Impressionism*. The word came about when an outraged art critic referred to an obscure artist's painting, *Impression, Sunrise*, in a mocking fashion. The critic considered it a mere "impression" of a painting, and not a finished composition. The obscure artist was Claude Monet. Ironically, Monet and fifty-four other fine artists were taking part in an exhibition in the studio of a French photographer after the official Salon of Paris had rejected their works. Another critic later referred to the group "as a bunch of lunatics and a woman." The woman was Berthe Morisot, a painter who was the sister-in-law of Manet. The shimmering luminous *Impression, Sunrise* painting by Monet is displayed in figure 2.4.

Artists that embraced the classic Impressionism movement—signified by applying pure, unmixed colors with short brush strokes that emphasized an overall atmospheric effect rather than elaborate details—were responsible for bringing to an end the dominance of the major academies of fine arts in defining what style, technique, or subject matter of art was acceptable for painting, exhibiting, and collecting. For instance, in breaking from the serenity of painting quiet landscapes or embellishing religious icons, Edgar Degas depicted lively scenes from dance halls, theaters, and cafes. The American printmaker and painter, Mary Cassatt, befriended Degas

Figure 2.4. *Impression, Sunrise,* **Claude Monet.** *Photo image courtesy of Kimball Art Museum.*

and exhibited her images of the social lives of children and their mothers with the Impressionists in Europe. As Cassatt and Morisot were women, it was socially unacceptable for them to paint in public with an easel. They relied upon domestic scenes from their own families and friends as their primary subjects.

Another major influence during this era besides the birth of the camera was the phenomenon of Japanese printmaking which gained a foothold in America and Europe. In the early 1900s, the women comprising the Provincetown Printmakers guided by Blanche Lazzell learned their white-line woodblock technique from Japanese printmakers, and established their own printmaking colony on Cape Cod. Prints made from oil-based ink designs on stone (lithographs) and from designs etched with acid in metal allowed the Impressionist artists to make and sell multiple copies of their decorative works to an audience that eventually recognized the brilliance of their works.

Another major development that propelled painting was the invention of packaging paint in metal tubes. This innovation enabled artists to paint outside their studies. Also, new techniques of creating colors from artificial pigments and mixing of paints by automation instead of delegating the activity to apprentice artists arose.

The market for buying and selling works of art by the Impressionist artists would not have developed were it not for the son of a paper shopkeeper in Paris, Paul Durand-Ruel. Beginning in the mid-1860s, Durand-Ruel progressively began to exhibit and financially support artists from the Neoclassical movement that branched off into the *Barbizon* period, such as Corot, Delacroix, Millet, and Courbet. Durand-Ruel had established a reputation as an expert appraiser and curator. Yet, his initial endeavors led to the first of his bankruptcies because of the strong opposition to this movement which had rejected traditional aesthetic standards from official art circles and the public.

A decade later, Durand-Ruel opened art galleries in London and Brussels, in addition to his Paris gallery. Despite financial woes, he continued to organize and exhibit the next wave of avant-garde artists, the Impressionists. He paid monthly stipends to these artists in advance to permit them to continue to develop their techniques.

Durand-Ruel was the first art dealer to bring financial leverage into the art market. He borrowed money from banks and private investors to buy hundreds of paintings by Monet, Renoir, Degas, Cassatt, and Manet. By controlling the market, which also included the practice of bidding up works of art he put up for sale at auctions, he worked to brand these artists at the numerous gallery exhibits he staged in Philadelphia, New York, Moscow, Chicago, and other major cities. Durand-Ruel marketed these artists whose sketch works concentrated on images of daily life and modern contemporary society to the newly minted moneyed industrialists and middle class. Instead of traditional large group exhibitions, he was the first art dealer to conduct solo exhibitions of artists.

Durand-Ruel disrupted the historic role of the salon in defining what was acceptable as "high art." His innovative marketing techniques to cater to a new audience of collectors linked with his moral and financial support for visual fine artists, established an enduring model of the modern art dealer that remains today.

In 1900, at the age of nineteen, the Spanish artist Pablo Picasso arrived in Paris. He joined a world of painters—Seurat, Matisse, and Cézanne—that went from painting what their eyes were seeing to now doubting what they were seeing. Any understanding of the next art movement, *Post-Impressionism*, led by the art and life of the greatest painter of the twentieth century, must start with Gertrude Stein.

Three years after Picasso first arrived in Paris, Gertrude Stein, who was trained as a medical doctor, moved there with her brother Leo to embark on a writing career. The Steins' home doubled as a literary and artistic salon at 27 rue de Fleurus. For the equivalent of about $100 the Steins purchased a non-natural color painting by Henri Matisse from a gallery. One critic referred to this work that separated the color of a painting from its representational purpose, as the lair of "fauves," or wild beasts. By hanging this "notorious" painting in their apartment, the Steins stamped themselves as serious financial and moral supporters of Matisse and other key members of the first modern art submovement of the twentieth century, *Fauvism*. The Steins held weekly gatherings at their apartment that brought together visual fine artists and writers, including writer Guillaume Apollinaire.

For many years the Steins were the patrons that cultivated the increasingly adventurous works by Picasso and emotionally colorful paintings by Matisse. Picasso, in particular, courted Gertrude by painting her portrait, as seen in figure 2.5. These two uniquely talented geniuses became admiring friends particularly after Leo left to return to the United States. In 1938, Gertrude Stein published her intimate memoir, aptly named *Picasso*, about her relationship to him as cofounder along with Georges Braque of the next modern Post-Impressionism movement, *Cubism*.

The writer Apollinaire was one of the most original and influential poets of the early twentieth century. The undisputed leader of the avant-garde authors of that period, he penned critical studies on Cubic artists whom he admired as "singers of a constantly new truth" (see Genova, *The Poetics of Visual Cubism*, 2003). According to Peter Read, author of an authoritative text on the lives of these two close friends, Apollinaire's lyric writings shaped many of Picasso's drawings, sculptures, and paintings (see Read, *Picasso and Apollinaire*, 2010).

Meanwhile, in the United States, the 1913 Armory Show held in New York City introduced thousands of visitors to the newest trends in European art and marked the dawn of modern art in America. The public loved what the New York critics hated: a blue-colored nude by Matisse that defied all classical perceptions of a nude painting and a Marcel Duchamp Cubist-inspired nude that descended a staircase that deconstructed old ways of thinking about art. The latter painting by Duchamp eventually sold for $324 before commission, or over $7,500 in today's dollars. This was an enormous sum of money for an unknown French artist. The Armory Show then traveled to Chicago, where the art critic Harriet Monroe wrote, mimicking the insight of Apollinaire, "These radical artists are right. They represent a search for new beauty" and "a longing for new versions of truth observed" (see "Listen to the Story" on National Public Radio at www.npr.org/2013/02/17/172002686/armory-show-that-shocked-america-in-1913-celebrates-100).

Figure 2.5. *Gertrude Stein,* Pablo Picasso. © *Estate of Pablo Picasso/Artists Rights Society (ARS), NY, photo image courtesy of Metropolitan Museum of Art.*

Four years later in Paris, Apollinaire coined the term "Surrealism" after watching the performance of a play that began when a large woman entered center stage and unbuttoned her blouse to reveal two gas-filled balloons serving as breasts. She then flung the balloons into the audience. Initially a literary movement, the *Surrealism* movement spread to the art world. Loosely defined as the tapping of the unconscious mind to reveal the power of imagination, André Breton, Salvador Dalí, and Joan Miró were the visual artists most closely associated with this free association art movement. Their influence extended beyond the framed canvas to commercial work in advertising, fashion photography, and film.

Breton, the writer and artist, frequently organized and curated exhibitions for his fellow *Dada* and Surrealist artists. After World War II, Dalí and Breton left Europe, where the movement had dissolved, for the United States. The New York philanthropist and art collector, Peggy Guggenheim, organized exhibitions at her museum/gallery there that revitalized the Surrealism movement. Shortly thereafter, Breton organized a group showing of Surrealist artists in Mexico City that included two Mexican artists loosely affiliated with this group, Frida Kahlo and Diego Rivera. Breton later collaborated with Cuban Surrealist Wilfredo Lam.

The unconventionality of these deeply symbolic imagistic paintings swayed the next generation of post–World War II fine artists, who engaged in their own modern form of "action painting" known as the *Abstract Expressionism* movement.

By now readers are aware of the serious obstacles to understanding the relationship among artists, art movements, critics, dealers, and collectors based solely on an "ism" label. The artistic currents of the twentieth century are particularly hard to distinguish. The ending of one significant art movement, such as Surrealism, and the beginning of the next, such as Abstract Expressionism, which is composed of early forms of distinct arts—expressionism and abstraction—are interrelated, and not mutually exclusive. Yet, presented in this chronological manner, it gives the history of art a sense of order and a directional GPS.

Regardless of the titles to the art movements discussed, the excitement of the public's fascination with art still lies in the preoccupation with the imaginative fabrication and arrangement of lines, colors, spaces, textures, and shapes.

One woman, though, significantly impacted the course of the post–World War II modern art: Peggy Guggenheim. Her Medici-like patronage and quest to collect great art was based on her own personal sense of what she liked. Unlike the high-roller buyers of postmodern art, never purchased art as an investment. Her European friendship with artists like Duchamp and Jean Cocteau supplied her with access to the leading radical fine artists of the time. In 1938, Guggenheim opened her first gallery in London. Her contemporary exhibits featured sculptures by the British artist Henry Moore and American artist Alexander Calder. Also, she was the first person to exhibit the abstract works of Wassily Kandinsky.

Guggenheim asked one of the foremost art critics of the day, Henry Read, to help put together a list of artists whose works she should collect. It is said during the war years she bought a painting a day of works by Braque, Picasso, Mondrian, Fernand Léger, Miro, and Max Ernst, her husband for a short period. Hitler's military invasion of France forced her to return to her home in New York City.

In 1942, she opened her museum/gallery, Art of This Century. It was there where she first displayed her Cubic, Abstract, and Surrealist art collection. Similar to Picasso's wooing of Stein, artists created unique works of art especially for her to augment her grand opening. For example, Ernst and Breton helped in the design of a notable exhibition catalog that featured her assortment of top-tier European art and the works of a new generation of American artists, such as Janet Sobel, Robert De Niro Sr., Mark Rothko, and Robert Motherwell. The star of the opening exhibition, however, was a young, former construction worker whom Guggenheim put on a monthly allowance to financially support: the American Abstract Expressionist drip painter, Jackson Pollock.

The Abstract Expressionist movement was shaped by the legacy of the Social Realism artists of Norman Lewis's era and Surrealism. Remarkably, it signaled the beginning of America, not Europe, as the primary source of the next wave of avant-garde art. The center of this expressive art movement was firmly rooted in lower Manhattan. It was there where Pollock and William de Kooning located their art studios, and the Art Students League-educated German born artist Hans Hofmann taught his color-field push-pull theories.

A major art merchant shepherded the careers of numerous modern artists: Samuel Kootz. As a young advertising executive in New York, he commissioned artists like Stuart Davis and Arthur Dove to design patterns for clothing. By the wartime years, after he established his own gallery, he financially subsidized Motherwell and William Baziotes so long as they each met their quota of producing seventy-five paintings a year. Artists like Motherwell and Hofmann signed exclusive representational contracts with Kootz's gallery.

A masterful promoter of artists that he represented, Kootz was shrewd in enlisting the assistance of Clement Greenberg, an influential visual art critic, and Meyer Schapiro, an art historian, to select new artists for an upcoming exhibition and to curate the show. The group exhibition brought a new level of public appreciation for the art of the Abstract Expressionists. Greenberg's book, *Art and Culture* (1969) became a significant cultural record of his view of the role of avant-garde and rear-guard artists of Paris and America whose works he reviewed as an art critic.

Not to be neglected, photography eventually found its identity as a recognized art form in the twentieth century in America, starting with Alfred Stieglitz. His image of street scenes laid the foundation for documentary photography that stirred emotion. During the 1930s, Edward Weston began working with different camera lens openings to fuse together Abstract and Realism images. One of his followers, Ansel Adams, became one of the most admired nature photographers in the world.

Also, in the 1930s, Dorothea Lange's Social Realism photographs established her as one of America's premiere chronologists of the depths of poverty. Her images of starving migrant workers in California served as a clarion call for government assistance to a segment of society that had been ignored. Figure 2.6 is one of Lange's most famous gelatin-silver print images, now owned by the Library of Congress.

Figure 2.6.   Dorothea Lange, Migrant Mother, California. *Photo courtesy of History.com.*

In the 1950s, the work of the Swiss-born photographer, Robert Frank, signified a new form of what artists called "straight" photography. A compilation of eighty-three of his stark black and white images focusing on race and alienation in cities and rural communities was elegantly captured in the book *The Americans*, with a foreword by beat poet Jack Kerouac. His book, which established museums like the Museum of Modern Art refused to sell, changed how Americans saw themselves. It also altered the way future photographers looked through their viewfinders.

Frank's work so influenced a young advertising art director, Joel Meyerowitz, that he decided to quit his job and become a photographer. In 1962, Meyerowitz's use of color photography ushered in the dominance of a media capable of reproducing colors over monochromatic photography. The technological wizardry of fine art print makers like Bob Korn enhanced the completion of the glorious dye-transfer color prints of Meyerowitz, and portraits of fashion icon, Robert Avedon.

The Leica camera favored by Frank was the same instrument that allowed photojournalist Rowland Scherman to capture signature pictures of immense social impact and historical import during the 1960s. Many of his iconic works of pop stars and Civil Rights heroes that appeared in the leading periodicals of the day are seen in the book *Timeless: The Photography of Rowland Scherman* (Jones and Jones, 2014).

Meanwhile, three women photographers independently pushed the boundaries of what is acceptable art. Sally Mann famously depicted her own young children in provocative, non-pornographic poses at her family's rustic cabin. Cindy Sherman's untitled photographs used herself as a canvas to comment on her self-identity. Carrie Mae Weems's controversial photographs and multimedia images challenged viewers to contemplate provocative social, gender, and racial issues. All three of these established photographers are enjoying long professional careers highlighted by countless major museum retrospectives and superior gallery representation. Additional recognition has occurred by having their works displayed for sale to prosperous buyers at the world's premier art show for modern and contemporary art: Art Basel.

Still, all three of these photographers suffered indignation from critics. Mann was accused of exploiting her children for personal artistic purposes. Jed Perl's review of Sherman's exhibit at the Museum of Modern Art was characterized as "more of a wake than a coronation" ("The Irredeemably Boring Egotism of Cindy Sherman," *New Republic*, March 14, 2012). The African American photographer Carrie Mae Weems was accused of infringing upon Frank's moral rights and copyrights when she sought to give new meaning to his art by adding the "N" word to some of the original images from *The Americans* series that she appropriated.

Nonetheless, technology continues both to threaten the practices of established photographers and also to enable the creation of novel images. New "light-field photography" cameras contain hundreds of micro lenses merged into a single device to capture both two- and three-dimensional digital cube images.

The revolution in digital photography that allows for the altering of reality is not unlike similar epochal changes that have occurred in other forms of visual arts. In the mid-1950s, many artists felt squeezed by the works of commercial artists, printmakers, and comic strip illustrators. In a break from leading artists that were exploiting the emotional and symbolic value of colors, groups of artists on both sides of the Atlantic began to experiment with the saturated mass media images found in the everyday commercial culture of film, advertising, and comics.

Abstract Expressionism was considered suitable art for intellectuals. Visual artists such as Richard Hamilton, Peter Blake, Pauline Boty, Richard Smith, Jasper Johns, and Roy Lichtenstein tapped into an insatiable hunger by the British and American public for art they could understand. The common person did not care whether art critics considered this new art "low brow" or "high brow" nor did these original Pop Artists. The genius of the *Pop Art* movement was to use recognizable pictures and metaphors from popular culture, music, and literature and translate them into an accessible, easy to read, fun, ironic, and humorous art form that blurred the boundaries between commercial and fine art.

The prince of the Pop Art movement who made his name with his Campbell's Soup Can exhibition, held at the Ferus Gallery in Los Angeles was Andy Warhol. For that 1962 exhibition, he oil painted thirty-two identically sized soup cans and placed them in a manner similar to how they would be found on a supermarket's display shelf. After first hand-painting his soup series, he turned to commercial printing techniques like silk screening. His engagement in mass-producing art imitated the commercial world he was appropriating. Warhol transformed familiar images, such as Coca-Cola bottles, dollar bills, Brillo boxes, Elvis Presley, and Marilyn Monroe, into lasting forms of art that soon found public acceptance and curatorial recognition.

One of Warhol's later Campbell Soup silkscreen posters, as seen in figure 2.7, was produced specifically for Campbell Soup. The packaged soup product promotion was launched at a "special members only" event at the Whitney Museum in New York City. Warhol autographed individual copies of the print for attendees. The product itself was developed to compete against the commercial success of Ramen noodles.

Before his death in 1987, Warhol set the standard for the classic business artist. He was an ambitious and masterful self-promoter. His studio, the Factory, became a playground for hip visual artists, such as David Hockney, and music performers, such as Mick Jagger, while serving as an assembly line

Figure 2.7. Andy Warhol, *Campbell's Soup Box 1985*. © 2016 The Andy Warhol Foundation for the Visual Arts, Inc./ Artists Rights Society (ARS), New York.

for his silkscreen prints. Corporate clients beckoned him to design advertisements for products ranging from Mercedes Benz cars to Absolut Vodka.

The acknowledged dean of contemporary Pop Art art dealers, Leo Castelli, helped to organize art shows in New York for emerging fine artists. Castelli's first major exhibit, after ending his deal making relationship with the art dealer Sidney Janis, featured the new *Pop Op* styles of Jasper Johns and

Robert Rauschenberg. Not surprisingly, it was the Leo Castelli Gallery that sold Warhol's original 1962 *Campbell's Soup Can* painting.

Another of Castelli's early clients was the Princeton University–educated Frank Stella who helped usher in a new aesthetic art reduction movement called *Minimalism*. The point of this American nonobjective style that featured Sol Lewitt, Donald Judd, and Richard Serra was to reduce painting and sculpture to its essential components.

Perhaps no current artist represents a synthesis of the traditions of Pop Art, Minimalism, and *Conceptualism*, which focuses on the idea of art not the object, better than the German painter Gerhard Richter. Training originally as a Realist painter at the Düsseldorf School of Art, his latest works contain layers of heavily textured paint scraped off leaving a blending of unpredictable colors that defy easy classification.

Today, Richter's works are sold through major art dealers throughout the world, such as the Gagosian Gallery, Marian Goodman Gallery, and Galerie Maximillian. In 2013, a painting of his was commissioned by the electronics firm Siemens sold for $37 million at a Sotheby's auction. It set a record for the highest price ever paid for a living artist at auction.

This German heavyweight painter is not without his critics. The highly regarded British painter David Hockney remarks about Richter's paintings nearly echoed the scathing comments another critic made about Whistler in the nineteenth century. The art critic Ruskin, in published court documents in a defamation lawsuit, said this about Whistler's works, "Sir Coutts Lindsay ought not to have admitted works into the gallery in which the ill-educated conceit of the artist so nearly approached the aspect of willful imposture." Hockney's reported comments about Richter have a similar and familiar bite, "He always makes the same stuff with the squeegee, which is okay, but I don't see what's so great about it" (Henri Neuendorf, "David Hockney Delivers (Another) Scathing Criticism of Gerhard Richter," in *Artnet*, June 29, 2015). Historically, narrative transitions in painting from one art movement to another in the search for meaning of art beyond simple beauty are consistently the source of stimulating commentary and stinging censure.

SUMMARY

Labeling historic art movements in a chronologic order is not a seamless activity. The Middle Age artists learned their skills and techniques in apprentice workshops. Guilds served as the primary source for controlling the display and sale of their religious and historic works. The teaching of acceptable principles of art shifted to the salons of Europe during the Renaissance period. Eventually, their disciplined form of instruction was undermined by a series of vanguard movements in conjunction with avant-garde writings. The growth of the middle class that corresponded with the Industrial Revolution provided a new source of collectors. The invention of the camera spurred interest in creating visual art that did not compete with this new medium. Artists began applying unmixed colors in short brush strokes to create an atmospheric condition in a twentieth-century movement called Impressionism. Initially, critics spurned these radical artists, until dealers like Paul Durand-Ruel helped command public recognition and acceptance. The development of unconventional art from Surrealism to Abstract Expressionism followed by Pop Art set the stage for the latest art movements of the twenty-first century. Mega-art-dealers like Larry Gagosian continue to act in shrewd and daring ways to influence the public's sense of cutting edge art by offering innovative gallery exhibitions and developing scholarly catalogues to appeal to well-heeled buyers. Of course, the critics try to have the final word.

WORKS REFERENCED

Ruth Brandon, *Surreal Lives*, New York: Grove Press, 2000.
Mark Brown, "Gerhard Richter Work Sells for $37m, Setting New Record for Living Artist," in *The Guardian*, May 15, 2013.
Anda M. Corn and Tirza True Latimer, *Seeing Gertrude Stein*, Berkeley: University of California Press Foundation, 2010.
Holland Cotter, "Lost in the Gallery-Industrial Complex," in the *New York Times*, January 17, 2014.
Kelly Crow, Sara Germano, and David Benoit, "New Masters of the Art Universe," in *The Wall Street Journal*, January 23, 2014.
Susan Greenberg Fisher, *Picasso and the Allure of Language*, New Haven, CT: Yale University Art Gallery, 2009.
Olivia Fleming, "Why the World's Most Talked-About New Art Dealer is Instagram," in *Vogue*, May 13, 2014.
Pamela A. Genova, "The *Poetics* of Visual Cubism: Guillaume Apollinaire on Pablo Picasso," in *Studies in 20th Century Literature*, 27:1, Article 3, 2003.
Clement Greenberg, *Art and Culture*, Boston: Beacon Press, 1969.
H. W. Janson, *History of Art*, New York: Harry N. Abrams, Inc., 1969.
Ken Johnson, "Paul Durand-Ruel, the Paris Dealer Who Put Impressionism on the Map," in the *New York Times*, July 22, 2015.
Michael Jones and Christine Jones (ed.), *Timeless: Photography of Rowland Scherman*, Portsmouth, NH: Peter Randall Publisher, 2014.
The Kootz Gallery, *The Art Story Foundation*, http://www.theartstory.org/gallery-kootz.htm# , 2015.

Erin Landry, *Whistler v. Ruskin: Morality in Art Versus Aesthetic Theory*, http://www.loyno.edu/~history/journal/Landry.htm.

Norman Lewis: American Painter, http://www.theartstory.org/artist-lewis-norman.htm

Arthur Lubow, "An Eye for Genius: The Collections of Gertrude and Leo Stein," in *Smithsonian Magazine*, January 2012.

Jill Markwood, "Photography's Influence on Painting," in *Agora*, http://www.agorajournal.org/2010/Markwood.pdf, no. 19, Spring 2010.

Philip McCouat, "Early Influences of Photography on Art—Part 1," in *Journal of Art in Society*, 2015.

Nadine Kathe Monem (ed.), *Pop Art Book*, London: Black Dog Publishing, 2007.

Henri Neuendorf, "David Hockney Delivers (Another) Scathing Criticism of Gerhard Richter," in *Artnet*, June 29, 2015.

Allison Lee Palmer, *Historical Dictionary of Neoclassical Art and Architecture*, Plymouth, UK: Scarecrow Press, 2011.

Jed Perl, "The Irredeemably Boring Egotism of Cindy Sherman," in *New Republic*, March 14, 2012.

Elizabeth Prettejohn, *Interpreting Sargent*, London: Stewart, Tabori & Chang, 1998.

"The Priceless Peggy Guggenheim," in *The Independent*, October 21, 2009.

Provincetown Printing Blocks, *The Provincetown Art Association and Museum*, Provincetown, MA, 1988.

Peter Read, *Picasso and Apollinaire*, Oakland, CA: Ahmanson-Murphy Fine Arts Book, 2010.

Mark A. Reutter, "Artists, Galleries and the Market: Historical Economic and Legal Aspects of Artist-Dealer Relationships," in *Jeffrey S. Morad Sports Law Journal*, 8:1, Article 4, 2001.

Ingrid Schaffner, *The Essential Andy Warhol*, New York: Harry N. Abrams, Publishers, 1999.

Frances Spalding, *Whistler*, Ann Arbor, MI: Phaidon Press Limited 1979.

Gertrude Stein, *Picasso*, New York: Dover Publications, Inc., 1984.

John Walker, *Turner*, New York: Harry N. Abrams, Inc., 1983.

Rob Walker, "The Revolution in Photography," in *The Atlantic*, December 2011.

3

Art, Artists, and Museum Law

"Give me a museum, and I'll fill it."

—Pablo Picasso (*Letters of the Great Artists—*
From Blake to Picasso)

The relationship between artists, their art, and a museum is complex. Artists, whether living or dead, serve as intermediaries between the display of art and the public that encounters it. There are a variety of means and methods for the public to become engaged depending on the nature of the art, and the skill and talent of the director-like exhibit organizers in conveying a message or fostering an interactive learning experience. A text label on the wall, a two-dimension Quick Response (QR) bar code, a gallery talk by a curator, the sequence of the displayed works, architecture of the exhibit area, use of multi-media, existing public exposure of the artist, and a concise catalog are all contemporary forms of giving context to art.

A few years ago, the Art Institute of Chicago hosted a 100-year retrospective on the most preeminent fine artist of the twentieth century, Pablo Picasso. The reason for the 250-piece reflective exhibition was to celebrate the special relationship between Picasso and the museum that began in 1913. It was then that the Art Institute became the first American museum to exhibit Picasso's work, as part of an international exhibition of European Modernists. Interestingly, according to the catalog that announced the opening of this controversial exhibition, many of the displayed works were also offered for sale. Nowadays, it is less common for a fine arts museum to actually serve as a selling agent for artists unless it is a museum members' exhibition. These member/artist-museum events frequently serve as an institutional fundraiser. The pioneering mutually constructive relationship between a trendsetting artist and a museum (especially when it embodies showcasing a contemporary artistic practice like Picasso's was in 1913) is a model that continues today.

An artist, however, may not always strictly be the transitional third party between the museum and visitors. The leading member of the Young British Artists (YBA), Damien Hirst, spent $40 million to build his own public museum located near the Tate Modern Museum in London. The YBA is a diverse mixture of painters, sculptors, visual installation artists, and photographers educated at Goldsmith's College of Art at the University of London during the mid-1980s.

Hirst's principal intent in opening the museum is to display his own vast collection of works of art by modern and contemporary artists, such as Francis Bacon, Richard Prince, Sarah Lucas, Jeff Koons, and Pablo Picasso, for free. In this instance, the artist by acting as designer, administrator, curator, board member, donor, exhibitor, artist, and visitor is in a unique position to both structure and mediate the relationship between the visiting public and the works of art situated in a modern cultural arts building. In an utterly unique way, Hirst has a direct influence on how the public engages in dialogue with the fine art displayed in his museum.

The focus in the chapter is both to examine the relationship between art and the fine arts museum and to highlight the functions and organizational legal challenges of these museums starting with a history of fine arts museums in America.

BRIEF HISTORY OF FINE ARTS MUSEUMS IN THE UNITED STATES

Historically speaking, fine arts museums are a relatively recent invention. Unlike in Europe, where the world's first public museum—the Louvre—had its origins tied to the emergence of bourgeois power to end aristocratic dominance, the history of fine arts museums in America is different. In the United States, the development of fine arts museums was closely bound to the desire of men and women of enormous wealth, privilege, and cultural acumen, wanting to preserve their genteel status. The May 9, 1925, edition of the *New York Times* captured this state of affairs when it reported the Metropolitan Museum of Art was "not so much an institution for the instruction and the pleasure of the people as a sort of joint mausoleum to enshrine the fame of American collectors." The post–Civil War business brokers and financiers that were living in the major cities of Boston, Chicago, and New York privately founded, and funded, the first major art museums in America.

Figure 3.1. Channel your inner Camille Monet and try on a replica of the kimono she's wearing in *La Japonaise. MFA Boston, via Facebook.*

The aforementioned Metropolitan Museum of Art was incorporated in 1870 largely through the philanthropic efforts of members of the Union League Club of New York City, a civic group formed in 1863 to preserve the union. The Museum of Fine Arts Boston (MFA) was organized under the leadership of members of Boston's elite class. Six years later, in 1876, the MFA's art school was established by the museum. In 1879, in a cultural and economic development directly related to the aftermath of the Great Fire of Chicago in 1871, the Art Institute of Chicago and its school for the fine arts was founded by its board of trustees. Each of these museums reflected the capitalist ethos and ambitions of the times, that is, magnificent edifices often adorned with images of Greek gods or with the names of famous Western European artists carved into the exterior of grand marble buildings, constructed in the evolving commercial centers of these vibrant post–Civil War cities.

In contrast to the goal of creating national institutions of art by the larger museums, a number of factors contributed to the growth of art colonies in remote areas that led to the development of smaller, regional fine arts museums. By way of example, in 1873 the New Haven Railroad began taking passengers to Provincetown, Massachusetts, on the tip of Cape Cod. Inspired by stories of the wind-swept dunes, piers of the Portuguese fishing community, and shimmering light reflecting off the ocean waters, during the summer months artists flocked to Provincetown to paint plein air. By the early 1900s three major artists led by Charles Hawthorne opened schools for painting that attracted aspiring artists. In 1914, local artists and business people collaborated to form the Provincetown Art Association and Museum (PAAM) to exhibit and collect works of art by Provincetown artists. A year later, and two years after the famous Armory Show in New York that introduced avant-garde modernist painters to America, PAAM organized the first annual Provincetown exhibition in a local town hall. The *Christian Science Monitor* praised the exhibition for "avoiding the dullness of academicism" that was typified in the recent exhibitions in museums in Boston and New York (see Tony Vevers, *The Beginnings of the Provincetown Art Association and Museum*, *Provincetown Art Association and Museum*, 1999).

Over time, fine arts museums have grown from private collections of the gentry's class and artists' colonies raising funds to secure buildings for exhibiting native art to public institutions that educate and assemble a wide-ranging collection of fine art characterized by aesthetic quality and dynamic exhibitions. They vary dramatically in size, purpose, and delivery. Museums are popular with the public whether they are privately owned and operated or publicly funded and managed. According to the American Alliance of Museums (AAM), every year there are more visitors to museums then the attendance for all major sporting events and theme parks combined. The Louvre

Museum in Paris remains the most frequently visited art museum in the world with over 8.5 million turnstile guests annually. In the United States, the Metropolitan Museum ranks first in guest popularity with over 5 million visitors per year followed by the Museum of Modern Art, the J. Paul Getty Museum in Los Angeles, and the Art Institute of Chicago. Collectively, the varied museums that encompass the Smithsonian Institution unofficially count over 28 million free "visits" yearly. The development of online museum experiences linked with new digital technology and software applications to cultivate remote access to collections is on the rise. The AAM is championing the digital online experience via its Center for the Future of Museums program.

THE MUSEUM ORGANIZATION AND LEADERSHIP

Regardless of the size, location, or vision of a museum in the art world they all have one thing in common: they are for the benefit of the community of people they serve. The International Council of Museums (ICOM) proffers an official definition of a museum:

> A museum is a non-profit, permanent institution in the service of society and its development, open to the public, which acquires, conserves, researches, communicates and exhibits the tangible and intangible heritage of humanity and its environment for the purposes of education, study and enjoyment.

A fine arts museum is one that focuses its activities specifically on painting, drawing, watercolors, prints, posters, graphics, sculpture, interactive mixed media, photography, ceramics, textile art, conceptual art, and the like. By serving the public, they occupy an inimitable position of contributing to the preservation and conservation of varied forms of visual art that represent the history and culture of a range of artists and art practices; providing access to learning places and exhibition spaces; collaborating in partnership with emerging artists and cultural institutions to develop multiparty projects; conducting outreach programs to engage underrepresented audiences; serving as centers for professional expertise; and keeping the museum experience enjoyable, educational, and meaningful.

The attributes of museums organized as nonprofit, charitable institutions existing to reflect change and continuity in traditional cultural values place them in a unique, and sometimes difficult, position. In 2015, a young white man entered a church in Charleston, South Carolina, and horrifically shot nine African Americans engaged in a bible study. The assailant, after his capture, is seen in widely distributed photographs holding the Confederate battle flag as a banner of admiration. At the time of the killings, the Confederate flag appeared at state houses and on license plates in various ways in numerous states south of the Mason-Dixon line. President Obama, in response to the slayings, called for removing the Confederate flag from South Carolina's state capital and putting it in a museum because of its link to the cause of slavery (Ben Davis, *Why the Confederate Flag Should Not Be Placed in an American Museum*, *Artnet*, June 29, 2015). Consternation over some of his remarks ensued. For countless Americans of all races and creeds, the Confederate flag is emblematic of racist identity and hatred. Placing it any museum may be offensive to many citizens, and its presence could give credence to perverted and outdated notions of "Southern pride and heritage."

Any discussion about artifacts or art in a museum begins with a brief understanding of the various leadership roles in a museum. The board of trustees or directors is responsible for overseeing a museum's policies, executive management, and assets. They must conduct the museum's affairs consistent with a *fiduciary duty* to ensure that it fulfills its primary goal of responsibly serving and educating the public. On a practical level, the day-to-day decisions regarding a museum's collection including what to collect and exhibit is relegated to senior staff, such as the executive director, collections manager, and curator.

Here is the cultural and political rub facing museum leadership that has a Confederate flag in its collection: By failing to remove or deaccession the flag does it endorse this unmistakable mark of white supremacy, slavery, and oppression? On the other hand, do museums have an instructional obligation to display the flag in its historical context by acknowledging it as a symbol of "civil war heritage" and emblem of "hatred"?

Assuredly, these are complex issues left largely to resolution by museums that are classified by collections as historical museums. Yet, the Board of Trustees at the Virginia Museum of Fine Art (VMFA) located in Richmond confronted its own Confederate flag dilemma. More than a dozen years ago the VMFA board entered into an arrangement to lease a chapel it owned adjacent to the museum to the Sons of Confederate Veterans. This group then began to fly a confederate flag at the chapel, which was once the site of infirmed and dying Confederate soldiers. In 2010 the board, concerned about its public image especially in light of its newly designed arts building that stands as a beacon to the city arching forward, asked that the flag be removed. In response, led by social media bloggers, organized groups *against* the flag's removal protested weekly on VMFA's grounds by waving the Confederate flag. The museum's board and executive leadership balanced the right of the public to freely assemble and express their views on state-funded property versus public safety and public relations concerns before forcing its removal.

After the VMFA incident but before the Charleston shooting, an award-winning artist, Sonya Clark, offered an artistic metaphor for America's racial tolerance and healing. Her art involved the Confederate flag. In an exhibition, framed by the curator of the Institute of Contemporary Art museum at Virginia Commonwealth University, Clark and gallery visitors worked together to undo the seams of the flag in an exhibition titled *Unravelling*.

The Clark exhibit was part of a group show that served to demonstrate how a *curator* helps an artist engage the audience in conversation with her art on a controversial subject. One of the roles of a curator is to work with an artist for the purpose of assembling an exhibit that requires the viewer to be responsible for half the work in creating art's meaning, as Marcel Duchamp insisted.

Exhibition spaces are rarely neutral or natural organic sites for discourse. And contentious exhibitions are not limited to the display of artistic relics from the south. The Museum of Fine Arts Boston (MFA) experienced organized Facebook protests when it invited visitors to dress up in a kimono in front of Claude Monet's canvas featuring Camille Monet in a Japanese costume (*La Japonaise*, 1876). The painting, which highlighted the wife of the painter wearing a blond wig and holding a tricolor paper fan, was meant to serve as a comment on the Parisian fad for all things Japanese, according to the MFA's website (http://www.mfa.org/collections/object/la-japonaise -camille-monet-in-japanese-costume). Social media outrage preceded any formal art critic's commentary. Online chatter centered on the lack of education from curators on the painting's context and a failure to describe the meaning of the kimono in Japanese society. The group Stand Against Yellow-Face online posted its objection to this interactive museum experience, "The act of non-Japanese museum staff throwing these kimonos on (visitors) as a 'costume' event is an insult not only to our identities, experiences, and histories as Asian-Americans in America, but affects how society as a whole continues to deny our voices today" (see Brian Boucher, "Outrage at Museum of Fine Arts Boston over Disgraceful 'Dress Up in a Kimono' Event," the *Boston Globe*, July 6, 2015).

A day after the *Boston Globe* exposed social media alarm over what some observers viewed as an inconsiderate interactive exhibition, the MFA apologized for offending any visitors and decided to no longer allow visitors to try on a kimono. The museum stated on its website that when the Monet painting traveled to Japan, visitors there could try on an authentic replica kimono. In the future, the MFA promised to increase the frequency of its museum educators engaging the public about culturally sensitive works of art. Seen in figure 3.1 is a museum visitor in front of the painting that sparked social media indignation.

Returning to the subject of a museum's organizational structure it is, in most instances, either incorporated as a nonprofit company or chartered as a public trust or a hybrid combination. In any case, each entity must follow the statutory filing and recording requirements in the state where it generally conducts museum business. A museum organized as a corporation must have articles of incorporation, by-laws to guide its internal operations, and a board of directors. In a similar fashion for a public trust, the governing body, to wit the board of trustees or directors, must follow the museum's *public purpose* articulated in its charter. All museum board members are obligated to subscribe to the rule of protecting and enhancing the museum's collections and programs, while responsibly managing its physical, human, and financial resources to support the museum's mission. The board must conform to rules, statutes, treaties, and other legal obligations that relate to its operations and collection management. Nearly every museum board has promulgated a *code of ethics* that serves to guide institutional conduct over the activities of board members, executive leadership, staff, and volunteers. The AAM has enacted a Code of Ethics for Museums that its member-organizations generally follow.

Another professional organization, the Association of Art Museum Curators (AAMC), has enacted the following general principles statement as part of a recommended code of ethics or conduct for curators:

> Members of the Association of Art Museum Curators (AAMC) believe that the core mission of art museums is to collect, preserve, study, interpret, and display works of art for the benefit of the public. As dedicated professionals trained in the history of art, curators have a primary responsibility to carry out this mission, in close collaboration with the museum director and other members of the staff. Curators must consider the well being of the museum in which they are employed. These responsibilities must be balanced with the ethics of their scholarly disciplines. Whenever allegiance to ethical standards poses the risk of conflict with the interests of the museum, curators must seek direction from an appropriate authority (their director, department head, or museum counsel). Curators must recognize that they hold positions of trust and should act with uncompromising integrity.

The AAMC's broad code then identifies a curator's chief professional responsibilities and fundamental role as it relates to the museum's collection, exhibitions, scholarship, intellectual property, staff development, works of art, board members, dealers, auction houses, private collectors, artists, personal collecting, the public, and potential conflicts of interest.

Museum-related codes of ethics whether drafted for directors, trustees, curators, or other staff are considered non-legally binding *guidelines* that tend to drive museum practice and assist courts in evaluating questionable policies and conduct. In a later chapter, a museum's compliance with its articulated policies and procedures related to the sale of art from its permanent collection (known as deaccession) and how the proceeds may be used is reviewed in detail. A museum's failure to comply with these standards may lead to a loss of professional institutional accreditation.

An example of questionable ethical practices by one of the world's fore-most public museums recently spilled into the media arena. In 2014, the co-median Bill Cosby and his wife Camille Cosby fully funded the Smithsonian Museum's 50th anniversary tribute to African American art. In addition to their originally undisclosed financial support, they also loaned the National Museum of African Art nearly one-third of all the quilts, paintings, sculpture, and mixed media on display.

Mrs. Cosby sits on this museum's advisory board. She is not a member of its governing board, the Board of Regents. Technically, the Smithsonian's ethical guidelines for accepting an art loan do not apply to non-Regent Board members. However, a popular art-museum blogger, Lee Rosenbaum, has sug-gested her service on the advisory board is a sufficiently strong enough con-nection to have required the museum to have followed the *conflict of interest* review standard required under its code of ethics for Regents. Rosenbaum further observes that the Cosbys are likely to find their art has appreciated in value should they choose to sell it because of its exhibition at the Smithsonian (see Lee Rosenbaum's July 13, 2015, cultural commentary at www.artsjourn al.com/culturegrrl). Additionally, instead of the exhibition serving its stated purpose of inspiring "conversation about the beauty, power and diversity of African art and culture," the public discourse has shifted to the public ac-cusations of rape and drugging against Mr. Cosby. Despite criticism directed toward the Smithsonian on multiple levels including lack of transparency, the Cosby works of art remained on exhibit.

The nonprofit public purpose of museums is a distinctive characteristic of this form of organization that distinguishes it from for-profit entities that exist for the benefit of its shareholders or owners. A museum can obtain tax-exempt status by complying with the filing requirements of the before-mentioned Internal Revenue Service (IRS) Code. As discussed in chapter 1, there are advantages to a museum qualifying for the Section 501(c) (3) charitable organization exemption from federal and state income taxation status. One benefit is that individuals and organizations that donate property, goods, services, or money to the museum might then be eligible to acquire a charitable deduction for the value of what was given. Another reason for a museum to garner this status is that many charitable foundations and grant organizations require cultural institutions to be tax exempt as a condition for receiving funding.

It is significant to recognize that not all the activities of a 501(c) (3) mu-seum are necessarily exempt from taxation. The revenues earned from gift shops, cafes, and licensing of copyrighted art are all potentially subject to income taxation by the government. In addition, some larger municipalities and cities frequently "ask" nonprofit museums to make a contribution for access to public services in lieu of paying a real estate tax.

The character of a museum is not solely dependent on its organizational charter or legal status. The board is duty bound to devise managerial and financial policies for the museum. The executive director and staff put the policies into practice. The governing body for the museum hires the executive director. In turn, the executive director, guided by the board, is responsible for the day-to-day management of the museum enterprise including hiring staff, recruiting and training docents (visitor tour guides), and developing community membership partnerships.

THE BOARD, BANKRUPTCY, AND BAILOUT

The fiduciary challenges of museum board officials to hold onto an art collection, worth billions, held not as an asset but a *public trust*, was never more evident than in the city of Detroit. In 2013, after decades of economic deterioration, Detroit filed for bankruptcy protection against all its creditors in the nation's largest case of its kind. The city suffered from $18 billion in long-term obligations to banks and pensioners it could not repay. In the midst of this legal fight was the Detroit Institute of Art (DIA).

The DIA had its original inspiration not unlike the story told earlier in this chapter about how the rich and cultured business elite of the Gilded Age contributed to the building of permanent museums. In 1883, a board of directors was established in Detroit to help establish a home for significant works of art that had already been donated to an art loan exhibition committee. The success of the thriving auto industry during the first half of the twentieth century matched the expansion of the DIA's fine arts collection and commitment to the community.

The city owned the DIA's physical building and *part* of its extensive collection of fine art from around the world that included murals by Mexican artist Diego Rivera. Originally, Detroit's emergency managers contemplated requiring the Board of DIA to sell off $500 million of its collection to assist the city in working its way out of bankruptcy. In contrast, the bankruptcy judge viewed the DIA as an "invaluable beacon" and thought that if the leaders of DIA were forced to sell off some of its art, Detroit would be forfeiting its future. The court viewed the presence of the DIA as an invaluable cultural and civic tool to attract business, retain citizens, and enhance community pride.

Ultimately, in what was referred to as the "grand bargain," the leaders of DIA at the behest of the bankruptcy judge raised around $800 million from board members, corporate executives, philanthropic leaders, and charitable foundations in return for the transfer of the city's ownership of its share of the art collection to the nonprofit charitable trust that operates and manages the DIA.

Unfortunately, though, in what many observers considered a lesson in fiscal irresponsibility, if not an outright breach of its fiduciary duty, the board handed out significant raises to the museum's most senior managers in the midst of this debilitating statewide financial crisis. This lapse in judgment led to community calls for the resignation of these executive leaders from their positions. In response, members of the board personally reimbursed the museum for the bonuses paid.

Detroit Free Press chronicled the remarkable story of how Detroit was saved by its art in a lengthy report titled "How Detroit was Reborn: The Inside Story of Detroit's Historic Bankruptcy Case" by staff writers Nathan Bomey, John Gallagher, and Mark Stryker.

THE SHEPHERD MUST NOT
BECOME A WOLF: FIDUCIARY DUTIES

Justice Benjamin Cardozo eloquently described the fiduciary duties that apply to a trustee in a landmark decision issued long ago. He wrote that:

> Many forms of conduct permissible in a workaday world for those acting at arm's length, are forbidden to those bound by fiduciary ties. A trustee is held to something stricter than the morals of the market place. Not honesty alone, but the punctilio of an honor the most sensitive, is then the standard of behavior. (*Meinhard v. Salmon*, 164 N.E. 545 [N.Y. 1928])

Cardozo's declaration translates into a legal duty for trustees to be loyal to the institution they serve, act openly and honestly in the best interest of the museum's mission and guiding principles, make full disclosure whenever they have a conflict of interest, care prudently for its core functions, and avoid self-dealing. The charter of a museum is significant as it relates to fiduciary duties. The law recognizes a lower standard of care for directors serving on a nonprofit corporation than trustees serving on a charitable public trust.

Issues related to the fiduciary duties of museum officials are not always simple. For instance, a county-owned fine arts museum in Greenville, South Carolina, was party to a civil lawsuit by a citizen living in the county who believed museum officials breached their duties to the public.

In brief, a long-standing patron and donor had lent twenty-six paintings by Andrew Wyeth to the museum under a standard loan agreement. The agreement acknowledged the unequivocal ownership of the paintings by the museum supporter, Arthur and Holly Magill. Mr. and Mrs. Magill had purchased the paintings privately under a condition that they were to be "donated" to the museum "where they will be preserved for public exhibition." After an eleven-year public display, the museum was informed that they were terminating the loan agreement because the couple had decided to sell the paintings.

The appeals court determined, based largely on an affidavit supplied by a former director of the museum, that the museum did not abuse its discretion in failing to pursue ownership in the paintings. The court further acknowledged statements by museum officials of not wanting to spoil the ongoing positive relationship with the family and their foundation, which included a loan of a group of 230 drawings and sketches by Andrew Wyeth (*Owens v. Magill*, 419 S.E. 2d 786 [S.C. 1992]).

In a resolution that did not lead to a judicial finding, but a negotiated settlement, the Attorney General of New York sued the trustees and executive officers of the Museum of the American Indian-Heye Foundation for breach of the public trust. An independent investigation of museum practices determined trustees had acquired art and artifacts from the museum's gift shop that the executive director had removed from its collection. In another instance of self-dealing, a trustee received over-valued tax deductions and art in exchange for art gifted to the museum. In the aftermath of the investigation, the museum's executive director was removed, and the board of trustees was reformed (see Jason R. Goldstein, "Deaccession: Not Such a Dirty Word," *Cardozo Arts & Entertainment Journal* 15 [1997], 219).

More recently, in 2015, the city of Boston was in an uproar after two drawings, one by Rembrandt worth about $25,000 and another by Dürer estimated to have a value of more than $600,000, had gone missing from the special collections of one of the city's most venerated cultural institutions, the Boston Public Library. These works are among 350,000 prints and drawings, and one million photographs in the library's world-renowned collections held in public trust.

Staff members had known the artwork had disappeared for nearly a year before informing the library's president, Amy Ryan. The day after Ryan submitted her resignation to the library's board of trustees, the lost drawings were found having been merely misfiled. Her resignation followed the commencement of a criminal investigation and the mayor's office publicly criticizing the volunteer trustees for failing to properly conduct oversight over Ryan and her staff. Meanwhile, during Ryan's tenure full time staff in the collections department had fallen by 25 percent. The board's chairperson during the furor over the arts' disappearance strongly supported the library's executive leader. He, too, was forced to resign at the request of Boston's mayor, notwithstanding his earlier donation to the library of more than $750,000. City politicians cited the need to make the library more accountable to the taxpayers of Boston. Soon after both resignations the library commenced safety inspections, inventory control audits, and collection management overhauls.

Both the library's president and chairperson of its board of trustees unconditionally are held to the highest standard of institutional care and management. The failures of Ryan's staff to timely inform her of the missing drawings was ultimately her undoing, and by extension, the reason for the departure of the chairperson of the board of trustees. This case illustrates the *subjective* nature of reviewing decisions of museums officials by public officials, where there are no obvious indications of misconduct or criminal behavior. ⌐

SUMMARY

The advance of fine arts museums in America coincided with the increase in fortunes of post–Civil War industrialists. Unlike in Europe, where museums are usually owned and operated by governments, the model in the United States is for private individuals or foundations to transfer assets into a private nonprofit corporation or public charitable trust chartered as a museum. These entities are nearly always tax-exempt 501(c) (3) organs under the IRS Code, which then permits donors to deduct the fair-market value of their gifts.

All museums function as partners with the community they serve. A fine arts museum's identity frequently turns on the nature and quality of the art collected, preserved, and exhibited along with the esteem of the artists represented. Taken as a whole, a museum's collection reflects the institution's cultural values. The manner in which a museum engages the public by serving as a community focus, organizing accessible exhibitions, outreaching to underrepresented groups, and collecting and preserving interesting and inspirational fine art is the responsibility of museum officials. These officials are obligated to act in the best interests of the public under ethical guidelines, and operate consistent with the legal fiduciary duties that are imposed on trustees and directors.

WORKS REFERENCED

Tony Ambrose and Crispin Paine, *Museum Basics*, 3rd ed., New York: Routledge, 2012.

Charles Bryan Baron, "Self-Dealing Trustees and the Exoneration Clause: Can Trustees Ever Profit from Transactions Involving Trust Property?," in *St. John's Law Review*, 72:1, No. 1, winter 1998, and updated March 2012.

"Bill Cosby Art Exhibit Will Go On at Smithsonian Despite Sexual Assault Scandal," in the *Associated Press*, July 13, 2015.

"Code of Ethics for Museums," *American Alliance of Museums*, Washington, DC, n.d.

Matthew Dolan, "In Detroit Bankruptcy, Art Was Key to the Deal," in the *Wall Street Journal*, Nov. 7, 2014.

Leonard DuBoff and Christy King, *Art Law*, 3rd ed., St. Paul, MN: West Publishing, 2000.

Hirakyama Hina, "The Boston Athenaeum and the Creation of Boston's Museum of Fine Arts," in *The Boston Athenaeum: Bicentennial Essays*, ed. Richard Wendorf, Boston: Boston Athenaeum, 2009.

Martin Kemp, *The Oxford History of Western Art*, New York: Oxford University Press, 2000.

Elaine King and Gail Levin, *Ethics and the Visual Arts*, New York: Allworth Press, 2010.

Robert Lind, Robert Jarvis, and Marilyn Phelan, *Art and Museum Law: Cases and Materials*, Durham, NC: Carolina Academic Press, 2002.

Brian MacQuarrie, "Library Chairman Set to Step Down," in the *Boston Globe*, June 11, 2015.

Marie Malaro and Ildiko Pogany DeAngelis, *A Legal Primer on Managing Museum Collections*, 3rd ed., Washington, DC: Smithsonian Books, 2012.

Paula Marincola (ed.), *What Makes A Great Exhibition*, Philadelphia: Philadelphia Exhibitions Initiative, 2006.

John Henry Merryman, Albert Elsen, and Stephen Urice, eds., *Law, Ethics and the Visual Arts*, 5th ed., Frederick, MD: Kluwer Law, 2007.

"Museum Definition," *International Council on Museums*, Vienna, 2016.

"Museum Facts," *American Alliance of Museums*, Washington, DC, n.d.

"Picasso and Chicago," *Art Institute of Chicago*, Chicago. 2013.

"Professional Practices for Art Museum Curators," *Association of Art Museum Curators*, New York, 2007.

Roberta Smith, "When Exhibitions Have More to Say Than to Show," in the *New York Times,* April 13, 2003.

Tony Vevers, *The Beginnings of the Provincetown Art Association and Museum*, *Provincetown Art Association and Museum: The Permanent Collection*, Provincetown, MA: Provincetown Art Association, 1999.

"Visitor Statistics," *Press Room of the Smithsonian Institution*, Washington, DC, n.d.

4

Acquisitions
Good Title, Theft, Forgery, and Authentication

"We are inclined to believe those whom we do not know because they
have never deceived us."

—Samuel Johnson (*The Works of Samuel Johnson*)

Acquiring fine art, sculpture, or cultural artifacts is not always a straightforward process. Unlike the purchase of living room furniture from a department store, just because you bought a work of fine art for value does not necessarily mean you own it. Establishing good title before exercising a transaction by searching its provenance or history of ownership is an important first step for a collector, auction house, dealer, or museum. An art object may possess an impeccable chain of ownership, however, it is not the exclusive answer to the issue of good title. In the United States a person cannot acquire good title from stolen art. The work itself may be a forgery and not be authentic. An art expert that issues a certificate of authenticity might change his or her opinion based on new facts or revelatory technology. A buyer relying upon one expert's professional judgment that is disputed by a different art appraiser or art historian expert might cause the value of the acquired art to decrease dramatically, which might lead to breach of warranty claims. Another concern, especially for works of antiquities and even postmodern art, is that because of their rarity they may have acquired a unique intrinsic, and sometimes sentimental, "inflated" value. In a celebrity-driven commercial world, art connected to the social status of the seller may impact the work's market value. A fundamental duty exists for a buyer of an object d'art to examine the work's provenance, authenticity, and value before making a purchase. It is also imperative to know and trust the party that is selling or brokering the art transaction.

Chapter 5 addresses the specific ownership concerns including provenance of cross-border art transactions dealing with cultural property and fine art, in particular, Nazi-era art. The material in this chapter focuses on title, theft, forgery, and authentication issues related to acquiring works of art.

GOOD TITLE AND THEFT

In his book *Master Thieves*, Pulitzer Prize–winning reporter Stephen Kurkjian attributes the 1990 nighttime theft of thirteen works of art from the Isabella Stewart Gardner Museum in Boston to two low-level career criminals who gained entry into the museum disguised as police officers. The never-recovered priceless paintings and sketches by Rembrandt, Vermeer, Degas, and others vanished apparently because of poor museum security. The loss of these irreplaceable works of art resonates with the public because of the magnitude of the financial harm and the cultural value associated with the purloined masterpieces. In many countries, it is not uncommon for the public to perceive thefts of cultural objects and treasured art as a "national disgrace," according to Kurkjian (see figure 4.1).

The motives for the Gardner Museum heist, along with works stolen in similar fashion from other museums, are rarely fully known or understood. It is clear that in the United States a party that steals art can never pass good title to a subsequent acquirer. The proper protocol for a gallery, auction house, museum, or individual interested in acquiring fine art and cultural objects is to first check the database of the Art Loss Registry, the world's largest database of art theft, to determine whether it is listed as stolen property.

The Isabella Stewart Gardner Museum robbery led to the passage of the **Theft of Major Artwork Act** (18 U.S.C. section 668, effective 1994). This act makes stealing objects of art older than 100 years and worth more than $5,000 or any work of art valued in excess of $100,000 from a museum a federal crime. Those parties that knowingly receive, conceal, or dispose of stolen art are equally subject to a felony charge that carries the possibility of twenty years of incarceration and a substantial fine. The statute of limitations for this offense is twenty years.

Admired artists are not immune to theft. In 2015, a longtime assistant to the American painter and printmaker Jasper Johns pled guilty to having sold dozens of works of art he had stolen from the artist to a New York gallery. In an elaborate scheme of betrayal the assistant, James Meyer, filched incom-

Figure 4.1. *Christ in the Storm of the Sea of Galilee,* Rembrandt. *Photo image courtesy of Isabella Stuart Gardner Museum, Boston.*

plete artworks from Johns's studio. He then falsely established certificates of authenticity identifying himself as the lawful owner stating the works were gifts from the artist. A conditional requirement imposed on those that purchased the art from the gallery was that they were prohibited from loaning, exhibiting, or reselling the works for at least eight years as a way to elude discovery. A federal court ordered Meyer to forfeit all proceeds from the sales, which amounted to about $4 million, and sentenced him to eighteen months of incarceration.

Whether a museum acquires works of art by gift or purchase, a *best practices* policy, in addition to reviewing the appropriate art-loss registries and examining provenance, is to keep detailed records related to the acquisition. For objects of significant value another consideration is to publicly release a watermarked digital image of the object so the community of art experts, directors, collectors, and archivists may scrutinize the new acquisition.

In general, there are three defenses advanced to prevent a party that has lost art through theft from recovering it: *statute of limitations*, *doctrine of laches*, and *adverse possession*. The affirmative defenses of laches and statute of limitations are sometimes raised in those situations when museums seek to hold on to Holocaust-era acquired art with a disputed title. These blocking strategies are thoroughly discussed in the following chapter on Nazi-era art. The third defense, adverse possession, is more a real property legal action that historically has little application in the personal property museum-art world. However, a museum or collector that possesses an object of art of unclear ownership could attempt to perfect title by demonstrating to the world that it has held this property openly, visibly, exclusively, notoriously, and continuously for twenty or more years. The time period required depends on the applicable state statute.

The few courts that have addressed the application of the doctrine of adverse possession with works of art have pointed out the practical difficulty of determining what constitutes open and notorious possession. Simply put, to establish title in this manner the issue may boil down to whether displaying a work of art in a person's home or having a work of art being a part of a museum's collection without actually exhibiting it gives satisfactory notice to the owner. The Supreme Court of New Jersey addressed these concerns in a case where Georgia O'Keeffe sought the return of paintings apparently stolen from her. The art dealer who possessed the paintings asserted he purchased them for value, and acquired title by adverse possession (*O'Keeffe v. Snyder*, 416 A.2d 862 [1980]).

Somewhat surprisingly, a loophole for a recognized museum to acquire good title by adverse possession exists under the **Convention on Cultural Property Implementation Act** (19 U.S.C. 2601, amended 1987). This federal statute was enacted to help eliminate the smuggling of stolen cultural property into the United States. It has a provision that prevents the seizure of cultural property, and archaeological and ethnological materials imported after April 1983 that were acquired by a museum in good faith without knowing they might have been illegally stolen, and have been publicly exhibited and properly catalogued, and held for a period of not less than three consecutive years. Apart from this provision there are other enumerated statutory time periods available for a museum to acquire valid ownership by adverse possession. There are no reported cases of museums employing this method to establish good title.

The **1970 UNESCO Convention** promulgated a code of ethics that requires its member states to stop acquiring any object illegally removed from its country of origin. In the United States, this declaration applies only to federal agencies responsible for museum collections, such as the National Park Service (National Park Museum), Smithsonian, US Postal Service (National Postal Museum), American Art Museum, and National Portrait Gallery among many others. For private museums and cultural institutions there is no similar legislative compliance requirement to avoid purchasing or accepting by donation illegally removed objects from foreign countries. Nevertheless, museums that adhere to the policies and protocols of the Association of Art Museum Directors (AAMD) are now obliged to assume undocumented cultural objects are deemed title deficient unless provenance research can demonstrate the objects in the collection were outside the country of foreign origin before 1970.

GOOD TITLE AND FORGERY

Authors Laney Salisbury and Aly Sujo chronicle one of the most astonishing and far-reaching frauds in the history of art forgery in the book *Provenance*. The ultimate con man, John Drewe, in concert with the affable former British art teacher John Myatt, exploited the upper echelons of the *archives* of the most esteemed fine art museums in England, such as the Tate Museum and London's Institute of Contemporary Art, to legitimize hundreds of paintings they forged.

The conspiracy began in the 1980s when Drewe, a collector of Myatt's nineteenth and twentieth-century "Genuine fakes" paintings, began consigning them as original art to prominent auction houses like Christie's, Phillips, and Sotheby's in the major art markets of New York, Paris, and London. Myatt perfected his painting technique to resemble the style of master artists such as Le Corbusier, Dubuffet, Matisse, Nicholson, and Giacometti.

Their first successful art scam occurred in 1986 when Drewe purchased Myatt's reproduction of Albert Gleizes's Cubic pencil sketch *Portrait of an Army Doctor* and took it to Christie's in London. The auction house authenticated the portrait as real and its experts valued it at more than $70,000 in present dollars. Drewe then began to rely upon middlemen dealers to help unload the forged art that was now accompanied by a copy of a falsified bill of sale, bogus exhibition label on the hardboard, or fabricated mention of the work in a handwritten letter from the original painter. In some cases the provenance material was stamped "For Private Research Only/Tate Gallery Archive," which lent even greater credence to the hoax.

Provenance this perfect especially for a flawless Giacometti about to be acquired by a Japanese collector ultimately was their undoing. Extensive and diligent fact-finding work by a Giacometti scholar responsible for his catalogue raisonné led to the discovery that Drewe was revising a painting's history. The investigating Art and Antique Squad, Scotland Yard, were less offended by Myatt's role. The chief police detective in the case was quoted as saying art forgers were a "healthy component to the art system" because they forced dealers, collectors, auction houses, and museums to look more closely at the works they elected to authenticate (*Provenance* p. 242). Drewe's offense of deliberately tampering with a painting's cultural heritage was the greater crime.

By 1990 the ruse was over. Myatt confessed to giving Drewe over 240 fake paintings and drawings. Sixty of the forgeries were found leaving nearly 200 remaining in museums, art dealers, and the homes of private collectors. Myatt served four months in jail for his role. Drewe spent two years incarcerated for conspiring to alter provenance to fake paintings sold as genuine works of art.

In the aftermath of the deception perpetrated on the art community by John Myatt, and more recently, Mark Landis, the International Art and Artists society designed a groundbreaking traveling exhibition. The purpose of the exhibition was twofold: to illuminate the audacity and occasional bizarre charm of the forgers and to ask whether the uncovering of a work of art's unpalatable history makes it any less of a work of art. Figure 4.2 is Myatt's copy of Vermeer's *Girl with a Pearl Earring* exhibited at the Ringling Brother Museum of Art.

Figure 4.2. Exhibit cover catalog featuring John Myatt's copy of Vermeer's *Girl with the Pearl Earring. Photo image courtesy of Colette Loll/artfraudinsights.com.*

After serving his time in jail, Myatt, the man Scotland Yard claims committed "the biggest art fraud of the 20th century," became a successful commercial visual fine artist. The BBC hired him to host a TV show *Fame in Frame*, where he paints celebrities in different styles. Myatt has even appeared on the popular *Antiques Roadshow* program.

An American counterpart to the skilled copycat painting talent of Myatt and the deception techniques of Drewe is Mark Landis. He, too, forged works of well-known art and falsified ownership documents to create a believable paper trail. Unlike other forgers, Landis was not motivated by financial gain. Under the guise of various aliases, Landis approached numerous museums, such as Oklahoma City Museum of Art and Hillard University Art Museum in Louisiana, offering to donate counterfeit art on behalf of his deceased mother and father. Law enforcement investigators never charged Landis with a crime because he received no economic benefit and the museums were deemed neglectful in failing to take steps to authenticate the artworks before accepting them into their collection. In 2014, Landis was featured in the well-received film documentary *Art and Craft*.

GOOD TITLE AND AUTHENTICATION

The ability of art forgers and even thieves to fool curators and art experts points out a weakness in the system for *authenticating* works of art. Historically, a two-prong approach is used to authenticate art: an *art expert* stating that the work reflects the artist's style, technique, and signature, and *provenance* based on the paper trail of ownership, exhibition, and sales history. A third technique known as *technical analysis* is coming into vogue. This technique relies upon a variety of scientific methods to determine the age and composition of an artist's materials, such as radiography, electron microscopy, and chemical analysis. It is a helpful approach in determining whether a work of art is genuine or not. However, its use is limited because it cannot verify whether the work is by a given artist. These three approaches when used together help create a consensus of evidence for determining authentication in an area of law and ethics fraught with confusion and frustration.

Increasingly, mathematicians are playing an intriguing, but not always consistent, role in looking for patterns to assist art experts in verifying the authenticity of a painting or drawing. For instance, in a study published in the *Proceedings of the National Academy of Sciences* (Online edition November 22–26, 2004), scientists at Dartmouth College used high-resolution digital images of drawings by Bruegel to encapsulate data about stroke patterns and signatures. These data were then compared against other artworks attributed to Bruegel to look for

64 *Chapter 4*

inconsistencies and consistencies. The hypothesis is that this same technique could be applied to other artists where there is no dispute about a work's genuineness against works attributed to the same artists to determine authenticity.

The International Council on Museums (ICOM) International Observatory on Illicit Traffic in Cultural Goods provides excellent online examples at pbs-traffic.museum/authentication on the use of sophisticated scientific analysis to help uncover fake cultural objects. *Fake* art is generally described as an object or work of fine art that is not what it is held out to be, as opposed to *forged* art, which involves falsifying documents to support a stolen or fake object or art form's provenance. Courts, though, frequently use these terms interchangeably. The International Foundation for Art Research conducted the x-ray imaging in the photograph in figure 4.3 that illustrates the existence of modern soldering pins in a cultural object that was presented as an ancient Assyrian bronze statuette. Distinguish this case, though, from a situation

 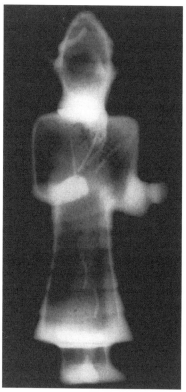

Figure 4.3. Image on left Assyrian bronze statue. Image on right modern soldering pins. *Photo images courtesy of International Foundations for Art (IFAR).*

where for conservatorship purposes highly skilled professionals engage in remedial and preventive conservation to halt the deterioration of an object. In these instances, detailed records by the conservator including photographs should accompany the object or painting to document its history to prevent any future confusion or misrepresentation over authenticity.

In 2007, Harvard University completed a yearlong scientific examination of the chemical makeup of the pigments found on three recently discovered paintings purportedly by the Abstract Expressionist artist Jackson Pollock. Pollock died in a car crash in 1956. Some of the pigments analyzed were not commercially available until after his death, thereby calling into question the likelihood that the paintings were genuine. On the other hand, critics retorted that someone might have added paint to the original paintings after his death.

A few years earlier, these three and other acknowledged Pollock works collectively referred to as the "Matter" paintings were subject to a different study by a physicist at Case Western Reserve who employed a mathematical practice referred to as fractal analysis. This process requires programming a computer to look for replications of geometric drip patterns. According to the professor's criteria, none of the undisputed Pollock paintings were deemed authentic. Upon the reporting of these findings, the consensus among scientists was that fractal analysis is not a reliable tool for deciding the authenticity of paintings or at least Pollock's paintings.

An example of a lingering dispute on legitimacy occurred when Boston College's McMullen Museum enlisted another Case Western University professor, Ellen Landau, to authenticate the same three Pollock paintings that Harvard's researchers had studied. Their groundbreaking exhibition explored the inspirational and personal relationship between Pollock and the photographer Herbert Matter, and their respective artistic spouses. Professor Landau, who is considered one of the leading Pollock scholars, curated the exhibition. Meanwhile, the Pollock-Krasner Foundation retained an art historian who authored the complete work (catalog raisonné) of Pollock's art and is a well-recognized art dealer to publicly dispute the authenticity of these exhibited paintings. Ironically, all three of the so-called art experts had at one time served together on the now-dissolved foundation's Pollock-Krasner Authentication Board.

Similar authentication disputes occur in Europe. The innovative Dutch-based Rembrandt Research Project relied upon forensic evidence, documentation, and painting techniques to determine the genuineness of works by Rembrandt and contemporary artists who worked in his studio. The project reduced the number of genuine Rembrandt self-portraits in half. Yet, the decades-long project raised serious doubts about the ability of some of the world's most progressive technology to conclusively determine authenticity.

In 2011, the project was abandoned after completing its final survey or corpus of Rembrandt's works that was published in 2014.

AUTHENTICATION LAWSUITS: EUROPE

Disputes over the accuracy and validity of authentication opinions offered by art experts, estates, foundations, and findings from technical compositional analysis have led to an explosion in lawsuits in the United States and Europe. In some European countries, only members of a deceased artist's immediate family are authorized to authenticate. The basis for this power rests in the *moral right of paternity*. This is a legal status conferred on an artist, and after death passes to the artist's heirs or close friends, under international law, the **Berne Convention**. In other countries, courts designate an art historian or a scholar that compiles a catalogue raisonné as the "expert" to decide on authenticity. Regardless of the country and the circumstances, it is evident that there is no absolutely undeniably objective nor infallible test to determine authenticity. At best, those that authenticate are offering an opinion that can be challenged on ethical conflict of interest grounds, personal motivation, or inadequate legal exercise of judgment.

Figure 4.4.　Image *The Cardsharps*, Caravaggio. *Kimball Art Museum.*

One of the most recent legal disputes over authenticity took place in a courtroom in England. Mr. Lancelot William Thawytes sued Sotheby's for auctioning off the painting depicted within, see figure 4.4, as by being by a follower of one of the great Italian painters of the Baroque period—Michelangelo Merisi (1571–1610), known as Caravaggio after his birthplace near Milan.

In 2006, heeding Sotheby's advice on authorship, Thwaytes sold the painting for £42,000. The buyer was a straw man for an art collector and renowned Caravaggio scholar, Sir Denis Mahon. He had the painting cleaned and restored, while conducting research on its authenticity. Relying upon the opinion of an Italian scholar, Mina Gregori, he declared the painting an original Caravaggio dating back to 1595, and not a copy. Furthermore, Mahon claimed it has a market value of £10 million or more than $15 million. The painting was lent to the Museum of the Order of St. John at Clerkenwell in London, where it was insured for the full value, as though it was an authentic painting by Caravaggio.

The Thwaytes lawsuit was filed in England. There the High Court of Justice Chancery Division held that Sotheby's in-house experts and outside consultants exercised reasonable due care in determining that the quality of the painting was insufficient to determine that it might be a painting by Caravaggio. In a side-note that relates to the question of who is equipped to determine authenticity, the judge in this civil suit was criticized in some legal quarters because she actively participated and interjected her own thoughts over authenticity. The prevailing English view on this matter, as articulated in a Queen's Bench decision, *Drake v. Thos. Agnew & Sons Ltd.* (2002) EWHC 294 (QB), is that magistrates are not experts in art history and are supposed to judge the experts, not the art (*Thwaytes v. Sotheby's* [2015] EWHC 36 [Ch]).

An additional European case is worth evaluating because it serves as an instructive guide on how a court distinguishes between the opinions of art experts who examine an artist's style and technique versus a scientist who conducts chemical analysis on the painting. A Dutch Court of Appeals was asked to rule on the authenticity of initially five paintings, later two. In reviewing the evidence on genuineness offered by the art experts, the court noted that it was primarily based on "experience and intuition" making it difficult to explain, and arguably, hard to accept. In contrast, the forensic research findings of a painting conservator that evaluated the paint pigments had determined the ground layer paint did not match the artist's other paintings and a pigment was detected that did not exist before the date of the creation on the painting. Based on the conservator's scientific investigations the two paintings were deemed forgeries by the court.

Shortly after this 2012 judicial verdict, Milko den Leeuw, the art conservator whose opinion the Dutch Appeals Court trusted to confirm that the two paintings were counterfeit, cowrote a masterful article on authentication issues. He posted the piece on the website for the newly established nonprofit organization Authentication in Art (see www.authenticationinart.org/about -us/aia-foundation).

den Leeuw lays blame for the mercurial increase in authenticity lawsuits to multiple causes: the greed to acquire original works by new, wealthy buyers is so massive that the market cannot keep pace with the demand; art forgers familiar with master artists' painting techniques and using appropriate materials working with corrupt art dealers and experts have stepped forward to fill this insatiable demand; buyers eager to purchase old masters and contemporary paintings bank upon these hearsay recommendations; and old-school art experts state opinions that frequently conflict with new material scientists' findings leaving courts in a dilemma regarding whose opinion to believe. Meanwhile, collectors are susceptible to purchasing fakes that look genuine and genuine works that may be fakes, and honorable dealers and auction houses can find themselves responding to civil complaints for financial reimbursement from unhappy purchasers. In den Leeuw's view, the challenge to the profession is to respond to these remarkable changes in buying high-end art for an investment rather than its aesthetic appeal is by agreeing to "rigorous analytical protocol based on objective technical investigation in combination with the painting and technique of original paintings and art historical research." Of course, this approach is not without considerable outlay in time and money that may be beyond the budget of many collectors, dealers, and museums.

Meanwhile, in 2014, a French court upheld an art expert's right *not* to authenticate a work of art. In this instance, the expert possessed the legal moral right to authenticate works by the French painter, Jean Metzinger. The owner of the painting believed the work was by Metzinger, and needed a certificate of authentication to complete the sale. The painting's owner sued the Metzinger expert for failing to authenticate the work. At the lower court level, the court-appointed expert opined that the painting was worthy of authentication as a work by Metzinger. The authorized Metzinger expert refused to comply with the court's order to authenticate. She appealed the decision, including the assessment of damages and fines. The appeals court relied upon Articles 9 and 10 of the **European Convention on Human Rights** in reversing the original holding. The higher court recognized her right not to authenticate as a basic element of freedom of thought and expression.

Authentication Lawsuits: United States

A long-ago federal court decision summarized the basic posture in the United States regarding whether an art expert is expressing an opinion on authenticity based on evidence known at the time or stating a fact that a subsequent purchaser may trust even to his or her detriment. In *Reeves v. Corning* (51 F. 774 [C.C.D. Ind. 1892]), the court stated that it "will take into consideration the intelligence and situation of the parties, the general information and experience of the people as to the nature and use of the property [art], the habits and methods of those dealing in or with it, and then determine, upon all the circumstances of the case, whether the representations ought to have been understood as affirmations of fact, or as matters of opinion or judgment."

The issue of *fact versus opinion* and *justifiable or reasonable reliance* by a buyer or museum patron who seeks advice from a museum curator regarding a work's authenticity not surprisingly has led to litigation. In some instances, the cause of action is negligent or intentional *misrepresentation*, or *defamation*. A museum that offers authentications gratis or for free usually will not be liable for damages in the event the opinion offered is incorrect because there is no financial gain from the relationship. To avoid any whiff of liability, though, many museums follow the stated practice of the Montgomery (Alabama) Museum of Art, which is, "Museum personnel do not appraise or authenticate works of art. The Museum has a non-circulating reference library of publications related to art and art history that is available for use by Museum staff and Docents, College and University Professors or students (with current valid ID or other credentials) and Members of the MMFA Association. The library holdings are available for use by appointment only." In contrast, an in-house auction expert, appraiser, or dealer who mistakenly or purposefully expresses a false opinion, where there is a direct pecuniary gain, runs the risk of civil liability. A disclaimer release form that requires the party seeking an appraisal or authentication opinion to hold harmless and indemnify the museum for any opinion rendered is a way to limit exposure to a lawsuit based on a negligent misrepresentation claim.

An attempted application of a gross negligence claim against an auction house occurred when a buyer purchased at auction a painting attributed to Mary Cassatt at $650,000. Terms of the purchase, written in Sotheby's auction catalogue, indicated the painting would be sold accompanied by a letter from a leading Cassatt expert "discussing" the work. Included in the sale was an express warranty from Sotheby's guaranteeing the authenticity of the painting for five years. About five years after the auction the buyer asked to receive a copy of the letter regarding the painting's authenticity. The expert cautioned that her opinion was based on reviewing a transparency, not the original painting. A year later, after the five-year conditional guarantee period had expired, Sotheby's informed the buyer that the Mary Cassatt Authentication Committee questioned the work's genuineness. The court dismissed the claim for failure to demonstrate justifiable reliance on Sotheby's representations regarding the painting's authenticity (*Foxley v. Sotheby's*, 893 F. Supp. 1224 [S.D.N.Y. 1995]). Apparently, the buyer's own negligence in not seeking the "authentication" correspondence earlier led to the case's discharge, which is a fairly heavy burden in light of the buyer's presumptive reliance on the overall good reputation of Sotheby's.

Sotheby's, like all the major fine arts auction houses, spells out its written guarantee or express warranty in its Terms of Agreement provision, which is found in all of its auction catalogs. Reviewing the key definitional catalog terms and conditions delivers insight into how the industry has attempted to self-regulate the opinion-versus-fact authenticity controversy. Sotheby's conditional pledge to guarantee authenticity or authorship for five years for the original buyer at auction follows:

TERMS OF GUARANTEE

As set forth below and in the Conditions of Sale, for all lots Sotheby's guarantees that the authorship, period, culture or origin (collectively, "Authorship") of each lot in this catalogue is as set out in the BOLD or CAPITALIZED type heading in the catalogue description of the lot, as amended by oral or written sales-room notes or announcements. Purchasers should refer to the Glossary of Terms, if any, for an explanation of the terminology used in the Bold or Capitalized type heading and the extent of the Guarantee. Sotheby's makes no warranties whatsoever, whether express or implied, with respect to any material in the catalogue other than that appearing in the Bold or Capitalized heading and subject to the exclusions below.

In the event Sotheby's in its reasonable opinion deems that the conditions of the Guarantee have been satisfied, it shall refund to the original purchaser of record the hammer price and applicable Buyer's Premium paid for the lot by the original purchaser of record. This Guarantee does not apply if: (i) the catalogue description was in accordance with the opinion(s) of generally accepted scholar(s) and expert(s) at the date of the sale, or the catalogue description indicated that there was a conflict of such opinions; or (ii) the only method of establishing that the Authorship was not as described in the Bold or Capitalized heading at the date of the sale would have been by means or processes not then generally available or accepted; unreasonably expensive or impractical to use; or likely (in Sotheby's reasonable opinion) to have caused damage to the lot or likely to have caused loss of value to the lot; or (iii) there has been no material loss in value of the lot from its value had it been in accordance with its description in the Bold or Capitalized-type heading. This Guarantee is provided for a period of five (5) years from the date of the relevant auction, is solely for the benefit of the original purchaser of record at the auction and may not be transferred to any third party. To be able to claim under this Guarantee of Authorship, the original purchaser of record must: (i) notify Sotheby's in writing within three (3) months of receiving any information that causes the original purchaser of record to question the accuracy of the Bold or Capitalized type heading, specifying the lot number, date of the auction at which it was purchased and the reasons for such question; and (ii) return the Lot to Sotheby's at the original selling location in the same condition as at the date of sale to the original purchaser of record and be able to transfer good title to the Lot, free from any third party claims arising after the date of such sale. Sotheby's has discretion to waive any of the above requirements. Sotheby's may require the original purchaser of record to obtain at the original purchaser of record's cost the reports of two independent and recognized experts in the field, mutually acceptable to Sotheby's and the original purchaser of record. Sotheby's shall not be bound by any reports produced by the original purchaser of record, and reserves the right to seek additional expert advice at its own expense. It is specifically understood and agreed that the rescission of a sale and the refund of the original purchase price paid (the successful hammer price, plus the buyer's premium) is exclusive and in lieu of any other remedy which might otherwise be available to the original purchaser of record as a matter of law, or in equity. Sotheby's and the Consignor shall not be liable for any incidental or consequential damages incurred or claimed, including without limitation, loss of profits or interest.

In addition to authentication disputes, a unique "failure to appraise" case demonstrates a linked picture of the sordid underbelly of the global art world. In this instance, the National Gallery of Art in Washington, DC, was charged with failing to conduct *due diligence* to make sure that the art it acquired from a dealer was *not* purchased under fraudulent conditions. The family of the prior owner of paintings by the Russian-born French artist Soutine alleged two Soutine experts falsified the true market value of the paintings. The experts then, working with other intermediaries, turned around and acquired the paintings, and flipped them to the National Gallery for twice their original $1 million purchase price. In an out-of-court settlement, the two New York–based experts agreed to pay the family $210,000, while the National Art Gallery settled the case by returning the paintings to the heirs and receiving a small profit (see www.blouinartinfo.com/news/story/274126/soutine-suit-settled-over-bargain-beef).

Interestingly, a major player in the art world who is well known for operating a large art facility that stores and transports art, frequently tax free, in Geneva, Switzerland, allegedly was part of the art expert group that tricked the elderly owner of the Soutine paintings to sell them for below market value, according to a report by *Forbes* (March 12, 2015). This same art broker, Yves Bouvier, was arrested in 2015 for complicity with money laundering and criminal fraud in an unrelated case in the Principality of Monaco.

Authentication boards, such as the Pollock-Krasner Foundation and the Andy Warhol Authentication Board, have been sued by collectors for anti-trust

restraint of trade violations, conspiracy to create a monopoly, and unjust enrich-
ment grounds for failing to authenticate. In general, these civil suits have failed;
however, they do draw attention to a fault-line in having a cadre of self-serving
authenticators effectively control the supply market, and therefore impact
the value, of already authenticated works of art (see 890 F. Supp. [S.D.N.Y.
1995]). In defending itself in one civil lawsuit, the Andy Warhol Authentication
Foundation spent nearly $7 million in defense fees, leading it in 2012 to cease
conducting authentications.

An alternative claim that has occasionally arisen in the "fact versus opinion" authentication process is the civil action tort of *defamation*. Historically,
spoken words causing harm to one's reputation are referred to as *slander*,
whereas written words or symbols that invade a person's interest in his or her
good name is known as *libel*. Today, defamation is used as the catch-all term
for libel and slander.

An example of an arts-related defamation dispute occurred when the Keith
Haring Foundation, acting in its capacity as authenticator and protector of the
integrity of works by the social activist painter, Keith Haring, was sued for
defamation over a press release. The controversy began when collectors exhibited two hundred works of art, ostensibly by Haring, for public sale. Some
of the drawings and paintings had been previously adjudged not authentic by
the foundation. Originally, the foundation sued the organizers of the "Haring
Miami" show to enjoin or prevent the group from displaying the allegedly
forged works. Initially, the parties reached an out-of-court settlement that
included destroying all catalogues and brochures. The foundation issued a
press release that announced the group agreed to remove any "fake Haring
works" from the show.

The organizers then turned around and charged the foundation with defamation in a New York federal district court. The collectors argued one of the
reasons behind the foundation's disparaging statement was to hurt sales at the
Miami Design District's show. Additionally, the aggrieved group argued that
the foundation acted in its own self-interest and benefited at their expense
by failing to fully evaluate the disputed works. The civil complaint stated
that many of the works were acquired directly from close friends of Haring,
including a former lover. It valued the so-called fakes at $40 million. The
foundation disclosed it would cease conducting authentication evaluations
presumably to avoid similar litigation headaches.

For the nine collectors that brought suit against the foundation to prevail in
their defamation suit they will have to prove, under state law, that the press
release statements made about the "fakes" are construed to reflect badly on
their reputations as the owners of the disputed works. The requirements to
prove a defamation case vary from state to state. In general, though, the collec-

tors must show that the factual statement was false; the statement injured their reputations; the statement was published to a third party and a third party would recognize the false statement as referring to them; and they have been injured.

Frankly, these kinds of defamation cases are difficult to win. The foundation's position is that its public announcement clearly regarding the "fakes" was mere opinion. And, even if its opinion is false, that is, some or all of the so-called "fakes" are actually real works by Haring, it was its opinion at the time that they were not genuine. On the flip side, the collectors acknowledge that while the **First Amendment** grants the foundation some leeway in addressing issues of public concern regarding protecting the integrity of Haring's oeuvre and not misleading the public about their authenticity, in this case the foundation was derelict in its duty. Specifically, according to the complaint filed, the foundation acted irrationally and irresponsibly be operating "in secret, with little or no explanation and often without ever physically inspecting the works."

STATUTORY PROTECTION

Finally, unlike the prior cases where a purchaser or collector seeks a remedy from the seller of a fake or forged work of art under a breach of warranty contract theory or a misrepresentation or fraud tort related cause of action, **Article 2** of the **Uniform Commercial Code** (**U.C.C.**) allows for a different type of warranty relief. Specifically, under section 2-313, buyers of goods, and sales of works of art are considered goods under the statute, and may recover the difference between the value of the non-genuine work and the value of the work had it been real. To win, the buyer must have relied upon representations regarding the genuineness of the work as a basis of the bargain. The advantage to this reprieve is that the buyer does not have to accept a substitute offer because of the unique nature of artworks. This section of the sales law protection for buyers generally has a four-year warranty from the time of sale, which is a year less than most major auction houses grant. A different section of this sales law permits the parties to rescind their bargain when it is difficult to determine the art was a counterfeit before the sale was consummated, as explained below.

In light of the inconsistent, and sometimes difficult, application of the U.C.C.'s *express warranty* provision to the opinion versus fact authentication controversy the state of New York passed a specific law to address the issue more precisely. The **New York Arts and Cultural Affairs** statute also deals with the classic *mutual mistake* situation. The landmark mutual mistake case, as told by many contract law professors to their students, occurred when both the buyer and seller mutually believed the cow that was being transferred for consideration was barren. The cow was to sell for about one-tenth the price of a fertile cow. Before the deal was consummated the seller discovered the cow was with calf. The court agreed with the seller's request to rescind the sale based on the mutual fact that both parties were mistaken about the fact that the cow was not barren.

In the art world context, this doctrine often deals with a claim that both parties were mutually mistaken as to a painting's authenticity or authorship. Not all courts are quick to rescind art purchase contracts and put the parties back to where they were before they entered into the agreement under this legal theory. New York's statute, which has been followed by a handful of other states including Florida, imbues the buyer with stronger rights than he or she might otherwise possess. For example, the non-dealer purchaser of art is given an *express warranty*—and not an opinion statement—of authenticity or authorship whenever the sale includes a "certificate of authenticity or any similar written instrument" as a basis for the transaction. Under this specific New York art market legislation, a buyer is also protected from seller's remorse when it is discovered after the sale that the work of art, instead of having been painted by an insignificant artist, was in reality created by a much sought-after master painter.

It is not uncommon for major art purchasers to include additional contract protection. Generally it includes a rescind provision against the dealer merchant for a mutual mistake in authenticity with a six-year statute of limitation term granted under New York law. In the following chapter the U.C.C. is examined further in terms of its use to secure an interest in art including intellectual property interests.

TITLE INSURANCE

Unlike in the traditional mortgage lending industry, where the norm for real estate buyers is to acquire title insurance to protect against the risk of a defective title, there is not a similar requirement for purchasing art. The difficulties in assuring good title detailed in this chapter, coupled with a one-time premium fee ranging from 1.5 and 3 percent of the purchase price, serve as practical limits on acquiring title insurance for most purchasers of art.

SUMMARY

A global art market where the demand by wealthy buyers to acquire Old World masterpieces and contemporary art by cutting-edge artists has outstripped the supply, and has encouraged the creating and selling of fake and forged works of art, and even stolen art. The difficulty of detecting counter-feit art is compounded by the lack of standards among authenticators. Increasingly, forensic scientific methods are available to augment the scholarship of art experts to help collectors, dealers, and museums to accurately identify authorship and authenticity. Unfortunately, it is often an imprecise practice that has difficulty distinguishing between fact and opinion, which has led to numerous lawsuits in Europe and the United States.

Unscrupulous and unknowledgeable art dealers and professed experts seeking a fast dollar return are all too eager to rig the system for their own self-interests at the expense of innocent buyers. Authentication boards and foundations that seek to protect the integrity of an artist's oeuvre are subject to charges of conflict of interest, conspiring to create a monopoly, and defamation. New York has taken the lead in carving out statutory express warranty protections for non art-dealer purchasers of art.

WORKS REFERENCED

Authentication in Art, *Newsletter*, February 2015.

John Browning and Lawrence Weinstein, "It's a Complete Red Haring: Court Dismisses Wide Ranging Art-Authentication Lawsuit against Keith Haring Foundation," in *JDSUPRABUSINESS Advisor*, March 19, 2015.

Leonard D. DuBoff and Christy King, *Art Law*, 3rd ed., St. Paul, MN: Thomson-West, 2000.

Augustino Fontevecchia, "Steve Cohen's Modigliani in the Middle of Art Market War: Billionaire Rybolovlev vs Yves Bouvier," in *Forbes*, March 12, 2015.

Sophie Gilbert, "Why Are Art Heists So Fascinating?," in *The Atlantic*, March 18, 2015.

Daniel Grant, "What Happens When an Artist's Own Work Is Stolen," in *Huffington Post*, July 15, 2014.

Stephen Kurjian, *Master Thieves*, Philadelphia: Perseus Books, 2015.

Marie C. Malaro and Ildiko Pogany DeAngelis, *A Legal Primer on Managing Museum Collections*, 3rd ed., Washington, DC: Smithsonian Books, 2012.

Mitchell Martin, "Soutine Suit Settled over Bargain Beef," in *BlouinARTINFO*, June 1, 2009.

John Henry Merryman, Albert E. Elsen, and Stephen K. Urice, *Law, Ethics and the Visual Arts*, 5th ed., Kluwer Law, Alphen aan den Rijn, The Netherlands, 2007.

Anne-Marie Rhodes, *Art Law & Transactions*, Durham, NC: Carolina Academic Press, 2011.

Laney Salisbury and Aly Sujo, *Provenance*, New York: Penguin Books, 2009.

5

Ethical and Legal Challenges of Nazi-Era Art and Cultural Property

"Remembering is a necessary and noble act."

—Eli Wiesel ("Hope, Despair and Memory")

The recent media revelation by *Focus* magazine, followed by a lengthy article in *Vanity Fair*, that a hidden cache of nearly 1,500 paintings, drawings, and prints worth more than a billion dollars was located in the Munich and Bavaria apartments of a frail, reclusive gentleman with family ties to Nazi Germany caused an international uproar. This discovery renewed conversation about the dark legacy of looted art, complex laws related to restitution, and the living memory of the ghosts of the Holocaust. Legitimate concerns that the legal system in place to resolve ownership of looted Nazi-era art may favor the wrongdoers over the original Jewish property owners is not limited to Germany, Switzerland, or Austria. In particular, Russia—with its vast holdings of looted art captured after World War II by the Red Army Trophy Brigades that are in the State Hermitage Museum in St. Petersburg and the Pushkin Museum in Moscow—claims ownership justified as war bounty in exchange for the damage Nazi Germany inflicted upon its people and property. Meanwhile, Germany considers this art as cultural property, part of its national heritage, and wants it returned. Elsewhere, the major Western democracies of Britain, France, the Netherlands, and the United States, after signing a protocol about how to deal with the provenance of Nazi-era art, are still struggling with designing and implementing legal and moral restitution policies and practices.

While the main focus of this chapter is on art looted by the Nazis, it falls within a larger framework of ownership disputes over ancient artifacts and cultural property. For example, the bitter controversy between Yale University and Peru over ownership of the thousands of objects of pottery, ceramics, metal textiles, and bones taken from Machu Picchu by an academic scholar and then donated to Yale remains current. The classic marble sculptures removed from what is now Greece by the 7th Earl of Elgin and British Ambassador to the Ottoman Empire at the time, and now owned and exhibited by the British Museum, continue to stir passionate historical, cultural, and legal arguments regarding plundering, ability to protect, and title to cultural property. The wanton destruction of Mesopotamian sculptures in the Mosul Museum, obliteration of ancient Christian art, and burning of rare books and manuscripts in a library in northern Iraq by the Islamic State—all objects of the record of a shared past that reflect who we are as humans—remind many of the senseless criminal effort by the Nazis decades ago to eliminate the culture heritage of the Jews in Europe.

NAZI-ERA ART

In the mid-1990s, two books dealing with the fate of art looted by the Third Reich during the Second World War—*The Rape of Europa* and *The Lost Museum*—for the first time provided vivid documentation of the methodical and systematic pillaging, appropriating, concealment, and smuggling that took place in Germany, Austria, and France. These publications guided international conversations and conferences on the moral imperative to assist the descendants of persecuted families in locating and recovering art and objects lost during the Holocaust period. A number of task forces by governments, private nonprofit groups, and museums were enlisted to establish largely aspirational guidelines to assist in determining whether a work of art was unlawfully confiscated and offered solutions to restitute or resolve adverse claims of ownership.

In 1998, the US Congress enacted two statutes related to Nazi-era confiscated property. The **Nazi War Crimes Disclosure Act** called for the declassification of records related to crimes and looted property. The **Holocaust Victims Redress Act** encouraged all governments to undertake "good faith" efforts to assist in the return of looted secular and religious property. Shortly thereafter, a US government–led multi-day conference was held in Washington, DC, attended by more than forty countries and scores of private organizations from around the world. The general consensus (although *never legally binding on any nation*) that arose from the conference was that based on *moral principles*, cultural property, such as religious objects, books, paintings, photographs, and drawings, illegally seized from Holocaust victims should be returned to them or their lawful heirs consistent with national laws to achieve just and fair resolution of claims. The eleven major guiding principles of the Washington Conference now known as the Washington Principles, extracted from the *Washington Conference on Holocaust Era Assets*, are:

WASHINGTON PRINCIPLES:

1. Art that had been confiscated by the Nazis and not subsequently restituted should be identified.
2. Relevant records and archives should be open and accessible to researchers, in accordance with the guidelines of the International Council on Archives.
3. Resources and personnel should be made available to facilitate the identification of all art that had been confiscated by the Nazis and not subsequently restituted.
4. In establishing that a work of art had been confiscated by the Nazis and not subsequently restituted, consideration should be given to unavoidable gaps or ambiguities in the provenance in light of the passage of time and the circumstances of the Holocaust era.
5. Every effort should be made to publicize art that is found to have been confiscated by the Nazis and not subsequently restituted in order to locate its pre-War owners or their heirs.
6. Efforts should be made to establish a central registry of such information.
7. Pre-War owners and their heirs should be encouraged to come forward and make known their claims to art that was confiscated by the Nazis and not subsequently restituted.
8. If the pre-War owners of art that is found to have been confiscated by the Nazis and not subsequently restituted, or their heirs, can be identified, steps should be taken expeditiously to achieve a just and fair solution, recognizing this may vary according to the facts and circumstances surrounding a specific case.
9. If the pre-War owners of art that is found to have been confiscated by the Nazis, or their heirs, cannot be identified, steps should be taken expeditiously to achieve a just and fair solution.
10. Commissions or other bodies established to identify art that was confiscated by the Nazis and to assist in addressing ownership issues should have a balanced membership.
11. Nations are encouraged to develop national processes to implement these principles particularly as they relate to alternative dispute resolution mechanisms for resolving ownership issues.

A year later, the Office of the Special Envoy for Holocaust was established to assist institutions and organizations in addressing formal looted asset claims.

Around the same time, the Association of Art Museum Directors (AAMD) and the American Association of Museums now called the American Alliance of Museums (AMA), implemented guidelines that serve as a Code of Ethics to assist museums in dealing with legal claims over ownership of works of art. Non-litigation or alternative methods of dispute mechanisms of resolving title issues, including a call to waive *statute of limitations* and the *doctrine of laches* as affirmative defenses, are embedded in these principles, codes, and guidelines.

Internationally, Europe established the Commission for Looted Art to assist families and institutions in the research and location of looted art. Registries, such as the previously mentioned Art Loss Register created by the private International Foundation for Art Research (IFAR), and the National Archives and Records Administration in the United States, serve as databases that provide information to help families match documented losses of art against art images and provenance records identified at museums, galleries, or auction houses.

One of the grave difficulties that face the heirs of Jewish victims of the Holocaust in the United States is the lack of any formal legal authority to require the restoration of looted "degenerate" art to the original owners. This is because most of the contested works are in the hands of private collectors, private dealers, and private museums, and not owned by government-run museums. Many of the major museums in Europe and Russia are publicly owned and managed. However, even in these situations, as in the case of Russia where museum immunity from the seizure of looted art is provided, or in the case of Germany where a thirty-year statute of limitations from the time of the loss exists, recovery by heirs of Holocaust victims is difficult. In many cases, the children, grandchildren, nieces, and nephews of the victims of Nazi looting are left with no choice but to file civil claims against museums, auction houses, and private owners whose ownership of contested art has become publicly known.

HOLOCAUST-ERA ART LITIGATION

Prior to the symposiums and conferences that led to the passage of the Washington Principles and establishment of Holocaust-era lost art registries, there were a handful of World War II seized art cases that came before US courts. The term *Holocaust-era art* refers to works that might have been illegally seized during the Nazi era with unexplained gaps in provenance from 1933 to 1945. *Provenance* refers to the documented chronology of ownership, custody, and location of objects of art frequently related to authenticity.

Price v. United States—Hitler Watercolors

One historically intriguing decision arising from an ownership dispute during this period is *Price v. United States* (707 F. Supp. 1465 [1989]). It concerned ownership of four watercolor paintings by Adolf Hitler, and the role of the Monument Men. In 1936, Hitler gifted these paintings to Heinrich Hoffmann, Sr., who stored them during the war until they were discovered by army troops and transferred to the central collection location for pillaged art established by the Monument Men. The Monument Men were 345 professional artists, academics, historians, architects, and curators from thirteen countries that served as part of the Monuments, Fine Arts, and Archives section of the Allies war effort. These men and women saved tens of thousands of priceless works of art that had been plundered by the Nazis. Ultimately, Hitler's watercolors were transferred to the United States and stored in a warehouse where they were marked as "property of the state of Germany." After the war, Hoffmann was adjudged a war profiteer at a Nuremberg trial and lost title to many of his works of art, but not these four paintings. Hoffmann's children had no knowledge of the location of this art until 1982. After the United States refused to return the paintings, a lawsuit for recovery was brought to the United States In denying the government's claim that it could keep the art because they conveyed a "propagandistic message" which the army was authorized by statute to combat, the federal court ordered the return of the four "innocuous, pleasant scenes" to Hoffmann's heirs.

Menzel v. List

One of the earliest reported cases dealing with the restitution of Holocaust-era art looted by the Nazis is *Menzel v. List* (267 N.Y.S.2d 979 [1966]). In summarizing this decision, it is important to recognize that the litigation took place in the state of New York. Unlike many other jurisdictions, New York applies a "demand and refusal" rule for deciding when a cause of action arises for applying the statute of limitations defense. The term *statute of limitations* refers to the amount of time a person has to file a lawsuit before that action is barred. Once the statute of limitations has expired, and the period generally runs from one to six years, then no lawsuit may be successfully filed. The tricky legal issue for Holocaust-era stolen art is when a court should begin to calculate the starting point for the cause of action.

The facts in *Menzel* are undisputed. In 1941, the Menzel family was forced to flee Brussels because of the oncoming Nazis. Their art collection, including a painting by Marc Chagall, was seized as "decadent Jewish art." In 1955, a collector, Albert List, purchased the Chagall in "good faith" for value from a reputable gallery in New York City. Earlier that year this gallery, as a bona fide purchaser, had acquired the Chagall from one of the leading galleries of Paris. The custom in the trade is that art sold between galleries constitutes a representation of authenticity and good title. Mrs. Menzel had been searching for the lost Chagall, and discovered its location in 1962 in the possession of List. She demanded its return, and List refused citing he was a good faith buyer and the complaint is barred by New York's statute of limitations affirmative defense.

In ruling for Menzel, the court held good title could not be conveyed to List through the galleries because Menzel was the sole and rightful owner and never abandoned ownership. In the matter of the statute of limitations argument, in a powerful statement that stands as a "bulwark against the handiwork of evil," the court determined that *the cause of action for bringing a civil lawsuit begins "not upon the stealing or the taking, but upon the defendant's (List) refusal to convey the chattel (Chagall) upon demand."*

The court's opinion in *Menzel* emphasized that both galleries involved in the commercial transactions were reputable. While this factor did not help the good faith buyer List retain the Chagall, in later cases the reputation of galleries is significant. One of the post–Washington Principles disclosures from various task forces and committees researching the provenance of Nazi-era art is that there were certain dealers that purchased art from Nazi party officials and then resold the art, in many cases, to support the Nazi government's war effort.

Provenance Research

The Nasher Museum of Art at Duke University, formerly the Duke University Museum of Art, as part of its provenance research project, learned that prominent objects of art it received as donations that helped establish the museum's base collection were acquired from a dealer in New York City that was suspected of collaborating with the Nazis while operating a gallery in Paris. It deaccessioned the art and sought to return the objects of art to their original owners.

The Nasher Museum's statement on provenance drawn from its website, emuseum.nasher.duke.edu/collectionoverview, states that its "aim is to compile all known provenance information for works in its collection created before 1946, transferred after 1932 and before 1946, which were, or could have been, in continental Europe during the Nazi era." It posts all of its research findings from the Holocaust era on its website in a fashion similar to other museums that are members of the American Alliance of Museums. As the museum points out, gaps in provenance are quite common and "do not in themselves constitute evidence of looting from archeological sites or seizure by the Nazis." Any person with information about the museum owning suspect art from this era is encouraged to contact one of its senior curators.

The Nasher Museum conducts research on disputed Nazi-era art the way most American museums do. Curators with expertise in specific areas or periods of art study its provenance when called upon. Budgeting the time for research while performing other curatorial responsibilities such as organizing exhibitions or acquiring new works limits the ability of museums to timely and thoroughly respond to requests. In contrast, the Museum of Fine Arts in Boston is the first museum in the United States to employ a full-time provenance curator, Dr. Victoria Reed, to perform detective work that can resolve art ownership challenges.

The second major lesson learned from the *Menzel* case is that the answer to the complex question of who owns Nazi-era art depends on whose law applies, as is demonstrated in statutory law and later cases.

The general rule followed by *Anglo-American nations*, such as English speaking Canada, the United Kingdom, Australia, New Zealand, and the United States is that *a thief cannot pass good title* regardless of how many subsequent purchasers buy in good faith for value. At one end of the spectrum are the New York courts that protect the right of ownership from whom objects and works of art have been stolen. The original owner must seek demand for the return of the stolen art and should the possessor of the works refuse, then the original owner has three years from the time of the *demand* to file suit and *refusal*. After three years New York's statute of limitations bars recovery. Contrast this view with that of many *civil law countries* in Europe. Switzerland, for example, *presumes that all good faith innocent purchases of art, whether looted, stolen or not, acquire superior title to that of the original owner*. The original owner or heirs must prove that there were dubious circumstances surrounding the sales transaction that would have led the buyer to inquire further about its origins and details related to its acquisition and proposed sale. Moreover, *Switzerland's five-year statute of limitations period begins to run at the time of the theft or loss*. This is unlike in *New York, where the statute of limitations term starts after the possessor of the art refuses the demand for its return so long as the delay in seeking the return does not unreasonably delay the request*. These two jurisdictions impose sharply contrasting presumptions and burdens making it exceptionally onerous for families to recover stolen Nazi-era art now located in civil law countries such as Switzerland. New York is alone among common law states and nations in applying its strict demand and refuse rule.

New York City's status as a leading international cultural center for exhibiting art, while dealers, galleries, and auction houses conduct thousands of sales transactions annually, enhances the importance of this state's judicial decisions. The harshness of the demand and refuse rule on innocent purchasers was ameliorated in another New York case decided by a state appeals court. This case did not involve art stolen during the Nazi era; however, the ruling could apply to disputes over ownership of art stolen during this period.

Solomon R. Guggenheim v. Lubell

In *Solomon R. Guggenheim v. Lubell* (569 N.E. 2d 426 [1991]), the court considered whether the Guggenheim museum waited too long in seeking the return of a gouache by Marc Chagall that had been stolen from the museum in the mid-1960s. Embarrassed by the theft, the museum never reported the loss to law enforcement authorities nor did it inform other museums, galleries, auction houses, or art experts. Meanwhile, in 1967, the Lubells acquired the painting for $17,000 from a dealer. Twenty years later the Guggenheim demanded the return of the stolen painting, which the Lubells refused. The court acknowledged the demand and refusal statute of limitations standard established in *Menzel*. However, the court recognized the application of the doctrine of *laches* in remanding the matter back to the lower court for a decision. Laches is a rule that *protects innocent purchasers of art when the original owner unreasonably delays in seeking the return of the property to the prejudice of the good faith buyer for value.* Many observers thought the Lubells, as innocent purchasers, were entitled to retain the Chagall on the grounds that the museum forfeited the right to claim ownership by not undertaking a timely diligent search to seek the return of the stolen art. The parties resolved the dispute privately before the subsequent lower court rehearing.

The prevailing law regarding when the *statute of limitations* begins to run in the *United States* is *when the owner knew or should have known the facts needed to seek recovery of the stolen art*. This is also known as the *discovery* rule.

The issue of where to litigate art ownership quarrels between an innocent purchaser versus the original owner usually occurs in the buyer's domicile, which is generally where the disputed art is situated. It is possible that the forum of the original owners or heirs may claim significant contacts or connection to the dispute to support a lawsuit. In those circumstances where the art is on loan at a museum or consigned for sale in a jurisdiction different from the original owner or innocent purchaser, the host state of the site of the art might also serve as the interested place for judicial intervention or resolution. The various sources and differing interpretations of governing law over stolen Holocaust-era art makes this area of the law ripe for "forum shopping" by the litigants. The law selected may lead to dramatically different outcomes.

Bakalar v. Vavra—Seated Woman with Bent Leg

For instance, in 1963, a Boston philanthropist David Bakalar purchased a drawing by Egon Schiele, whose works along with Marc Chagall's art figure prominently in many Holocaust looting disputes, from a dealer in New York. The drawing was referred to as *Seated Woman with Bent Leg*. In 1956, the dealer had acquired the drawing from a Swiss gallery. In 2005, Bakalar elected to consign the Schiele for sale at a Manhattan auction house. The provenance of the drawing was questioned, so Bakalar filed a lawsuit in New York that sought to declare him as the lawful owner. Heirs of the original drawing's owner, Fritz Grunbaum, also claimed ownership.

Fritz Grunbaum, a collector of Schiele's art, lived in Austria before he was taken to a concentration camp where he died in 1941. Grunbaum's sister-in-law somehow came into possession of the drawing. The heirs, one of whom is a Czech citizen, alleged that Grunbaum's wife was driven to transfer the drawing by Nazi persecution, which was a common occurrence experienced by Jewish families during that period. In 1956, the sister-in-law sold it to a Swiss gallery before it arrived in New York.

This fact pattern presents a familiar *choice of law* dilemma, where depending on whether Swiss, Austrian, or New York law applies the end result could vary. After seven years of litigation the court determined that the art had *not* been stolen by the Nazis and had instead remained with the family. The court selected New York law to decide the outcome notwithstanding the traditional requirement that the law where the property was *located* at the time of the sale; Switzerland, with its five-year statute of limitations from the time of the theft, is the preferred choice. The controversial selection of New York law based on a finding of this cultural center having a stronger *interest* in determining the outcome of Holocaust-era ownership of art has been criticized because it compounds the confusion regarding what jurisdiction's laws are controlling.

Bakalar gained title after having to *disprove* the Schiele drawing was stolen by the Nazis. New York law prevents a good faith purchaser from obtaining title from a thief. The appeals court affirmed the lower court's ruling that the heirs were also barred from claiming ownership based on the family's lengthy delay in filing a claim, the equitable defense of laches (*Bakalar v. Vavra*, 619 F.3d 136 [2d Cir. 2010]).

Portrait of Wally

The tortuous journey of another Egon Schiele painting, *Portrait of Wally*, allegedly stolen by a Nazi art expert, Friedrich Welz, from a Jewish art dealer, Lea Bondi, forced to flee Germany and illegally imported into the United

States is arguably the most significant Holocaust-era opinion ever reached by an American court. After the war the *Wally* portrait ended up in the possession of the Austrian government when Allied Forces seized it from Welz. In a mix-up of a description of the work it ended up at the Australian National Gallery, mislabeled. Meanwhile, Bondi had spent years seeking the return of the Schiele painting. She enlisted the assistance of Dr. Rudolph Leopard, a collector of Schiele's art, who ultimately acquired the *Wally* for his personal collection, failing to return it to Bondi. In 1994, Leopard transferred the painting to the Leopard Museum, which lent it to the Metropolitan Museum of Modern Art (MoMA) in 1997. The painting was on exhibit for six weeks, and just before the exhibit was to close and the work was about to be returned to the Leopard Museum in Austria, the families claiming to be heirs of Bondi asked MoMA to hold onto the painting so that its provenance could be established.

MoMA refused the request citing **Section 12.03** of New York's **Arts and Cultural Affairs Law** that states:

> No process of attachment, execution, sequestration, replevin, distress or any kind of seizure shall be served or levied upon any work of fine art while the same is enroute to or from, or while on exhibition or deposited by a nonresident exhibitor at any exhibition held under the auspices or supervision of any museum, college, university or other nonprofit art gallery, institution or organization within any city or county of this state for any cultural, educational, charitable or other purpose not conducted for profit to the exhibitor, nor shall such work of fine art be subject to attachment, seizure, levy or sale, for any cause whatever in the hands of the authorities of such exhibition or otherwise.

The purpose of this statute, which is similar to the non-forfeiture museum loan laws in many other states, is to freely share the art treasures of the world without fear of seizure by foreign governments.

In what numerous publications referred to as a "stunning" decision, after thirteen years of litigation, an earlier 2000 holding that the painting ceased being stolen when recovered by US forces after the war, was reversed by the same court. In refusing to apply New York's civil restriction on seizing loaned art on exhibit as the court's early decision had done, Judge Mukasey relied upon new facts presented by the US government for a criminal seizure. The **National Stolen Property Act** (**NSPA**) authorizes the US government to confiscate imported property, including works of art on temporary loan for exhibition, worth more than $5,000 known to be stolen, converted, or taken by fraud. The court also found that under Austrian law Bondi's heirs more than likely owned the painting, and that under various statute of limitations and treaties the lawsuit is not barred (*US v. Portrait of Wally*, 663 F. Supp. 2d 232 [S.D.N.Y. 2009]).

Figure 5.1. *Portrait of Wally*, Egon Schiele. *Photo image courtesy of Wikipedia .com/media.*

Eventually, the parties settled their title dispute outside the courtroom. Reportedly, the heirs of Bondi received fair market compensation for the sale of the portrait painting to the Leopard Museum. The seventy-three-year-old drama became a documentary film favorite appropriately named *Portrait of Wally* (figure 5.1).

The analysis and application of law principles applied in the *Wally* decision stand as a landmark case for urging other nations to seek ways to advance the policies and principles of seeking the return of Holocaust-era art first envisioned in the 1998 Washington Conference. American museums interested in exhibiting works of art that might have questionable provenance can seek federal *immunity* from seizure from the US State Department. A grant of immunity, however, does not prevent deprived families from filing civil suits to recover stolen art.

Portrait of Block-Bauer

In an opinion written by Justice Stephen Breyer, the United States Supreme Court in *Republic of Austria v. Altmann* (541 U.S. 677 [2004]) ruled in favor of Maria Altmann in her quest to force the Austrian government to return five Gustav Klimt paintings that had been seized by the Nazis from her family in Austria. The court did not rule on the merits of her title claim under US or Austrian law. The issue was whether the **Foreign Sovereign Immunities Act**, which provides the exclusive jurisdictional route to file a lawsuit against a foreign nation in the United States, applies retroactively. The court authorized Altmann to proceed in her federal civil suit for recovery even though the Act had not been passed until 1976, years after the Nazi theft.

Maria Altmann's story was documented in the *Rape of Europa* book and *Woman in Gold* film. She had tried unsuccessfully to sue the government of Austria, where the Klimts were hung at the Austrian Gallery in Vienna. Under Austrian law the fee for filing a lawsuit is approximately 10 percent of the recoverable amount. The equivalent $1.5 million filing fee based on the estimated value of $150 million for the five paintings was a prohibitive expense even after the Austrian court reduced the filing fee to $350,000. She dropped her Austrian lawsuit and filed suit in her adopted home country, the United States, which led to the Supreme Court ruling.

In a calculated move, instead of proceeding in federal court in California, Altmann elected to submit her case to a binding three-person arbitration panel in Austria. The result hinged on whether language in the will of her uncle was a command to bequeath the art to the state galleries of Austria or a request. In finding that it was a request, Altmann was deemed the rightful owner of the five Klimts including the celebrated *Portrait of Block-Bauer*, the painting of her aunt. After taking title and possession of the Klimts, she sold the works for over $325 million.

The application of conflicting laws, standards, policies, and jurisdictions complicates the recovery of looted works of art to their rightful owner. Unlike the success of Altmann, in 2015 an Australian panel refused to return a famous Klimt frieze looted by the Nazis from its Jewish owner. In this case, after the war the stolen art was actually returned to the son of the original owner. The son was living in Switzerland, not Austria where the art was located. The art was subject to an export ban so the son could not physically remove the frieze from Austria. In 1972, he sold the Klimt at a bargain price. Meanwhile, in the 1990s Austria amended its restitution law to apply to property that was sold at a cut-rate price because of the export prohibition. Heirs of the son petitioned the arbitration panel for the return of the Klimt, which the Austrian panel denied.

NON-NAZI-ERA CULTURAL PROPERTY DISPUTES—PLUNDER

The conflict over *cultural property* is not limited to Nazi-era confiscated art. In Europe the British Museum continues to vigorously refuse the Greek government's plea to return the Parthenon/Elgin Marbles. In 1816, the museum acquired the classic marble sculptures, which were part of the temple of Parthenon in the Acropolis of Athens, when the British government purchased them from Lord Elgin. He was serving as British ambassador to the Sublime Porte at Constantinople when the ruling Ottomans allegedly consented to their removal a few years earlier. Elgin, acting as a private citizen, not as a British agent, transported them to England.

Even in the early 1800s controversy surrounded the removal and transmission of the marbles from one state to another. The English poet Lord Byron in *The Curse of Minerva* scorned Elgin for plundering and vandalizing cultural objects. Byron's objections to the British government's acquisition of "looted" property greatly impacted Western civilization's perception of cultural and patrimonial property.

Greece gained its independence from the Ottomans in 1832. However, it was not until the 1980s that Greece's minister of culture began a campaign for the return of the Marbles to Athens based on both legal and moral grounds. In 1984, the British government denied the formal request, although more recently they have proposed an access arrangement. In 2014, the United Nations Education, Scientific and Cultural Organization (UNESCO) offered to assist in the resolution of this dispute.

Sound arguments are made on each side of the cultural debate over whether the Marbles should be returned to Athens. The Marbles are exquisitely displayed in one of the most majestic museums in the world free of charge for all visitors. Their public exhibition gave rise to respect for Neo-Classic works of art that may not have occurred otherwise. They have resided in England for over two hundred years, where arguably they have become part of that country's national and cultural heritage. The Museum has diligently physically preserved them over time, whereas had they remained in Athens, exposure to environmental factors might have destroyed them. Over the past two centuries the Parthenon has substantially crumbled, while parts of it were removed and dispersed to different museums. In fact, the Greeks do not propose to return the Marbles to the Parthenon. Instead, despite a near total collapse of its economy, it spent precious euros to build the New Acropolis Museum, where it hopes to display the Marbles. The museum looks onto the ruins of the Parthenon.

For Greece the Marbles serve as a powerful cultural symbol related to its national identity. Today there are laws in place that would have prevented the pillaging of the Parthenon. By bringing the Marbles back to Greece, its people would have easier access to appreciate the cultural values associated with its classical heritage. Moral integrity and justice demand that the Marbles be returned to the original cultural site.

It is hard not to avoid the geopolitical debates that follow cultural and patrimonial controversies. This century the Taliban destroyed ancient statues of the Bamiyan Buddha and burned irreplaceable old manuscripts in an effort to cleanse Afghanistan of pre-Islamic art. In 2015, the militant Islamic State looted cultural artifacts and bulldozed ancient cultural heritage sites in northern Iraq, the site of where Assyria became the first true empire in world history, according to Yale scholar, Professor Eckart Frahm. Unlike past destructions of cultural objects and religious imagery, the Islamic State appear to be using these concerted acts of cultural vandalism as propaganda tools to recruit new zealot converts on social media by recording the acts of obliteration.

Of course, not all annihilation of cultural objects is committed on religious grounds. In the mid 1960s, Mao Zedong launched the Cultural Revolution to purge the country of the four "impure" elements of Chinese society: old ideas, old habits, old customs, and old culture. Also, African ethnic differences that mobilize one tribe against another in armed conflicts and war involving weak states and weaker economies frequently lead to intentional and collateral damage of cultural property, sites of religious worship, and national heritage icons.

The 1954 **Hague Convention for the Protection of Cultural Property in the Event of Armed Conflict (Convention)** requires countries to respect cultural property in their own territory and to refrain from exposing cultural property to damage, except in cases of military necessity. The general consensus is that the wanton acts of pillaging and vandalizing of cultural property by the Taliban and Islamic State are in violation of this Convention. UN Secretary-General Ban Ki-moon referred to the destruction of cultural property by the Islamic State as a "war crime." In 1998, the **Treaty of Rome** gave the International Criminal Court jurisdiction over war crimes against cultural property.

Since 2008, the US Immigration and Customs Enforcement Agency and Homeland Security have returned to the Republic of Iraq more than 1,200 cultural treasures illegally smuggled into the United States. Many of the cultural pieces ended up at international art auctions before working their way into the United States. Some of the items were posted for sale on Craigslist without any customs importation documentation. The cultural objects stolen included personal goods from Saddam Hussein's home and private airplane, and the Baghdad Museum. The most prominent antiquity repatriated was the head of Assyrian King Sargon II, a limestone fragmentary head of Lamassu, the winged bull, from the Palace of Sargon II. In what may be an unfortunate fate, these antiquities and artifacts were returned to their Iraqi homeland, where the Islamic State continues to wreck cultural havoc. Federal importation and customs laws give Homeland Security the legal authority to investigate, seize, and repatriate artifacts and works of art having a special cultural value to the country of origin.

In 2011, the government of Cambodia requested that the US government assist in the recovery of a thousand-year-old mythical warrior statue that Sotheby's was about to auction in New York. Cambodia alleged the sandstone masterpiece with an estimated value as high as $3 million was looted during the 1960s and 1970s Vietnam conflict. Cambodia passed a law in 1993 that nationalized cultural heritage property. Sotheby's responded that Cambodia has no legal claim to the statue and cannot identify when it may have been removed or looted from its original pedestal temple location. Cambodia found a 1925 French colonial law that declared that all antiquities from Cambodia's temples be part of its national domain and the exclusive property of its state applies even after Cambodia gained its independence in 1953. Homeland Security was about to seize the statue when a federal district court permitted Sotheby's to retain custody pending an investigation.

The US government charged Sotheby's of trafficking in stolen cultural property. The consignor of the statue, a woman from Europe, was alleged to have misled the artifact's provenance. In 2013, the US government agreed to drop all criminal charges in return for the Hindi warrior statue's return to Cambodia.

In response to increasing global concerns over the theft and trafficking of cultural artifacts and to prevent accusations of criminal activity, the Association of Art Museum Dealers declared that member museums should not acquire any post–November 1970 undocumented works removed from archaeological or historic sites without proper permits. In 1983, President Bill Clinton signed into law the **Cultural Property Implementation Act** (19 U.S.C. 2603), which implemented the US Senate's ratification of the 1970 **UNESCO Convention on the Means of Prohibiting and Preventing the Illicit Import, Export and Transfer of Ownership of Cultural Property** to curb archaeological pillage and illicit trafficking in cultural property.

The first instance in which a federal court, in a concurring opinion, acknowledged the potential applicability of this federal statute occurred in 1990. The case involving a dispute over title between an art dealer from Indiana and a Christian church in war-ravaged Cyprus. The dealer had purchased four Byzantine mosaics, created in the early sixth century, from dubious middlemen in Europe. They had acquired access to these religious relics after they had been unlawfully removed from the church following Turkish military forces invasion of Cyprus. Ultimately, the court granted the church's request to return the mosaics on the grounds that the American purchaser never acquired good title because the items had been stolen. The formal name for the action is *replevin* or the right to recover personal property wrongfully taken (*Autocephalous Greek-Orthodox Church of Cyprus and the Republic of Cyprus v. Goldberg & Feldman Fine Arts, Inc.* [917 F.2d 278]).

Clearly, the ethics, international conventions, and domestic laws related to ancient relics and repatriation of plundered art are changing. The increased flow of easily accessible information via the Internet, the growth of global tourism, and museums reaching out to audiences beyond the perimeters of their physical footprints, all have contributed to nations seeing social, symbolic, and economic value in ancient works of art. Cultural ministers are using calculated public relations tactics and social media as a means to pressure museums, art dealers, and auction houses to return looted cultural property.

In response to one of these demands, the Metropolitan Museum of Art returned two statues that Homeland Security investigators determined had been removed from the same Cambodian site as the Hindi warrior statue in dispute with Sotheby's. The Cambodian government continues to seek the return of pilfered statues in the collection of the Norton Simon Museum, Denver Art Museum, and Cleveland Museum of Art, among others.

On the other hand, directors from many of the world's leading museums, including the Art Institute of Chicago, the Museum of Fine Arts in Boston, the Museum of Modern Art in New York, the British Museum (London), State Museums Berlin, Philadelphia Museum of Art, Prado Museum (Madrid), and the J. Paul Getty Museum (Los Angeles), among others, declared themselves in 2002 as "universal" museums. Their collective position is that "the universal admiration for ancient civilizations would not be so deeply established today were it not for the influence exercised by the artifacts of these cultures, widely available to an international public in major museums." The declaration stresses the point that the objects and monuments acquired and installed years ago were done so under vastly different conditions that do not exist today, and, therefore, should be adjudged under a different legal, cultural, and ethical lens (www.thebritishmuseum.ac.uk/newsroom/current2003/universalmuseums.htm).

NATIVE AMERICAN GRAVES PROTECTION AND REPATRIATION ACT

Ownership disputes of cultural artifacts or patrimonial property can be a difficult concept for Americans who are not directly involved in the collection, exhibition, or sale of these works of art. Unlike countries like Greece, Syria, and Cambodia that are part of the continuous flow of ancient civilizations, the United States is a young immigrant nation that places a premium value on capitalism. As one writer for the *New York Times* put it, "(D)emanding the return of American art and artifacts to America sounds, well, un-American, not to mention bad for the bottom line" (Michael Kimmelman, the *New York Times*, "Who Draws the Borders of Culture?," May 9, 2010).

The one exception to this general notion of Americans believing they have no cultural property worth saving other than, perhaps, the Statue of Liberty or Liberty Bell relates to Native American artifacts. In 1990, President George H. W. Bush signed into law a federal statute, the **Native American Graves Protection and Repatriation Act (NAGPRA)**, that requires all museums and federal agencies that receive federal funds to identify Native American human remains, sacred objects, funerary objects, or cultural patrimony in their collection. The national Smithsonian Institution is exempt from this law because they were already subject to this requirement under the **National Museum of the American Indian Act of 1989**. The covered institutions are required to consult with lineal descendants or Native American tribes about how to handle and repatriate these culturally sensitive objects and remains. Additionally, the law made it a federal crime to traffic in these sacred objects without right of possession. The purpose of the statute is to return to the indigenous people of America culturally sacred and sensitive objects taken from current or former Native American homelands.

Since the passage of the Act, museums and federal agencies have returned thousands of Native American remains, sacred objects, and cultural artifacts according to the National Park Service, Department of the Interior. The statute was not passed without controversy especially by scientists that expressed concern on its negative impact on scientific study of ancient remains found on tribal lands. An example of this debate in action occurred in the well-documented Kennewick Man case.

The Kennewick Man is a 9,000-year-old skeleton found near Kennewick, Washington, in 1996. The area where it was discovered is classified as the ancestral land of the Umatilla, a federally recognized tribe, managed by the US Army Corps of Engineers. Three other tribes also claimed the skeleton remains as their ancestor. All four tribes wanted to bury him. Archeologists saw scientific value in studying the remains because it is one of the most complete early human skeletons ever discovered in the Western Hemisphere. The Indian tribes opposed scientific study of the remains on religious grounds.

In response, a group of highly regarded scientists brought suit in federal court on the grounds that the remains were a rare discovery of national and international significance that did not resemble skeletal traits of modern American Indians. The court ruled that the remains were not from any living Native American tribes and, therefore, were not NAGPRA cultural property. The court determined that the skeletal remains of Kennewick Man were covered under a different statute, the **Archaeological Resources Protection Act**, and under the permitting process of this statute the scientists are entitled to study the remains (*Bonnichsen v. United States*, 367 F.3d 864 [9th Cir. 2004]).

Ongoing research by scientists continues to reveal great and conflicting discoveries. For some time scientists thought Kennewick Man may not belong to any living population. Other scientists postulated that his closest relatives might be the Moriori people living in a remote island off of New Zealand. The latest DNA testing results released in 2015 indicate that the so-called Ancient One is more closely related to Native American populations when compared with any other known population groups. While the Kennewick Man still remains under the custody of the Department of Interior, this latest genome finding might spark a renewed court battle between scientists and tribes.

SUMMARY

Solving the puzzle of who owns art from the past, especially Holocaust-era art once deemed "degenerate," is complex and confusing. Thousands of works of art were systematically and methodologically confiscated or transferred under duress from Jewish owners by the Nazis. Dealers, collectors, and museums both in and out of occupied territories for below market value prices acquired many works by modern artists such as Chagall and Schiele. In many cases, good faith purchasers living in the United States acquired these paintings, drawings, and other cultural objects.

In the 1990s a concerted international effort gained steam to develop a set of guiding standards eventually known as the Washington Principles to promote the restitution of Nazi-looted or stolen art. Returning plundered cultural property to its rightful owner in practice has proven to be a difficult task. In part, the issue of who owns the art from European Jewish families turns on which state or country's law applies. In Anglo-American nations a thief cannot pass good title. However, the affirmative defenses of statutes of limitations and laches have limited the ability of heirs of missing art to successfully lay claim in many of the states in the United States, except New York. The state of New York as a major cultural center has taken the lead in limiting the application of these defenses.

Historically, plundered art more often than not has remained with the plunderer. Pressures brought by globalization, social media, and public relations campaigns have encouraged public museums and cultural institutions to consider returning to the "original" owner treasures taken from long ago. International treaties and national laws today work to prevent the removal and transfer of culturally sensitive objects from the site of origin.

WORKS REFERENCED

Bethany Bell, "Austria Panel Opposes Return of Klimt Frieze Looted by Nazis," BBC News, March 6, 2015.

"Cultural Property, Art and Antiquities Investigations," Department of Homeland Security, March 16, 2015, ICE.gov.

Geoff Edgers, "Research That Can Resolve Art's Ownership," in *Boston Sunday Globe*, December 11, 2011.

Laurie Frey, "*Bakalar v. Vavra* and the Art of Conflicts Analysis in New York: Framing a Choice of Law Approach for Moveable Property," (Notes) *Columbia Law Review*, 112:5, 2012.

Patty Gerstenblith, *Art, Cultural Heritage and the Law*, 2nd ed., Durham, NC: Carolina Academic Press, 2008.

Susan Gonzalez, "ISIS's Destruction of Cultural Antiquities: Q & A with Eckart Frahm," in *Yale News*, March 16, 2015.

Alexander Herman, "The Bern-Germany-Bavaria Agreement on Gurlitt Works," in *Institute of Art and Law Blog*, November 25, 2014.

Michael Kimmelman, "Who Draws the Borders of Culture," in the *New York Times*, May 9, 2010.

Jennifer Anglim Kreder, "Guarding the Historical Record from the Nazi-era Art Litigation Tumbling toward the Supreme Court," in *Univ. of Pennsylvania Law Review*, 159:25, 2011.

Andrew Lawler, "Can a Skeleton Heal Rift Between Native Americans, Scientists?," http://news.nationalgeographic.com/2015/07/150715-kennewick-man-dna-genome-lawsuit-archaeology/, July 15, 2015.

Tom Mashberg and Ralph Blumenthal, "Disputed Statue to Be Returned to Cambodia," in the *New York Times*, December 13, 2013.

Tom Mashberg and Ralph Blumenthal, "Mythic Warrior Is Held Captive in an International Art Conflict," in the *New York Times*, February 29, 2012.

John Henry Merryman, Albert E. Elsen, and Stephen K. Urice, *Law, Ethics and the Visual Arts,* 5th ed., Frederick, MD: Kluwer Law, 2007.

Jim Morrison, "The True Story of the Monuments Men," http://www.smithsonianmag.com/history/true-story-monuments-men-180949569/?no-ist, February 7, 2014.

"National NAGPRA: Documents and Publications," National Park Service, US Department of Interior, info@nps.gov.

Anne-Marie O'Connor, "The Nazi Art Theft Crisis in Europe," in *Time*, December 19, 2013.

Charles A. Palmer, "Recovering Stolen Art: Avoiding the Pitfalls," in *Michigan Bar Journal,* 82:6, June 2003.

Richard Perez-Pena, "Guggenheim Presses Case on a Stolen Painting," in the *New York Times*, December 27, 1993.

Douglas Preston, "Kennewick Man Finally Freed to Share His Secret," in *Smithsonian*, September 2014.

Patricia Youngblood Reyhan, "A Chaotic Palette: Conflict of Laws in Litigation Between Original Owners and Good-Faith Purchasers of Stolen Art," in *Duke Law Journal*, 50:4, February 2001.

Jessica Schubert, "Prisoners of War: Nazi-Era Looted Art and the Need for Reform in the United States," in *Touro Law Review*, 30:3, 2014.

Alex Shoumatoff, "The Devil and the Art Dealer," in *Vanity Fair*, April 2014.

Peter Welby, "Why ISIS Is Destroying Iraq's Ancient Heritage," in *Newsweek*, March 18, 2015.

Arabella Yip, "Stolen Art: Who Owns It Often Depends on Whose Law Applies," in *Spencer's Art Law Journal*, 1:1, Spring 2010.

6

Buying, Selling, and Consigning Art

"Making $ is Art."

—Andy Warhol (*The Philosophy of Andy Warhol: From A to B and Back Again*)

The visual arts are a powerful nonverbal language. An African tribal mask may convey the image of a face. Yet, depending on personal experiences, cultural background, and pictorial conventions the object may generate a host of associations and impressions. Some viewers may recognize the mask as a ceremonial object crafted by a particular tribe in Nigeria symbolizing strength and wisdom, while others focus on its material components. Besides the meaning expressed in the artistic language of the mask, it also serves as an abstract source of satisfaction from an appreciation of its visual elements: lines, texture, three-dimensional shape, space, and color. The aesthetic experience of examining and investigating the mask triggers reflection, creates dialogue, and offers a way of expressing, sharing, and even shaping insight. By constructing stories about the mask that are shared with others whether they are stories formed by curators, art historians, gallery directors, auctioneers, ad agencies, art advisors, members of the public, or the artists themselves, a value is being placed on the art.

In some cases, the cultural value placed on the tribal mask is translated into a monetary or commercial value by the chief operators in the world of the business of art: these same art galleries, art dealers, auction houses, exhibitors, museums, agents, publishers, advertising agencies, borrowers, collectors, and buyers. The wealthiest Americans, Chinese, Europeans, and South Americans are investing their money in fine art, not unlike buying stocks and bonds for asset growth. According to a survey by Deloitte and ArtTactic, three-quarters of all art buyers view their collections as a financial investment ("Art for Money's Sake," the *New York Times*, February 3, 2015). The art auction houses Christie's and Sotheby's together sold around $1.4 billion worth of art for the most recent year reported. The shift from fine art speaking a powerful nonverbal language to art representing a commodity that is bought and sold is disconcerting to many artists. This paradigm shift strengthens the need for all parties to understand the business side of commercial transactions in art.

The arrangement of rules required for a coherent systems of buying, selling, consigning, loaning, and even storing the mask or any object of fine art is the business of the law of *contracts*. The foundational examination of how contracts are formed and how they function is important because artists are constantly entering into agreements that impose specific duties, obligations, and risks on all signatory parties. A failure to perform as promised could lead to serious material and financial losses, and harm to reputation.

CONTRACTS

A contract is a necessary evil when a museum desires to enter into a relationship with a site-specific installation artist to construct and display the work on the museum's grounds; when an artist wants to consign art to a gallery and accept a commission on works sold; when a magazine seeks to reproduce copyrighted photograph images; when a collector lends an Impressionist painting to a museum for exhibition; when a benefactor intends to gift common stock to a history museum for a specific acquisition; when two lending museums need to insure against risk of loss or damage from transporting a delicate Native American headdress; when a museum wants to upload an art image on its virtual museum website; when a wealthy hedge fund buyer of art needs to store auction items for investment; or when an artist needs to lease studio space. All of these defined activities, and many others, constitute entering into a business association with legal ramifications.

The beginning point in any discussion on contracts is the requirement for all parties to know the person with whom they are conducting business. Check references. A successful art contract is built on personal trust. An effective contract is one where all parties to the deal have negotiated the key terms—length of the loan, which party pays for installation or transportation costs, commission rate, copyright assignment, selling price, delivery terms, payment schedule, warranty—in good faith at arm's length, and where the parties in advance have anticipated the vast majority of legal problems that could arise.

It is not unusual for artists to understate the value of their works. For instance, as chronicled in the book, *Timeless: The Photography of Rowland Scherman*, the renowned one-time LIFE magazine photojournalist, Rowland Scherman, delivered a single copy of a photograph he captured of a young Bob Dylan to a record company. On a handshake, Scherman was paid the sum of $300 for the "one time" use. The record company proceeded to re-produce the image millions of times. In 1967, the photograph appeared as the record cover for Dylan's "Greatest Hits Album," which did garner Scherman a Grammy Award. However, even decades later no additional compensation was received by Scherman.

Another name for "value" in an art transaction is *consideration*. The Scherman example illustrates the necessity of having a decent idea of what the art is worth before entering into a negotiation to license, loan, or sell. Consideration is one of the basic elements the parties must agree upon to forge a valid contract.

Basic Elements to Form a Contract

By definition a contract is an agreement that can be legally enforced. It requires two or more parties, which might be a person or an organization, that either agrees to do something or agrees not to do something. The two primary sources of law governing contracts are the *common law* and the **Uniform Commercial Code (U.C.C.)**. The latter is a state-by-state codification of the law of *sale of goods*. The term sale of goods refers to the *work product* or *final work of art* created by an artist that might be traded or lent. Whereas concerns or disputes related to *services* refer to activities such as an artist agreeing to construct a site-specific installation or a museum promising to publicize the opening of an exhibition. A contract for services is ruled by the case law derived from the common law of the individual state or states where the services were to be performed. Regardless of whether the issue debated between or among the parties concerns a sale of goods or a service the law of the state that is most involved should be consulted, preferably with the benefit of competent legal counsel in the field of arts or at least contracts. As a side note, many communities have a staff of trained lawyers similar to New York City's "Volunteer Lawyers for the Arts" that provide pro-bono contract assistance for low-income artists and nonprofit arts organizations in these matters.

These are the essential elements to the formation of a contract:

1. *Offer and Acceptance* – one party makes an offer and another party accepts the offer. Frequently, the parties engage in a back and forth negotiation of the material offer and acceptance terms, such as price of the

art, medium, size, frame, delivery date, and insurance coverage before reaching a "mutual meeting of the minds."

2. *Consideration* – is the bargained for exchange by the parties of receiving something of value for their respective promises to buy and sell, consign, license, or lend. For instance, when an artist agrees to paint a portrait for the sum of $50,000, the consideration is the exchange of money for the painting of the portrait.

3. *Legal Capacity* – the parties that are entering into the agreement must be of legal age, generally eighteen years, and of sound mind at the time of the *mutual assent* to contract. The French artist Jean Dubuffet coined the term "outsider art" to describe art created by artists not formally trained and institutionalized for mental illness. While today the term more generally refers to works of art produced by artists outside established art schools or whose works are not sold by galleries as evidenced by New York City's annual Outsider Art Fair, when applied in the original meaning those artists might lack the mental acuity to enter into legally binding contracts.

4. *Valid Purpose* – the reason for the contract must not be against public policy or for an illegal purpose. Two examples come to mind. A contract to forge the works of one of the grand dames of American Impressionism, Mary Cassatt, and sell these works as original works of art by her is not an agreement that the courts could enforce. The international movement of *cultural objects* or what some countries refer to as *patrimony art* can be restricted on public policy grounds. The French government prohibited the exportation and sale of a Vincent van Gogh painting on the grounds it was a national treasure. This same van Gogh painting, though, could be loaned outside of France for scholarly or exhibition purposes and not violate this French law. The United States does not have in place exports restrictions specifically for cultural objects; however, objects that fall within the protection of the **Native American Graves Protection and Repatriation Act** or **Archaeological Resources Protection Act** are prohibited from export.

Unfortunately, there is not a legal requirement that all contracts involving artists must be in writing to be enforceable. It is certainly the better policy to agree to write and sign a contract especially when memories fade over time or there are not witnesses alive to remember what the parties agree to do for one another. The writing to bind the parties may take different forms. An exchange of emails or text messages where the parties "agree" to do something in the future and consideration is exchanged may suffice to constitute a binding contract.

In some cases, contracts must be written to be enforceable. A transfer of an artist's *copyright* or the release of a *moral right* each requires written accords for a valid contract. The still applicable old English **Statute of Frauds** necessitates that contracts that could not be performed within one year must be in writing. Thus, a fresco artist retained by a homeowner to create a mural in the style of the Mexican artist Diego Rivera that will take five years to complete obliges the parties to spell out the terms of their agreement in writing to have a valid enforceable agreement.

Article 2 of the **U.C.C.** encompasses the sale of goods in commerce. This Article has a general condition that written evidence is needed whenever the price of goods, such as a sculpture, sketch, mobile, drawing, collage, and installation art, exceeds five hundred dollars ($500). An exception to this stipulation occurs whenever the goods, that is, a sculpture, sketch, photograph, or painting, for instance, are specially created for a place or buyer, then an oral contract might suffice.

Promises

Another name for a promise or guarantee that artists, galleries, and auction houses frequently make is a *warranty*. In legal parlance, a warranty is a fact, promise, or description of the art that the buyer relies upon as a basis for agreeing to enter into a contract. A warranty must be distinguished from "sales talk" or opinion conversation. An art gallery salesperson tells a prospective purchaser of documentary photographs by the contemporary African American artist Carrie Mae Weems that they are sure to appreciate in worth because past values have increased dramatically ever since she earned a MacArthur "genius" grant. The buyer who relies upon this salesperson's opinion cannot sue the gallery when ten years later Weems's artwork did not increase in value because no warranty was created. The doctrine of *caveat emptor* or buyer beware still prevails in the commercial world of art transactions.

On the other hand, an auction house, such as Swann, that specifically states in writing as a condition of sale, "unless otherwise indicated in the respective catalogue descriptions we warrant for a period of three (3) years from the date of the sale the authenticity of each lot catalogued herein," has articulated an express promise or warranty. In this instance, the buyer is not relying upon speculation about the authenticity of the object, but rather upon the express guarantee that the work is authentic as an inducement to bid and purchase.

The auction situation is an example of an *express warranty*. In certain situations an *implied warranty* is created. A talent agency known for representing actors like Johnny Depp and Angelina Jolie enters into the business of representing visual artists for the purpose of helping them sign corporate licensing deals, pledge art to fund major art initiatives, or consign their art. Any commercial enterprise or financing source that deals with this agency relies upon the implied promise that the agency actually has the legal authority to represent the visual artist in question and has the authority to convey title in the art.

The prestigious Gagosian Gallery on Madison Avenue in New York City came under "warranty" scrutiny not long ago when it advertised Bob Dylan's "The Asia Series" paintings were a "visual reflection on his travels in Japan, China, Vietnam, and Korea, people, street scenes, architecture, and landscapes." In fact, according to numerous major news accounts including David Itzkoff of the *New York Times*, several of the paintings were copied almost entirely from existing photographs taken by the likes of Henri Cartier-Bresson. Some of the images directly copy-painted are still protected under copyright. Dylan, and the gallery, failed to give credit to any of the photographers whose work he copied. Purchasers of any of the paintings had every reason to believe the implied and express representations that these paintings by Dylan were based on his travels to East Asia, and not reproduction paintings of existing photographs.

Excuse for Nonperformance, Breaches, and Remedies

A party to a contract that fails to perform as promised or does not live up to the warranties granted might be liable for damages. Every contract contains certain risks. An artist that covenants to paint a portrait of a celebrity actor and that person dies prior to commencement of the work is *excused* from performance. Similarly, should the artist die or become disabled prior to performance then the artist is excused from finishing the work. This rule of *impossibility of performance* applies to these situations because the artist's skill is deemed to be special and exclusive, and may not be *delegated* to another artist to fulfill the obligation. It is possible that performance may be excused, for example, when the party the subject of the portrait is unaccommodating in agreeing to mutually convenient times for a sitting or the backdrop of the painting is a unique structure that was demolished or damaged by an act of God thereby thwarting the ability to incorporate a vital symbolic component into the painting. Of course, the parties to the agreement could *modify* or *waive* the requirement to include the structure in the painting to allow the artist to complete the portrait. Preferably, any change in the duties and obligations of either party should or, depending on the terms of a written contract, must be in writing to be enforceable. While the performance of a visual artist's special skills cannot be delegated to another artist without approval of the other contracting party, the artist is generally permitted to *assign* or transfer any right to payment or compensation to another party or entity. A well-drafted contract contemplates and resolves in advance these and other potential risks to avoid future litigation.

The famously reclusive artist Cady Noland disclaimed authorship, under the **Visual Artists Rights Act (VARA)**, of a silkscreen print on 1/16" aluminum that Sotheby's was auctioning off. The owner of the work, Marc Jancou Fine Art Ltd., had entered into a *consignment* agreement with the auction house. A consignment agreement is a contract where an agency relationship is created in which the auction house, Sotheby's in this case, acts as the selling agent for the owner of the art (Jancou). Sotheby's withdrew the print from the auction based on a condition in the parties' contract that granted it the authority when "in its sole judgment" there is doubt about the authenticity of the art. Jancou sued Sotheby's for *breach of contract* for failing to put the work for sale at auction. In granting summary judgment for Sotheby's, the court held that as a matter of law there was a substantial and objective basis for casting doubt as to attribution based on Noland's assertion that because the print had been damaged after its creation her reputation and honor might be harmed by the sale. Jancou's claim for multi-millions of dollars in compensation was denied. Sotheby's was found not to have breached the terms of the consignment agreement nor did it violate its *fiduciary* agency duty to Jancou (*Marc Jancou Fine Art Ltd. v. Sotheby's, Inc.*, 2013 NY Slip Op 04901, June 27, 2013).

There are specific risks of consigning works of art that beg for a fair remedy when something goes wrong. In what has been referred to as "New York's Biggest Art Fraud Ever" by reporters, Kraken Investments Limited, consigned its Botticelli's *Madonna and Child* (1485) painting to the Salander-O'Reilly Galleries, LLC for sale. The terms of the one-year consignment dictated that the gallery would exhibit the painting worth upward of $9.5 million, use its best efforts to sell the painting, and refer all disputes between the parties to arbitration. Upon delivering the Botticelli to the gallery, Kraken was supposed to file a UCC financing statement registering its *security interest* in the painting in New York. It did not. Once the gallery fell into bankruptcy, Kraken was left with an unsecured claim, as opposed to a secured interest had it filed the proper paperwork to perfect the consignment. After nearly eight years of litigation, ultimately a New York federal district court settled the matter in favor of Kraken. The Botticelli was returned to its rightful owner, not without wistful lessons for all parties contemplating consignment.

The proprietor of the Salander-O'Reilly Galleries, Lawrence Salander, pled guilty to stealing more that $100 million from customers and investors. He used funds from consignment sales to acquire homes, high-end furniture, jewelry, and Renaissance works of art. John McEnroe and Robert De Niro Jr.

were among the well-known celebrities who suffered financial loss. Scores of artists and dealers who had consigned art are still awaiting compensatory damages for Salander's breach of his fiduciary duties to them.

The Salander episode reveals two different types of remedies that are frequently sought in consignment disputes. The party that refuses or fails to perform as promised potentially is liable for monetary damages. Typically, the party that was harmed seeks lost profits from a failed sale and out-of-pocket costs incurred to recover damages. Where the normal remedy of money damages is inadequate to protect the interests at stake, the court may seek to protect the harmed party by requiring specific performance on the contract. For example, a dealer who refuses to return a work of art after the term of the consignment is over may be judicially ordered to return the art immediately. For consigned art that is a secured interest under the UCC, specific remedies for the sale of art apply. In any event, as explained in an earlier chapter, each state has enacted a limitation period after which no lawsuit can be sustained. The period for filing a lawsuit for actions based on breach of contract generally ranges from three to six years. All artists are advised to become familiar with the statute of limitations in the state where they conduct their business activities.

It is common in the United States for artists to enter into consignment arrangements with galleries or dealers, where the galleries agree to act in the best interest of the artists (fiduciary duty) for agreed upon commissions, minimum sales prices, and responsibilities for losses or damages. By statute many states require artist-gallery consignment contracts to be in writing to assure minimal protection for the artist. All states do not offer the same level of safeguards from unscrupulous or unreliable dealers.

Below is a sample consignment agreement between an artist and gallery. It is presented solely as an example of the key or material terms the parties must be keenly aware of and precise in their negotiations about what is expected before entering into a consignment contract. Use this sample consignment agreement only as a guide, and whenever possible, seek appropriate legal guidance in advance of signing any contract.

SAMPLE CONTRACTS

SAMPLE CONSIGNMENT AGREEMENT

The Artist (name, address and telephone number): _____ (hereinafter referred to as "Artist") and the Gallery (name, address, and telephone number): _____ (hereinafter referred to as "Gallery") hereby enter into the following CONSIGNMENT AGREEMENT.

1. AGENCY. The Artist appoints the Gallery as **exclusive agent** for the Work(s) of Art consigned for the sole purposes of display, exhibition, and sale. The Gallery shall not permit the Work(s) of Art to be used for any other purposes without the consent of the Artist in writing.

2. CONSIGNMENT. The Artist hereby consigns to the Gallery, and the Gallery accepts on **consignment**, those Work(s) of Art listed below on the attached inventory sheet that is incorporated into this Agreement. (*Note the Artist may want to file a UCC-1 financing statement in the state of the contract to give notice to the public of this interest.*)

3. WARRANTY. The Artist hereby **warrants** that exclusively the Artist created the Work(s) of Art the subject of this Agreement, and that the Artist solely owns and possesses unencumbered legal title and copyright to the Work(s) of Art.

4. DURATION OF CONSIGNMENT. The Artist and the Gallery agree that the initial term of consignment for the Work(s) of Art is to be _____ (*select number of months*). Upon the conclusion of this term of assignment, unless the parties agree in writing otherwise, the Gallery shall return to the Artist all unsold Work(s) of Art.

5. TRANSPORTATION RESPONSIBILITIES. The responsibility for packing and shipping charges, insurance cost, other handling expenses, and risk of loss or damage incurred in the delivery of the Work(s) of Art from the Artist to the Gallery, and in their return to the Artist, shall rest with the _____ (*select either Artist or Gallery*).

6. RESPONSIBILITY FOR LOSS OR DAMAGE and INSURANCE COVERAGE. The Gallery shall be responsible for the safekeeping of all consigned Work(s) of Art while they are in its custody. The Gallery shall be strictly liable to the Artist for any loss or damage (except for damage resulting from flaws inherent in the Work(s) of Art); to the full amount the Artist would have received from the Gallery if the Work(s) of Art had been sold. The Gallery shall provide the Artist with all relevant information about its insurance coverage for the Work(s) of Art within ten (10) days after the execution of this Agreement. Any failure to provide this information is deemed a **material breach** granting the Artist the right to demand immediate return of the Work(s) of Art and the cessation of this Agreement. The parties have agreed to the value of the Work(s) of Art for purposes of this provision in the attached inventory sheet below.

7. FIDUCIARY RESPONSIBILITIES. The title to each of the Work(s) of Art remains in the Artist until the Artist has been paid the full amount owed for the sale of the Work(s) of Art. At that time, title then passes directly to the Buyer. All proceeds from the sale of the Work(s) of Art shall be held in **trust** for the Artist. The Gallery shall pay all amounts due the artist before any proceeds of sales can be made available to any creditors of the Gallery. The Gallery acknowledges its **fiduciary** duty to act honestly and in good faith in all dealings with and on behalf of the Artist.

8. NOTICE OF CONSIGNMENT. The Gallery shall give notice, by means of a clear and conspicuous signage in full public view, and on all sales' agreements to buyers that the Work(s) of Art are being sold subject to a contract of consignment.

9. REMOVAL FROM GALLERY. The Gallery shall not lend, encumber, trade, remove from the premises, assign to another person or entity including but not limited to another gallery, dealer, or auction house, or sell on approval any of the Work(s) of Art, without first obtaining written permission from the Artist.

10. PRICING; GALLERY'S COMMISSION; TERMS. The value of the Artwork for purposes of sale is \$_____.__ and the minimum price for the sale of the Artwork is \$_____.__; for multiple artworks the values and minimum prices may be listed on an attached Inventory. (*Note the values for insurance purposes may or may not be identical to the selling prices.*)

The Gallery and the Artist agree that the Gallery's commission is to be _____% of the retail price of the work of art. The Artist and the Gallery must agree to any change in the retail price or in the Gallery's commission, in writing in advance.

Payment to the Artist shall be made within thirty (30) days after the date of sale of any of the Work(s) of Art. The Gallery assumes full risk for the failure to pay on the part of any purchaser to whom it has sold a work of art by Artist.

11. PROMOTION. The Gallery shall use its best efforts to promote the sale of the Work(s) of Art of Artist. The Gallery agrees to provide adequate display of the Work(s) of Art, and to undertake other promotional activities on the Artist's behalf, including, but not limited to, an Artist's reception, social media communications, catalogue, and half-page advertisements in local and regional art magazines.

The Gallery and the Artist shall agree in advance on the division of artistic control and of financial responsibility for expenses incurred in the Gallery's exhibitions and other promotional activities undertaken on the Artist's behalf.

The Artist grants the Gallery the limited right to reproduce one or more of the Work(s) of Art for print and social media publicity, catalogue, and display purposes subject to the Work(s) of Art not being able to be reproduced by others and full acknowledgement of the Artist as creator and copyright owner. The Gallery may arrange to have the Work(s) of Art photographed for these limited purposes, at its expense unless the parties agree otherwise. Ownership of the negative or digital images shall be the property of the Artist.

The Gallery shall identify clearly all works of art with the Artist's name, and any copyright notice, and the Artist's name shall be included on the invoice or Bill of Sale of each of the works of art.

12. REPRODUCTION. The Artist reserves all rights to the reproduction of the works of art except as noted in the limited grant in **Paragraph 11**. In every instance of promotional use, the Artist shall be acknowledged as the creator and the copyright owner of the work of art. The Gallery shall include on each Bill of Sale of any work of art the following legend: "All rights to reproduction of the work(s) of art identified herein are retained by the Artist." There shall be no waiver of moral rights associated with any sale.

13. ACCOUNTING. The Gallery shall furnish a statement of accounts for all sales of the Work(s) of Art to the Artist on a quarterly basis. The Artist shall have the right to inventory his Work(s) of Art in the Gallery and to inspect any books and records pertaining to any sales of his Work(s) of Art, upon giving the Gallery ten (10) days advance notice in writing.

14. ADDITIONAL PROVISIONS. _____
_____.

15. TERMINATION OF AGREEMENT. Notwithstanding any other provisions of this Agreement, either the Gallery or the Artist may terminate this Agreement at any time upon giving fifteen (15) days of written notice. In the event of the Artist's death, the estate of the Artist shall have the right to terminate the Agreement. Any material breach of any condition within this Agreement constitutes grounds for termination. Within thirty (30) days of the notification of termination, all accounts shall be settled and the Gallery shall return all unsold Work(s) of Art to the Artist or assigns.

16. PROCEDURES FOR MODIFICATION. Any modifications or amendments to this Agreement must be signed by both Artist and Gallery, and attached to this Agreement. Both parties must initial any deletions or additions made on this Agreement.

17. MISCELLANEOUS. This Agreement represents the entire Agreement between the Artist and the Gallery. If any part of this Agreement is held to be illegal, void, or unenforceable for any reason, that holding shall not affect the validity and enforceability of any other part. A waiver of any breach of any other provisions of this Agreement shall not be construed as a continuing waiver of other breaches of the same provision or other provisions hereof. This Agreement shall not be assigned, nor shall it inure to the benefit of the successors of the Gallery, whether by operation of law or otherwise, without the prior written consent of the Artist.

18. TIME IS OF THE ESSENCE. Time is of the essence throughout this Agreement.

19. NONASSIGNABLE, NONDELEGATABLE. The duties and promises herein may not be assigned or delegated, except as provided, without the express written permission of both parties.

20. CHOICE OF LAW AND DISPUTE RESOLUTION. The laws of the State of _____ shall govern this Agreement. In the event either party has a dispute regarding any material term of the Agreement, the parties agree to seek resolution in good faith either through mediation or arbitration with each party paying any costs associated with utilizing this process, prior to seeking judicial relief.

This Agreement is entered into on the _____ day of _____, 20_____.

All parties to this Agreement acknowledge that they are of sound mind, not under duress, have had the benefit of legal counsel should they so choose, and are of legal age to contract.

WITNESS TO ARTIST: _____

ARTIST: _____

WITNESS TO GALLERY AUTHORIZED
AGENT:_____

AUTHORIZED AGENT OF GALLERY WITH PROVING DOCUMENT
ATTACHED:

_____

TITLE OF AUTHORIZED GALLERY AGENT:

The list and type of contracts artists may encounter or need in business transactions are vast. The range of agreements includes a contract for the sale of artwork, contract for creating a limited edition poster, contract for licensing copyrighted artwork, a model release form, and a lecture contract. Tad Crawford's *Business and Legal Forms for Fine Artists* handbook is an excellent starting point resource for ready-to-use forms. Meanwhile, by way of illustration one final chapter sample contract dealing with the design, construction, and exhibition of installation art between an artist and museum is provided. In light of the *MASS MoCA v. Buchel* installation art controversy is more fully discussed in chapter 8.1. It is presented as a sample form of how to avoid such a lengthy and costly dispute. It is significantly more detailed than the sample Consignment Agreement. It addresses concerns about free expression, obscenity, copyrights, and moral rights.

SAMPLE CONTRACT FOR DESIGN AND CONSTRUCTION OF AN EXHIBIT

Agreement made as of the _____ day of _____, 20___ by and between the Museum (hereinafter referred to as "MUSEUM"), located at _____, and Site Specific Artist (hereinafter referred to as "ARTIST"), with an address at_____ _____, and tax payer identification number of _____ _____, for the purpose of defining the ARTIST'S preparation of the **design** and **construction** of a site specific installation with an exhibition title _____ at MUSEUM. The **dates of the exhibition showing** commence on _____and end on_____.

WHEREAS, the ARTIST is a recognized and accomplished professional installation

Artist; and

WHEREAS, MUSEUM respects and admires the work of the ARTIST and wishes to enter into contract governing the terms and conditions for the design and construction of the site specific installation art (hereinafter "WORK") prepared by the ARTIST; and

WHEREAS, the parties wish to have the design, construction, and creation of this WORK governed by the mutual obligations and conditions herein:

NOW THEREFORE, for true and valuable consideration of the foregoing premises and the mutual covenants herein after set forth and other valuable consideration, the parties hereto agree as follows:

1. Preliminary Design. The ARTIST shall create the preliminary design for the WORK in the form of sketches, drawings or models described as follows: _____, and present them to MUSEUM on or before_____. The ARTIST agrees to develop the preliminary design according to the following description of the WORK as interpreted by the ARTIST:

Title: _____

Medium: _____

Size: _____

Value: _____

Description for exhibition catalog, if any, wall labels and publicity: _____
_____
_____

MUSEUM may, within ten business days of receipt of the preliminary design, demand changes in writing. The ARTIST has ten business days of receipt of demand changes to either accept the changes and redraft the WORK to MUSEUM's reasonable satisfaction or discuss the demand changes with MUSEUM to come to a mutual meeting of the minds regarding the WORK or not accept the demand changes and notify MUSEUM in writing, at which time the parties contract shall come to an end and be null and void. The parties agree to act in good faith in discussing the reasons for the demand changes and to negotiate a satisfactory resolution within thirty days of the original request for demand changes otherwise the contract shall come to end and be null and void. By mutual written agreement the parties may extend the time for discussion and preliminary draft performance.

MUSEUM respects the ARTIST's right to free expression and the ARTIST's artistic integrity in the design and ultimately creation of the WORK, and will not unreasonably object to the preliminary design unless MUSEUM in its opinion believes the WORK may constitute a WORK of "obscenity," "child pornography," or is otherwise inconsistent with MUSEUM's written mission statement.

2. Progress Payments. Upon MUSEUM's written approval of the preliminary design, the ARTIST shall proceed with the construction of the WORK, and MUSEUM agrees to pay the price of $_____ for the WORK as follows: _____% upon written approval of the preliminary design, _____% upon the completion of 50% of the construction of the WORK, and _____% upon the construction completion and installation of the WORK. MUSEUM agrees to promptly pay the following expenses incurred by the ARTIST, after receipt of invoices, in the course of creating the WORK: _____ _____, but in any event not to exceed: _____. MUSEUM shall pay the applicable sales tax, if any, with the final progress payment. ARTIST is responsible for all other costs and expenses related to the design and construction of the WORK not otherwise agreed upon. Completion of the construction of the WORK is to be determined by the ARTIST. The ARTIST shall use the ARTIST's professional skill and judgment to deviate from the preliminary design as the ARTIST in good faith believes necessary to create the WORK. If, upon the ARTIST presenting MUSEUM with written notice of any payment being due, MUSEUM fails to make payment with thirty days of receipt of notice, interest at the rate of three (3%) percent shall accrue upon the balance due. MUSEUM shall have right to inspect the WORK in progress upon reasonable notice to ARTIST.

3. Installation Participation and Completion. Upon acceptance of the Preliminary Draft, and completion of the construction, the ARTIST shall participate in the installation of the WORK, which shall be completed by _____ _____. This completion date may be extended at the option of MUSEUM in the event the ARTIST may be disabled by illness or injury preventing progress of the WORK. The completion date shall also be extended in the event of delays caused by events beyond the control of the ARTIST, including but not limited to fire, theft, strikes, shortage of materials, and acts of God. Time shall not be considered of the essence with respect to these conditions related to the completion of the WORK; **except under no circumstance may the time for completion extend beyond January 1, 2017, time being of the essence herein.**

The final decision of completion of the construction and installation shall rest with the MUSEUM.

4. MUSEUM Services and Expenses. MUSEUM shall provide and pay directly for services and expenses required for the preparation of the WORK that occurs in MUSEUM's location work site or actual exhibition area. These expenses may include carpentry, electrical, plumbing, construction material not acquired by ARTIST, and labor.

MUSEUM shall provide and pay directly for insurance covering fire and theft during the construction, installation, and exhibition of the WORK on MUSEUM's location work site or exhibition area. In addition, MUSEUM shall incur the costs and expenses related to creating content condition report, exhibit wall labels, catalog materials, publicity information, brochures, preview announcements, preview party, and promotional literature. The ARTIST shall bear the risk of loss until the WORKS are brought to MUSEUM's location site or exhibition area.

5. Images. The ARTIST agrees to permit MUSEUM to take photograph images, print or digital or otherwise, video, sound and audio recordings, or images of the WORK during its construction and upon installation for archival, promotional, educational, and such other purposes as MUSEUM shall determine now or in the future. The photographs and any reproductions of the photograph shall remain the physical and intellectual property of MUSEUM. The ARTIST grants MUSEUM the right to take and use photographs, and visual, sound, and audio recordings of the ARTIST on location at the work site or exhibition area for archival, education, and promotion purposes. The ARTIST specifically releases all rights of publicity related to these images. Appropriate copyright notice credit in the name of the ARTIST shall appear on the WORK and promotional and education materials related to the WORK, and in any reproductions of the WORK, where the copyright is in the name of the ARTIST.

6. Privacy and Publicity. The ARTIST gives to MUSEUM the permission to use the ARTIST's name, likeness, voice, signature, picture, portrait, photograph, and personal image in all forms and media and in all manners, including but not limited to this exhibition, display, advertisements, promotional materials, trade, education, and archival uses and purposes, without violation of the ARTIST's right or privacy or publicity or other personal or proprietary rights the ARTIST may possess in connection with the design, construction, installation, and exhibition of the WORK. Any reproduction or exhibition of the WORK produced shall be credited as follows: "Installation by (ARTIST), the MUSEUM at _____."

7. Design Ownership. The ARTIST shall retain the physical and intellectual property interest in any preliminary and final designs, plans, descriptions, drawings, instructions for construction and installation, and models created for the purpose of this site-specific exhibition. However, MUSEUM reserves the right to make copies of said property for the purpose of archiving and displaying these materials for research and education purposes.

8. Exhibit Title Ownership. The title of the exhibition shall remain with the ARTIST until the ARTIST has completed the construction and installation, and is paid in full, at which time the title of the exhibition shall transfer directly to MUSEUM.

9. Brochures. MUSEUM shall provide at no cost to ARTIST twenty (20) copies of any brochures and catalogs creating for the exhibition.

10. Repairs. In the event the WORK is damaged during exhibition the ARTIST agrees to make timely repairs to bring the WORK back to its original condition at the time of completion of construction and installation. MUSEUM will be responsible for any and all construction expenses related to the repair. In the event the ARTIST cannot or will not make said repairs within ten (10) days of written request, at MUSEUM'S discretion, it may make the repairs consistent with the site-installation's designs as provided by ARTIST. The ARTIST agrees to hold MUSEUM harmless for all repairs to the WORK.

11. Ownership. The WORK shall remain on MUSEUM's site from the date of completion and installation until _____, subject to earlier removal at the sole discretion and expense of MUSEUM. At such time, MUSEUM will dismantle and remove the WORK with or without the ARTIST's participation and shall deliver it to the ARTIST's premises unless the parties have made some other arrangements in writing. In the event the ARTIST fails to provide written instructions for the dismantling and removal of the WORK within ten (10) days upon receipt of notice to remove the WORKS, it shall become the property of MUSEUM, which may utilize or dispose of the WORK as it chooses. In no event, though, may MUSEUM sell, re-exhibit, or loan the work without the written permission of the ARTIST.

MUSEUM, consistent with the provision of **Paragraph 5** may photograph the dismantling and removal of the WORKS, and retain all rights associated with such images.

12. Inspection. MUSEUM will provide periodic on-site inspection of the construction and installation of the WORK and will maintain reasonable security during hours of operation open to the visiting public. MUSEUM's agents and employees shall not be responsible for or liable for any damage to or destruction of any equipment or tools supplied by ARTIST. MUSEUM will declare for insurance value the WORK at the value declared by ARTIST, subject to reasonable approval by MUSEUM, which will be presumed to be the replacement value.

13. Independent Contractor. The ARTIST shall be an independent contractor during the period of performance under this contract, and not an employee. The ARTIST shall be required to carry whatever insurance is necessary for the purpose of performance of this Contract. The ARTIST agrees to defend, indemnify, and hold harmless MUSEUM from any and all claims and liabilities arising directly or indirectly from the ARTIST's activities or acts or any assistant's or employees or persons under ARTIST's direction.

14. Waiver. The ARTIST waives any and all claims arising at any time and under any circumstances against MUSEUM as it relates to the WORK under the **Visual Artists Rights Act** (VARA) (17 USC Section 106(a) and 113(d)) or otherwise under any local, state, national, or foreign law that conveys the same of similar "moral rights" protecting the right of attribution and integrity of works of visual art.

15. Review. MUSEUM may conduct views and reviews, as it deems necessary during the construction and installation of the WORK on location site or exhibition area. Final acceptance of the WORK for purposes of payment and exhibition shall rest in the professional opinion of the **curator,** or his or her assigns, of this site-specific installation. The name of the curator is

_____.

16. Termination and Breach. This Contract may be terminated on the following conditions:

(A). If MUSEUM does not approve the final preliminary design pursuant to Paragraph 1. The ARTIST shall keep any and all payments made and this Contract shall terminate.

(B). The ARTIST shall have the right to terminate this Contract in the event MUSEUM is more than sixty (60) days late in making any payment due pursuant to Paragraph 2.

(C). MUSEUM shall have the right to terminate this Contract in the event the ARTIST fails to complete without cause any material condition of this Contract otherwise known as a **material breach** within the one year period for completion ending _____.

(D). This Contract shall automatically terminate in the event the disabling illness or injury of the ARTIST causes a delay of more than three (3) months or if events beyond the ARTIST's control cause a delay of more than six (6) months from the expected exhibition date; provided, that the ARTIST shall retain all payments made pursuant to Paragraphs 1 and 2.

(E). This Contract shall automatically terminate on the death of the ARTIST, provided, though, that the ARTIST's estate shall retain all payments made pursuant to Paragraphs 1 and 2.

(F). The exercise of any material breach of this Contract that leads to a termination or termination shall be written and set forth the grounds for termination.

17. Non-assignability. Neither party hereto shall have the right to assign this Contract without the prior written approval of the other party. The services provided by the ARTIST are **personal services** and are not to be transferred or assigned in any manner without this prior written approval by MUSEUM. The ARTIST, however, retains the right to assign monies due and payable to the ARTIST under this Contract subject to the terms and conditions of this Contract.

18. Time is of Essence. Time is of the Essence throughout this Contract unless otherwise specified.

19. Waivers. A waiver of any breach, material or non-material, of the provisions or conditions of this Contract shall not be construed as a continuing waiver of other breaches of the same or that are similar.

20. Notices. All written notices shall be given to the parties' addresses as described in the beginning of this Contract. Each party shall provide written notification of any change of address prior to the date of said change.

21. Integration. This Contract constitutes the entire understanding between the parties, and supersedes and replaces any previous documents, correspondence, conversations, or other written and oral understandings. Only an instrument in writing signed by both parties can modify its terms.

22. Dispute Resolution. The parties agree to attempt to resolve any dispute, claim, or controversy arising out of or related to this Contract by mediation. The parties further agree that their respective good faith participation in mediation is a condition precedent to pursuing any other legal or equitable remedy, including arbitration, litigation, or other dispute resolution procedures.

23. Governing Law. The laws of the State of ___ shall govern this Contract.

24. Counsel. The parties agree that there are important rights and responsibilities incorporated into this Contract. Each party acknowledges having had the opportunity to seek independent legal counsel and representation before executing this Contract.

IN WITNESS WHEREOF, the parties hereto have signed this Contract as of the date first set forth above, as their respective, free act and deed.

ARTIST _____ WITNESS _____

MUSEUM _____ WITNESS _____

Authorized representative's name and title:

SUMMARY

The culture shift from viewing visual art strictly as a means to nonverbally communicate an idea or expression about an object that is valued both for its aesthetics and its investment worth is a modern phenomenon. The growth in commercial art transactions involving artists, galleries, auction houses, insurance companies, financiers, collectors, and museums requires a basic understanding of contract law. Any contract creates legally enforceable duties and obligations between two or more parties. Contract law regarding the sale or consignment of art varies from state to state; however, to form a contract there always must be a mutual offer and acceptance, consideration, legal capacity, and a lawful purpose. There are risks associated with any agreement that relies upon mutual performance promises especially in the consignment arena. Whenever one or more parties to a contract fail to perform as promised a breach occurs that might lead to damage claims.

WORKS REFERENCED

William Alden, "Art for Money's Sake," in the *New York Times*, February 3, 2015.

Tad Crawford, *Legal Guide for the Visual Artist*, 5th ed., New York: Allworth Press, 2010.

John Murray, *Murray on Contracts*, 5th ed., San Francisco: LexisNexis, 2011.

Kevin Ray, "Botticelli's 'Madonna and Child': The Risks of Art Consignment," in the *National Law Review*, 2015.

7

Protecting Art

Copyrights and Reproduction Rights

"Obviously, creative ownership of art works is not a concept we have clearly defined, either in intellectual or in populist spaces, either in the white cube galleries of New York or the bureaucratic committees of Toronto. We thought we had, but our old definitions are disintegrating with every cellphone photo and every screen grab."

—Russell Smith, *The Globe and Mail*

The source of all the reproduction rights that an artist possesses in a work of art is a *copyright*. It, like other categories of intellectual property, refers to the exclusive intangible property rights of the mind granted to those who creatively express an original idea. It protects the *tangible expression of an idea, not the idea itself*. The copyright is a legal interest distinct from the right to possess or own the physical work of art. The laws of intellectual property encompass familiar topics such as patents, trademarks, trade dress, industrial design, trade secrets, and copyrights. Copyrights are relevant to the study of art law because these reproduction rights can be *licensed*, *assigned*, or even *sold*.

Inherent in any copyright is a tension that exists between public interests and private rights of the artist. By definition a copyright is an economic monopoly that grants certain exclusive rights to artists or rights holders for a limited time period. The justification for giving artists an economic incentive is to stimulate and reward artistic creativity. These property rights restrict the public from fully accessing and using the artist's protected images. Nearly all artists take some inspiration from the works of other artists. Yet there is a risk that this appropriation of an early work will infringe upon a copyright.

The suitable place to draw the line between these competing interests—term of protection, forms and features of art to protect, innovative means of storing and delivering art, first amendment freedom of expression—and how courts, legislative bodies, and cultural bodies address these conflicting concerns is the subject of this chapter.

A BRIEF HISTORY

The first oil-based printing press was developed around 1439 by the German blacksmith Johannes Gutenberg. This new printing technique was adopted throughout Europe. In England, for example, a system of regulation developed that delegated control of the printing presses to a guild of printers or "stationers" that enjoyed monopoly powers. Interestingly, the right to print or copy was granted not to the author or creator of the work, but to the authorized printer. The printer acted as a censor against the publication of materials offensive to the English government or Crown or heretical to the Church of England. An unauthorized or pirated copy published by a rival printer infringed upon the exclusive rights to copy granted to the printer by the Crown. The notion of paying royalties to the authors was unknown.

The exclusive printing powers of the "stationers" expired in the late 1600s as democratic values and norms began to take hold in England. The established printers sought legislative protection against their competitors. A statute enacted in 1709 became the foundational structure for copyright laws enacted in the United States. Named the **Statute of Anne**, it resulted for the first time in protecting the authors of works, not solely the printers.

While the reproduction of the written word was protected in England, it was not until 1735 that statutory copyright protection there was extended to images, that is, prints and pictures. Meanwhile, one of the founding fathers of the United States, Noah Webster, convinced each of the original twelve states to pass a law of copyrights. Ultimately, the **Federal Constitution** embraced this right in **Article I, section 8, clause 8** (the **Copyright Clause**) by providing that Congress shall have the right "to promote the Progress of Science and useful Arts, by securing for limited Times to Authors and Inventors the exclusive Right to their respective Writings and Discoveries." This Article expressly grants to Congress the legal authority to enact copyright legislation.

Pursuant to this power, Noah Webster persuaded his cousin Daniel Webster to convince the first Congress to enact the **Copyright Law of 1790**. The original duration for copyright protection was fourteen years, which was renewable for another fourteen years. Initially, the statute limited protection to maps, charts, and books. A dozen years later etchings and engravings of historical prints were added to the list. By 1870, the revised list of works subject to copyright was expanded to include photographs, negatives, drawings, sculpture, drawings, and paintings.

Over time, Congress has enacted several different copyright statutes that have not only increased the categories of works protected, but also enlarged specific rights for artists and lengthened the term of copyright protection. The most significant revision occurred when the **Copyright Act of 1976** was enacted, which took effect on January 1, 1978. A major change of the 1976 Act was to eliminate the involvement of individual states from the copyright system. Federal copyright law now preempts any state copyright law. A second important modification was to alter the presumption that an artist transferred copyright with a transfer of the original physical work of art. For works of art created after 1977 the term of copyright protection is now the life of the artist plus seventy years. For works of art created prior to 1978 that are subject to copyright renewal the maximum duration of protection is ninety-five years.

The Copyright Act of 1976 simplified the formalities for recognition of an artist's copyright. Copyright protection now begins the moment the original work of art is placed or fixed in some tangible form of expression. The strict regimen of notice of publication was relaxed, although the **1909 Copyright Act** previously exempted paintings, drawings, sculpture, photographs, prints, and maps from the full copyright notice requirement.

To bring United States copyright law in closer harmony with the main international copyright treaty, the **Berne Convention for the Protection of Literary and Artistic Works (Berne Convention)**, Congress enacted the **Berne Implementation Act in 1988**. Effective March 1, 1989, notice of copyright became permissive, not mandatory. It is highly recommended that artists aesthetically continue to use the traditional copyright notice, to wit the ©, year of first publication, and name of artist, to establish a public record of the copyright claim. By joining the Berne Convention artists in the United States automatically receive protection from the more than 100 countries that are members of the Berne Union. All Berne Convention countries must provide a copyright duration for at least fifty years after the death of the artist.

To more fully comply with a highly contentious aspect of the Berne Convention, two years later, Congress enacted the landmark **Visual Artists Rights Act (VARA)**. This federal legislation, which took effect on June 1, 1991, and was guided to law by Senator Edward Kennedy, protects *personality* aspects of the artist's creation. Personality rights are also described as *moral rights*. In general, they include the right to proclaim or disclaim authorship of a work of art and the right to protect the reputation of the work.

These are rights that are independent of pecuniary or economic copyrights. They last as long as the artist is living even if the artist has transferred a work of art and the accompanying copyright. The statutory definition of protected works under VARA is extremely narrow, thereby limiting its effectiveness. The scope and limits of VARA are more fully described in the next chapter.

While the Berne Convention is generally the governing international copyright treaty, in some instances another treaty—the **Universal Copyright Convention (U.C.C.)**—may come into play. The U.C.C. requires that all its member countries, including the United States, offer a minimum copyright term of at least the life of the author plus twenty-five years. The treaty also provides national treatment to any work first published in a U.C.C. member country or by a national of any U.C.C. member country. The term national treatment, as defined under the Berne Convention and U.C.C., means a member country extends the same copyright protection to nationals of other member countries that it provides to its own national citizens. Unlike the Berne Convention, the U.C.C. requires artists to use the long notice form, that is, ©, name of artist and date of first publication, for protection. In addition, another international law, the **Buenos Aires Convention**, extends copyright protection when the term "All Rights Reserved" is added to the notice language.

WHAT IS COPYRIGHTABLE?:
CREATION, SCOPE, AND BENEFITS

A copyright in a work of art whether a two-dimensional drawing or a three-dimensional sculpture grants the owner of a creative work the exclusive right to make copies, prepare derivative works, sell or distribute copies, and display the work publicly. The term "works of authorship" refers to pictorial, graphic, and sculptural works for our purposes. The artwork is automatically protected by copyright the moment it is created, that is, when it assumes a tangible form. It also gives the artist the correlative right to prevent others from unauthorized use of the art. To receive copyright protection all four of the following criteria are required:

1. It must be an original, not a copied, work of art or authorship.
2. It must be a copyrightable subject matter—literary works, musical works, dramatic works, pantomimes and choreographic works, pictorial-graphic-sculptural works, motion pictures and other audiovisual works, sound recordings, and architectural works.
3. It must be fixed in a tangible medium of expression—such as woodblock prints on paper, stained glass designs, tapestries, collage on paper

leaf, watercolor on stationery, charcoal comic strips on newsprint, artwork applied to clothing, gouache and crayon on paper over canvas, murals, screen-print posters, blush pen and ink on plastic sheet, tattoo drawn on skin, photograph saved digitally.

4. It must have a minimum degree of creativity produced by an exercise of human element—alas, a selfie, defined as a spontaneous photograph taken with a smart phone and an outstretched arm, by an ape lacks the human intellect component and therefore fails the creativity test. However, a selfie of Ellen DeGeneres taken at an Academy Awards ceremony and tweeted around the world does qualify. The creativity component is the framing of the image, selecting the angle, and composing.

These requirements for a work of art to receive copyright protection are set out in the Copyright Act of 1976 and are the subject of administrative law and judicial interpretation.

The degree of originality required for copyright protection only requires a minimum level of creativity independently conceived by the creator. The art work itself does not have to be new or unique. Two identical works of art created independently may each qualify as an original work of art so long as one was not copied from the other. Creativity can be found in nearly any work of art in large part because courts are reluctant to insert their own personal standards of what is art. However, in a landmark judicial decision, *Feist Publications, Inc. v. Rural Telephone Service Co., Inc.* (499 U.S. 340 [1991]), the US Supreme Court ruled that the original phone directory was not protected under copyright law. The Court made two significant legal points. First, the labor and expense required collecting and compiling material or information also known as the "sweat of the brow" test is insufficient on its own to amount to a creative effort. Second, listing names and phone numbers found in the public domain alphabetically fails to demonstrate a modicum level of creativity in the selection, coordination, and arrangement of the information required under the statute.

In a case more closely associated with creativity and museum or gallery art law in a digital world, a federal court in New York reached a fascinating cross-continental decision (*Bridgeman Art Library, Ltd. V. Corel Corp.*, 25 F.Supp.2d 421 [S.D.N.Y.1998]). The Bridgeman Art Library is a British company that commercially licenses high-quality photographic replicas of art works in cooperation with major museums and art galleries. A Canadian company Corel Corporation designs CD-ROMs that contain hundreds of digital reproductions of public domain works of famous paintings by European masters. Under US, Canadian, and European law once a copyright term has expired, the copyright to the work falls into the *public domain*, where anyone is free to use the work. Bridgeman sued Corel alleging copyright infringement for copying without permission or authorization Bridgeman's transparencies of works of art in museum collections that were found in a Corel CD-ROM.

Before reaching its decision, the judge in the case—Hon. Lewis Kaplan, a former Harvard Law professor who taught copyright law—acknowledged that photographic images are protectable under copyright law whether in print or digital format. Relying upon an earlier federal case, Judge Kaplan noted that "something beyond technical skill must be demonstrated in a photograph to be considered original, and, therefore, copyrightable." Another US Supreme Court case, *Burrow-Giles Lithographic Co. v. Sarony* (111 U.S. 53 [1884]), was cited because it held that a photograph could be copyrighted only if it displayed sufficient originality in "its pose, arrangement of accessories in the photograph, and lighting and expression in the photograph evoked."

In Kaplan's written ruling, he emphasized that the underlying works were two-dimensional paintings that were reproduced in two-dimensional images. The color transparencies were exact replicas of the original paintings, whose copyrights themselves were all in the public domain because the artists were long since deceased. Relying upon *Feist*, the court found that the lavish amount of time and energy, that is "sweat of the brow," expended by Bridgeman to create the transparencies was not the "creative spark" that is the *sine qua non* of originality. In adding further insult to Bridgeman's argument, the court likened the transparencies to a photocopy of a Michelangelo drawing, which is not copyrightable either.

The *Bridgeman* case was originally argued under US copyright law because the alleged infringement by Coral was said to have occurred in New York. In a highly unusual situation, the court agreed to rehear the case under United Kingdom copyright law. Judge Kaplan determined that whether the case is analyzed under the Universal Copyright Convention, Berne Convention, UK copyright, or US copyright law, Bridgeman's reproductions are not copyrightable for lack of originality (*Bridgeman Art Library, Ltd. v. Corel Corp.*, 36 F. Supp. 2d 191 [S.D.N.Y. 1999]).

The *Bridgeman* decision left unanswered the issue of whether a photograph of a three-dimensional work of art, such as a sculpture, is copyrightable. The implication is that when three-dimensional works are photographed there are more creative choices related to angles, positioning, and lighting thereby lending a sense of sufficient originality to qualify for copyright. Another unresolved question is whether a photograph of a portion of an art work in the public domain is copyrightable. To date no court has addressed either issue.

Keep in mind that copyright law does not protect facts or ideas. Instead, it protects the unique manner in which ideas or facts are expressed. For instance, an art gallery representing a professional photographer sued Korea Air because a color image of an island that appeared in a newspaper advertisement was similar to a black and white photograph of that same island taken by the photographer. The court held that copyright principles do not protect ideas or the choice of the subject matter. In this instance, where the subject matters are identical, copyright law cannot protect the two different ideas of deciding where and how to shoot the island. The outcome would have been different had Korea Air used the photographer's image without permission because the creator of the photograph is entitled to control how the work may be used by others.

Jean Anthelme Brillat-Savarin, the French philosopher and epicure, wrote, "Tell me what you eat, and I will tell you what you are." People everywhere impulsively reveal "what" they are by digitally photographing every leafy green salad and pork roast entree and posting it on Flickr, Twitter, Facebook, Shutterfly, and Foodspotting. Are you infringing upon a chef's copyright by taking that photograph? There is no copyright in food creations because food dishes are not considered an art form within the subject matter of protected works. The ideas, facts, and creation of prepared dishes are not copyrightable, although a cookbook including photographs of food and commentary related to recipes may be copyrighted.

Utilitarian objects are not copyrightable, however, a utilitarian object such as Marcel Duchamp's urinal that incorporates an artistic motif, is signed "R. Mutt," and titled *Fountain* is entitled to copyright protection. Geometric shapes are not copyrightable either, although a Kandinsky drawing combining circles, rectangles, and triangles floating freely on paper giving the viewer a sense of illusionistic space is copyrightable. Typeface designs are also not copyrightable, but a Jasper Johns lithograph that incorporates typeface in its artistic imagery is subject to copyright protection. Multimedia works that combine elements of visual art with non-visual art, such as mixing computer generated sound, video, or animation with objects of art in a physical space qualify for copyright protection. This form of art is increasingly found in science, computer, history, and fine arts museums, especially with the growth of virtual museums.

The Copyright Act of 1976 largely settles the question of who owns a copyright: *the person who created the initial work of art owns the copyright.* There are notable exceptions:

1. Works Made for Hire – when an employee creates a work of art in the regular course of employment then the copyright is owned by the employer. A range of circumstances is examined to determine work for hire status including whether the hiring party or employer has a right

to control the manner and means by which the art is produced, source of tools and materials, and level of skill required to prepare the art. The totality of the decisive legal tests for whether a work of art is "made for hire" or not is articulated in a US Supreme Court case, *CCNV v. Reid* (493 U.S. 730 [1989]). The duration of copyrights for work for hire is not the same as it is for copyrights for non-work-for-hire artists. It lasts the shorter of seventy-five years from date of publication or one hundred twenty years from the date of creation in the case of unpublished works. Unpublished works of art are those that have not been made available to the general public without restriction.

2. Pre-1978 Commissioned Works—in general, the copyright to a commissioned work of art by an independent contractor belongs to the party that retained the independent contractor, such as the Detroit Institute of Art commissioning Diego Rivera to create a series of frescos in 1932 and 1933 or Harvard University commissioning Mark Rothko to create murals in the early 1960s.

3. Post-1978 Commission Works—so long as the artist is not an employee of the commissioning party the copyright belongs to the creator of art. For instance, when a museum commissions a non-employee artist to paint a mural the artist owns the copyright unless the parties by written contract agree otherwise. There is a statutory exception to this rule when the commissioning party, such as an art gallery, hires an artist to write an essay in an exhibition catalog known as a contribution to a collective work then the commissioning party, the gallery, owns the copyright to the essay.

4. Assignment—if the artist sells or assigns the copyright then the purchasing party owns the copyright.

5. Death—if the artist is deceased copyright interests may pass to an heir or beneficiary via a will, trust, or by inheritance.

A fascinating twist to the matter of copyright ownership was showcased in the film, *Big Eyes*, starring Amy Adams as the visual fine artist Margaret Keane. Her paintings, including the popular Keane Eyes or Big Eyed Waifs from the 1960s, were sold under the name of her purportedly domineering husband. She sued him for slander when he publicly claimed authorship. In court, each party was asked to paint a Big Eyed child painting. He begged off claiming a sore shoulder, while she finished her painting in under an hour. She was awarded a $4 million judgment.

The Copyright Act of 1976, **Section 106**, as mentioned earlier, grants to the copyright owner a bundle of five separate rights including the exclusive right to:

- reproduce or make copies of the art work
- display the art work publicly
- perform the art work publicly
- sell and distribute the art work
- prepare derivative art works

This provision provides the creator of the art, or the party to whom the work is assigned, transferred, or sold, with certain explicit rights to control how others may use it subject to various limitations. An example of a statutory limitation occurs regarding the right to display art. For example, a museum that owns a work of art or has lawfully borrowed the work has the right to display the art without further permission from the copyright holder. On the other hand, had the museum digitally made copies by creating commercial posters or greeting cards for sale online or in a gift shop without permission from the copyright owner then the museum is exposed to copyright infringement allegations. The "reproduction" and "sale and distribution" of the images are protected activities under the statute so long as the copyright in the work has not fallen into the public domain.

The protection of derivative or adaptation rights extends beyond mere shield against unauthorized copying to include the right to make other versions of the original art. A company that manufactured and sold ceramic tiles by incorporating transparent images it removed from a book that contained copyrighted images of art violated the exclusive right to prepare derivative images owned by the widow of the creator. The court denied the tile company's argument that by purchasing a copy of the book that contained the images it acquired the right to use the works under the "first sale" doctrine. The tile company was free to subsequently sell its physical copy of the book under this doctrine, but without a specific transfer of the copyright holder's exclusive right to prepare derivative, that is rearranging, recasting, re-versioning, or translating, works they remain with his widow (see *Mirage Editions, Inc. Albuquerque A.R.T. Co.*, 856 F.2d 1341 (9th Cir. 1988), *cert. denied*, 489 U.S. 1018 [1989]).

The opinion of the court in *Mirage* has come under criticism by advocates of those who find this interpretation of an artist's economic rights as too protective. Surely, not every use of a copyrighted work amounts to the production of a derivative work; exceptions do exist for libraries, archives, fair dealings, and fair use. Finding the right balance between ensuring consumers have reasonable access to copyright protected works and recognizing the scope of rights granted to artists remains complicated and challenging.

Digital technology makes available creative tools to both innovate new forms of paintings, sculpture, sounds, and movement, and also easily distribute them. In a world where a computer has to copy a work from a hard drive into memory to display it, are these transitory copies always-unlawful reproduction infringements? Generally, there are not. The extraordinary ability to manipulate, transform, meld, and merge old art into new digitally produced art presents detection difficulties for the artist that created the original protected work, while also testing the notion of the human hand in creativity.

INFRINGEMENT: PERMISSION, LICENSING, FAIR USE, AND PARODY

The owner of a copyright is free to give *permission* for others to use the artwork in the form of a temporary *license* or permanent *assignment*. Typically, a license or assignment occurs when a copyright owner is interested in commercially exploiting the work. The license may cover a precise geographic region, such as China, or a specific time frame, such as the month of June. Licenses may be *exclusive* where the party holding the license is permitted to exercise solely the copyrights or *non-exclusive* where others may be permitted to exercise the same rights. The transfer of all copyright interests unconditionally is referred to as an assignment. Monetary consideration in the form of royalty payments or an outright purchase agreement usually accompanies a license or assignment, respectively. Free licenses for those artists willing to share with the public their copyrights, while still retaining full copyright ownership and the ability to manage their copyright, is available through the Creative Commons (see www.creativecommons.org). A record of any license or assignment may be filed with the US Copyright Office to give notice to other parties of the existence of these property transfers.

The use of a work may become contentious when a person or entity without permission or authorization encroaches upon the exclusive bundle of intellectual property rights that a copyright holder enjoys. A stronger legal term for this encroachment is *infringement*.

The notion of what activities constitute an infringement is not always easy to decipher. Verbatim copying the work of another and claiming it is yours is rare, but does happen, as demonstrated in the *Keane* decision. The hard cases occur when material in the so-called new work takes protected elements from the first, original, copyrighted work. Justice Learned Hand summed it up well when he wrote "the test for infringement of copyright is of necessity vague."

The party that files a civil infringement action to protect a copyright is known as the plaintiff—usually the copyright holder or licensee. The plaintiff must demonstrate that the original creative effort is copyrighted, and the plaintiff is the one that owns the copyright or has acquired a license. Registry of the copyright or any assignment makes this first step easier. The focus is then on the activities of the alleged infringing party, the defendant. The defendant may be the actual party that directly or primarily infringed on one or more of the plaintiff's exclusive rights or an indirect or secondary infringer, where the allegation is that the defendant assisted another party in infringing.

The test for copyright infringement on paper is relatively straightforward: *whether an ordinary person, while examining the original work and the alleged copied work side by side, would conclude that the second work is indeed copied from the original work.* The copy does not have to be an exact reproduction of the first work. A finding of substantial similarity is sufficient. The copyright holder's case is frequently strengthened when it is shown that the alleged infringing artist had access to the original work, such as by proving that the original art work was downloaded by the defendant from the plaintiff's website. This type of evidence surfaced during the litigation proceedings involving the appropriation artist, Shepard Fairey, and the Associated Press (A.P.). Through forensic computer detective work the lawyers for the A.P. were able to show that Fairey had downloaded an A.P. photograph of Barack Obama that was subsequently used in his well-known "HOPE" posters.

The general observation test used by judges and juries to resolve copyright infringement claims requires an examination of both the qualitative and quantitative similarities between the contested works of art. There is no universal standard for guaranteeing that when more than some fixed percentage of the original protected work is altered, such as 10 or 20 percent, then a finding of non-infringement is assured. The case-by-case factual analysis required for infringement often comes down to the issue of whether the alleged infringing artist has merely used an idea from the original artistic creation, which is not a protected right, or infringed upon the basic expression of the art, which is a protected copyright.

Not all unauthorized uses of another artist's works of art qualify as infringements. Beyond the limits on the five basic exclusive rights of copyright holders found in Section 106 of the Copyright Act, as amended, there are a number of statutory exclusions. These so-called *affirmative defenses* and licenses are codified in **Sections 107 through 120** of this same Act.

In a broad sense the judicially crafted doctrine of *fair use*, as codified in Section 107, *permits uses of copyrighted works for purposes such as public criticism, news reporting, commentary, teaching, scholarship, or research.* This list is not complete because the law *allows for parody, appropriation art, and other uses* that are viewed as *transformative* of the protected work.

Artists from Pablo Picasso to Andy Warhol freely admit to having "borrowed" or "stolen" from the works of other pioneer artists. For example, Picasso's Cubist painting contained distinctive features of tribal masks from northern Africa. Similarly, Warhol's famous silkscreen image of Marilyn Monroe was based on a copyrighted photograph of the actress. The digital world allows musicians easily to remix songs and visual artists effortlessly to cut, paste, and collage from the works of others—a technique that began more than a century ago when Georges Braque initiated the practice of incorporating bits of emerging culture such as newspaper articles and typeface into his painting. At what point is the newly created art form legally sufficient to stand on its own as an original art form, as opposed to being challenged as infringing art?

To determine whether a particular use is a fair use or not there are four statutory factors to consider:

1. the purpose and character of the use, including whether such use is of a commercial nature or for nonprofit, education purposes;
2. the nature of the copyrighted work;
3. the amount and substantiality of the portion used in relation to the copyrighted work as a whole; and
4. the effect of the use upon the potential market for, or value of, the copyrighted work.

The role of the court is to assess each of these factors individually, and then view them all together in deciding whether the use qualifies for protection as fair use. For example, a museum that photographs an accessioned or formally acquired and recorded work of art by a living artist, such as a photograph of Cindy Sherman in costume taken by the artist Cindy Sherman, and stores the image on an internal museum database for archival purposes has more than likely engaged in a permissible use. Contrast that use with a museum that uses the same photograph for a non-education use, such as reproducing it on postcards or coffee mugs for sale in the museum's gift shop. How has the use changed? The character of the use is now commercial. There is very little creativity involved in taking a digital picture of a photograph and printing it on a mug or piece of paper. The totality of the original photograph is photographed even though it is downsized. And Sherman loses out on the opportunity to profit from the sale of her copyrighted photograph because the museum has not executed a royalty based licensing agreement with her. After inspecting each of the four fair use factors individually and examining them collectively this second use points to infringing conduct.

Returning to the Shepard Fairey example, this Rhode Island School of Design–trained artist altered the media from a photograph to a poster. That detail alone is not a sufficient defense to an infringement claim. Nor is the fact that the reworked painting is larger than the original work or that it is a version of the digital image that was cropped and then painted over in the colors red, white, and blue. A demonstration that Fairey had directly copied the original image from the Internet in the first place and an ordinary viewer's observation that he took more than a trivial amount of the copyrighted protected elements of the original work would warrant a finding of infringement. The A.P. is in the business of licensing its photographs. Although it may not be in the business of creating posters, it could license others to do so as a derivative right in the original photograph. Also, Shepard's change in use of his poster from a political statement that was given freely to state Democratic party members in support of Obama's quest for the presidency to a highly sought-after commercial poster, where the posters were individually numbered, signed, and sold on his www.obeygiant.com website, works against a non-infringing conclusion. The parties settled the major components of their civil dispute out of court. In the future, Fairey agreed not to use copyrighted A.P. photographs in his art without first obtaining a license.

In a side note to the Fairey copyright quarrel that also serves as an example of a legal concept discussed earlier, the person who took the 2006 photograph of Obama used by Fairey was Mannie Garcia, an established commercial photographer. The then-Senator Obama was captured on digital film at an event in Washington, DC, while Garcia was on assignment as a *freelance or work for hire* photographer for the A.P. Normally, Garcia would have owned the copyright to the image; however, by the terms of the parties' written contract, Garcia had assigned the copyright to the A.P. Otherwise the fair use dispute may have been between Fairey and Garcia.

Fairey is not the only repurposed or appropriation artist whose work exposes the tension between intellectual property rights and artistic freedom. In recent years, a handful of prominently exhibited artists whose works sell at auction and galleries for astronomical prices have all had their artistic integrity challenged. Federal courts have analyzed the weight and significance of each of the four fair use factors and the concept of transformative use differently making it difficult to draw any across-the-board conclusions about what is and is not copyright infringement that could be beneficial for emerging and current visual artists.

For instance, in *Rogers v. Koons* (960 F.2d 301 [2nd Cir.1992]), also known as the case of "Puppies" versus "String of Puppies," a for-profit commercial photographer, Art Rogers, successfully challenged a sculptor, Jeff Koons, who liberally made use of his copyrighted image. Rogers's photograph of a couple holding a line of puppies was licensed to a greeting card company that used the image in post cards and note cards sold to the public. Koons purchased one of the cards and promptly tore off the copyright notice. He then instructed his assistants to faithfully use the two-dimensional image

("Puppies") as a model or copy for a three-dimensional sculpture ("String of Puppies"). In finding *bad faith* infringement, the 2nd Circuit Court of Appeals ruled that Koons had meticulously copied the composition, pose, and expression of the original work. No original expression of a work of art was found in the four sculpture copies created. Koons's work was not sufficiently transformative to find protection against an infringement claim. The appropriation artist, Koons, was identified as the primary infringer. His gallery that sold three of the sculptures for $367,000 was a secondary infringer. Under the federal copyright statute because Rogers's work was registered with the US Copyright Office he was entitled to statutory damages or actual damages suffered plus any appropriated profits earned by Koons and his gallery.

Rogers's "Puppies" black and white photograph is the image on the top, and Koons's "String of Puppies" infringing rendition is on the bottom in figure 7.1.

In contrast to this decision, fourteen years later, the same 2nd Circuit Court of Appeals affirmed Koons's use of a copyrighted photograph that he had

Figure 7.1.   **Puppies vs. String of Puppies.** *Photo on top © by Art Rogers, Photo on bottom © by Jeffrey Koons.*

incorporated into a collage painting was fair use. The original photograph by the fashion photographer, Andrea Blanch, appeared in *Allure* magazine in 2000. In *Blanch v. Koons* (476 F.3d 244 [2nd Cir. 2006]), the court scrupulously examined all four of the fair use factors. In telling language, the court held that Koons's work, "Niagara," passed the transformative test "almost perfectly" because he changed the colors, background, medium, size of the objects, and their details with an entirely different purpose and meaning from the original commercial advertisement photograph. Koons had described his work to the court as one of using popular images for commentary on the "social and aesthetic consequences of mass media." The commercial nature of Koons's work—he had been commissioned to create a painting for an art gallery in Germany—did not defeat his fair use argument. Koons's painting on the right appears next to Blanche's photograph in figure 7.2.

In a highly controversial fair use case that saw a partial reversal of the original lower court holding, the 2nd Circuit Court of Appeals in a split decision ruled in favor of the appropriation artist Richard Prince, and the Gagosian gallery that sold the disputed work (*Cariou v. Prince*, 714 F.3d 694 [2nd Cir. 2013]). Twenty-five of the original thirty paintings that had been deemed copyright-infringing by a lower court are now fully protected as an entirely different aesthetic from the original copyrighted photographs by the French photographer, Patrick Cariou.

The court viewed the differences between the works as follows:

Where Cariou's serene and deliberately composed portraits and landscape photographs depict the natural beauty of Rastafarians and their surrounding environs, Prince's crude and jarring works, on the other hand, are hectic and

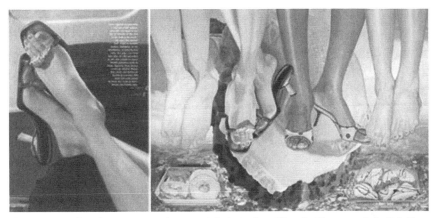

Figure 7.2.   Blanch vs. Koons. *Photo on left © Andrea Blanch, Photo on right © Jeffrey Koons.*

provocative. Cariou's black-and-white photographs were printed in a 9 1/2″ x 12″ book. Prince has created collages on canvas that incorporate color, feature distorted human and other forms and settings, and measure between ten and nearly a hundred times the size of the photographs. Prince's composition, presentation, scale, color palette, and media are fundamentally different and new compared to the photographs, as is the expressive nature of Prince's work.

What is critical is how the work in question appears to the reasonable observer, not simply what an artist might say about a particular piece or body of work. Prince's work could be transformative even without commenting on Cariou's work or on culture, and even without Prince's stated intention to do so. Rather than confining our inquiry to Prince's explanations of his artworks, we instead examine how the artworks may "reasonably be perceived" in order to assess their transformative nature.

These cases illustrate the complexities of judges subjectively analyzing the four controlling fair use factors, deciding how much weight to give each factor, when to ignore one or more of the factors, while simultaneously focusing on the global transformative nature of the entire work. Braque, a contemporary of Picasso and an outstanding twentieth-century painter, maintained that the intent of an artist is everything. Yet, the court completely ignored Prince's inability to articulate the reason or purpose behind his "transformative" art. Prince, similar to Koons in the *Rogers* decision, purchased a copy of Cariou's book and tore out copies of his Rastafarian images from which to create his new art. The court ignored this act, which an earlier court had found was evidence of bad faith.

Criticism of the 2nd Circuit Court of Appeals' approach to relying upon the transformative nature of appropriation art occurred in a 7th Circuit Court of Appeals that followed the *Cariou* ruling. In *Kienitz v. Sconnie Nation, LLC* (No. 13-3004 [7th Cir. Sept. 15, 2014]), penned by the respected judge, the Hon. Frank Easterbrook, the court emphatically noted that even though the US Supreme Court mentioned "transformative" use in its copyright decision in *Campbell v. Acuff-Rose* (510 U.S.569 [1994]), it is not one of the four factors listed in the fair use statute. Easterbrook expressed concern that the 2nd Circuit's approach to asking whether something is exclusively "transformative" amounts to overriding section 107 of the Copyright Act, which protects derivative rights. Easterbrook would have courts rely on the four stated factors, and reject the concept of transformative use. He also believes that the fourth factor, effect of the new work on the market value of the copyrighted work, is usually the most significant of the fair use considerations.

Time will tell whether other federal courts will embrace Easterbrook's belief that any new use of an original work transforms the copyrighted work. Which is to say it is a derivative work, and therefore infringes upon the protected work, unless the new work qualifies for protection under the fair use umbrella.

The US Supreme Court noted in *Campbell* that some works receive greater protection against infringement than others because they are "closer to the core of intended copyright protection than others." Works of art that are highly creative weigh against a judicial finding of fair use when copied. On the other hand, a humorous form of public comment called *parody* tends to be more favorably viewed as an *affirmative fair use defense* based on Justice Souter's unanimous opinion in the *Campbell* decision.

The legal issue in *Campbell* dealt with whether the commercial nature of a parody of Roy Orbison's hit song "Oh, Pretty Woman" by a rap band ("2 Live Crew") rendered the parody presumptively an unfair use within the meaning of the Copyright Act of 1976.

Souter wrote that a parody's commercial character is only one element to be weighed in a fair use analysis. In particular, the character and purpose of the use and the market harm must be reviewed, too. This decision watered down a prior US Supreme Court verdict—*Sony Corp. of America v. Universal City Studies, Inc.* (464 U.S. 417 [1984])—that held that every money-making commercial use is presumptively an unfair use. The high court noted that *context* matters and that parody (a "humorous form of public comment or criticism") even *commercial parody* could qualify for protection as a fair use.

Souter's fair use analysis worked to the advantage of the producers of a movie after being sued for copyright infringement by the famous celebrity photographer, Annie Leibovitz. Her photo of the naked and pregnant actress Demi Moore appeared on the cover of *Vanity Fair*. That particular magazine issue became an all-time best seller. Two years later in 1993, Paramount Pictures launched an advertising campaign that included a poster featuring a "pregnant" smirking Leslie Nielsen to promote the movie *Naked Gun 33 1/3: The Final Insult*. The movie starred Nielsen in a slapstick police caper. See the respective images in figure 7.3.

A federal judge in Manhattan dismissed Leibovitz's infringement lawsuit. The court ruled that the poster advertisement "took an image that had become widely known and added something distinctly new for humorous commentary," thereby fitting the definition of parody. This element weighed heavily in favor of a finding of fair use based on the film advertisement serving as a form of funny public comment on Moore's serious and pretentious expression. In the court's examination of all four of the fair use elements, it determined that although the poster drew heavily on Leibovitz's work including nearly identical poses and lighting, the Paramount image was actually a photograph of a different eight-month pregnant woman. There was no negative market effect on the sale or licensing of the Leibovitz photograph of Moore after the poster's

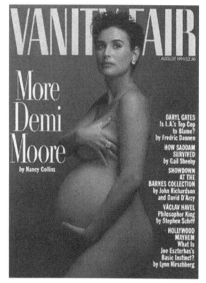 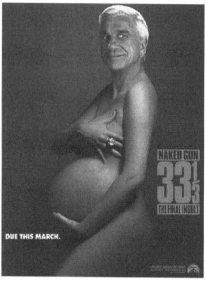

Figure 7.3. Leibovitz's *Vanity Fair* cover vs. *Naked Gun 33 1/3* poster. *Photo on left © Annie Leibovitz, Photo on right © Paramount Pictures.*

publication. Overall the poster image was a transformative work of protected art that contextually was used differently than the original photograph.

EQUITABLE AND STATUTORY DEFENSES: STATUTE OF LIMITATION, LACHES, ESTOPPEL, AND LICENSES

The *statutory defenses* and *licenses* are found in **Sections 108 through 120** of the Copyright Act of 1976. As discussed before, the doctrine of fair use is the most important and litigated defense. However, under **Section 507**, a civil action for copyright infringement must be filed within three years after the discovery of the infringement or after it reasonably should have been discovered. This rule, which is common throughout civil litigation, although the time length to bring suit may differ depending on the cause of action, is known as a *statute of limitations*. This three-year period also applies in legal actions to determine who owns a contested joint copyright.

Some federal courts recognize an old French legal concept, *laches*, a concept referenced in the chapter on contracts. It provides an equitable defense to an infringement claim by a copyright holder or licensee who unreasonably delays suing the alleged infringer. A copyright holder who has full knowledge of the infringing conduct is barred from recovering damages.

Another defense to an infringement claim is the doctrine of *equitable estoppel*. For example, a copyright holder who encourages, facilitates, or acquiesces in an infringing activity is barred under this doctrine from later on seeking monetary damages and equitable help such as *injunctive* relief.

The general rule that requires permission to reproduce, perform, or distribute a copyrighted work from the holder of the copyright is subject to a few exceptions. One of these exceptions is a *compulsory license*. It applies most often in the non-dramatic music industry, but does not incorporate lyrics to music because they are copyrighted as literary works.

An example of how a *non-compulsory license* does work is found in a recent dispute between James Cameron, the director of the movie *Titanic*, and the Artists' Rights Society, an organization that guards the exclusive rights of many prominent fine artists both alive and deceased. In Cameron's original epic romantic disaster film starring Kate Winslet and Leonardo DiCaprio depicting the fictional account of the sinking of the RMS *Titanic*, he displayed a rendition of Picasso's famous Pre-Cubism painting "Les Demoiselles d'Avignon" without authorization. Picasso painted it in 1907; and he died in 1973. Therefore, his exclusive copyright interests now held by his heirs but protected by the Artists Rights Society via an assignment last until 2043 under US copyright law. The actual physical painting still exists and is owned by the Museum of Modern Art in New York City.

Picasso's heirs were upset about Cameron's use of the painting for a handful of reasons: the movie depicts the loss of the painting when it was seen disappearing at sea; the painting was never on the ship; and it infringed upon their right to publicly display the image of *The Young Women of Avignon*. On behalf of the heirs, the Artists Rights Society successfully negotiated a licensing fee. And then, in 2012, the 3-D version of the original Titanic movie was released, which raises a host of new legal issues: is the 3-D version an adaptation or derivative form of the first Titanic film making it an entirely new movie that now requires a new licensing arrangement or is it, as Cameron believes, the same movie so it was already covered by the original licensing fee deal? In the absence of knowing the terms and conditions of the first licensing agreement the issue of monies owed, if any, is unknown until the parties amicably resolve their differences or a court decides.

DIGITAL MILLENNIUM COPYRIGHT ACT AND INTERNET COPYING, GOOGLE ART PROJECT

In response to copyright concerns created by Internet digital technology the **Digital Millennium Copyright Act (DMCA)** was enacted in 1998. This federal statute amended the Copyright Act of 1976 in two significant ways. It makes it illegal to attempt to circumvent processes, methods, or devices that limit or restrict copying of copyrigi¹ted works. This section of the statute, known as the *anti-circumvention* provision, also prohibits the production, promotion, or sale of products or services designed to circumvent systems, such as a digital rights management system (DRMs) that limits digital copying or downloading of photographs and other works of art. Numerous exemptions exist, such as for nonprofit libraries, museum archives, and educational institutions that need to override DRMs to protect works in their own collections. The statute prohibits the falsification of copyright management information and any distribution of works that contain false copyright information.

The second important change in copyright law is the section that limits Internet Service Provider (ISP) liability for primary or secondary copyright activities. Under its *safe harbor* provision, an ISP can avoid liability for transient routing or connecting of copyright infringing material that automatically flows through its computer. Copyright infringement claims are denied for permanently storing infringing material so long as the ISP promptly removes the material upon request from the copyright holder or licensee. The DMCA relieves an ISP from liability when it inadvertently links to a site that contains copyright infringing works. It is unclear how an ISP upon receiving a request to take down an alleged copyright infringing work considers the affirmative defense of fair use.

The DMCA permits statutory copyright damages, actual damages, and injunctive relief as civil remedies. *Willful* violations of the statute for personal or financial gain can lead to criminal charges and up to ten years of incarceration.

A little more than a dozen years ago the search engine Google devised an online feature called "Images." It offered viewers the ability to search the entire Internet for images based on a single inquiry. It works by storing snapshots of each image in a temporary storage area or cache available for fast retrieval upon request. It allows for access across the digital world of "thumbnail" samples of millions of photographs, paintings, logos, banners, and nearly any other image imaginable. Once the image is found online it is frequently easy to save the file and then print, copy, or edit the image.

Not long after Google launched its "Images" platform it was sued for copyright infringement by a men's magazine that demanded that Google stop storing photographs from its magazine in a cache and delete all "thumbnail" versions from its search engine. The 9th Circuit Court of Appeals held the "thumbnails" qualified as a non-infringing fair use under the Copyright Act of 1976. In similar cases, each time Google or any search engine employing this mathematical platform was sued for infringement it was deemed a passive participant in the search process. It is the *end users* who chose whether to view the cached images and save, print, and edit the copyrighted works that are the potential infringers depending on how the works are used.

In a sense courts have reasoned that search engines have an implied license to store images because technology exists that allows for a copyright holder to turn off the caching using codes and tags. A copyright holder who fails to incorporate this technology into his or her website may then lose the opportunity to claim copyright infringement. In an era of social networking sites, blogs, wikis, and sites such as Flickr, where amateur and professional photographers share photos and videos with the world, the impact on unsophisticated artists who lack the technological know-how or tools to protect themselves from unauthorized uploading is potentially devastating.

On the other hand, the global benefits of merging new technologies with making images of art more accessible are readily apparent in the Google Art Project. It is an interactive online showcase that allows viewers to "walk" through the interior of more than 150 museums from around the world. High-resolution images of artworks housed in these partner museums, including the Metropolitan Museum of Art, Tate Gallery-London, Hong Kong Museum of Art, and the Art Gallery of Ontario are available for easy online viewing. Nearly all of the artwork displayed in the Google Art Project is owned by the partner museums. In most cases the copyrights to these works have either fallen into the public domain or more contemporary artists have granted a license to have their works exhibited online. In a few instances, such as the Toledo Museum of Art, twenty-two works had to be removed from the online exhibition because the copyright holders complained.

EUROPEAN TRENDS

In 2015, a French photographer of furniture for auction catalogs, Stéphane Briolant, won a stunning monetary judgment against artnet, a publisher of auction house sales reports. Briolant successfully claimed in a French appeals court that he was entitled to copyright damages when reproductions of his images of furniture appeared in artnet's price database. The court held that artnet couldn't post the selling prices from auction furniture sales alongside his images without referencing his copyright and paying him his fee.

Factually, this case is fascinating on many levels. Interestingly, Briolant was paid for his original auction sales catalog photographs, which were taken at the sales offices. This is the first reported instance where a photographer successfully claimed a copyright in reproduction photography for reports of auction sales. Subscription-based services that report auction sales of fine art, decorative art, and antiquities now may be required to charge additional fees to their customers to cover reproduction copyright charges. The implications for all online auction databases, and even gallery catalogs, in a global art world are immense.

In the aftermath of this decision, artnet removed all images by Briolant from its database. A competitor of artnet, Artprice, also was found civilly culpable for a similar copyright infringement of the photographer's unlicensed images. The court was not swayed by arguments about the economic cost to pay for reproductions and how it might lessen market transparency.

In response to concerns about large-scale online piracy of copyrighted works and loss of royalty and licensing revenue, Britain revisited its intellectual property regulations. Effective in 2020, commercial copyright infringement may now be deemed a criminal offense subject to ten years of incarceration. The law's impact on artists who frequently "borrow" from the works of others, such as Jeff Koons, Bob Dylan, and Richard Prince, is unclear until British courts are asked to resolve a disputed copyright contest.

SUMMARY

The Copyright Act giveth and taketh away. The law grants the copyright owner a bundle of exclusive rights: reproduce, prepare derivative works, distribute copies, display, and publicly perform. A copyright protects the intangible creative expression of an original idea without actually protecting the idea itself. A copyright is a distinct, legal right independent from the right to own or possess a physical work of art.

A natural tension exists between the public's interest in creatively building upon the art forms of earlier artists and the private, constitutionally protected, economic rights of the original creator of the copyrighted art. Copyright holders are free to license their works or even give it away for free. In a digital age, where visual images and sounds are freely available and shared without complete regard for copyright restrictions, repercussions have led to civil law suits. In response to claims of copyright infringement, visual artists, and especially appropriation artists, look to the statutory defense of fair use. These artists argue their new works cause no economic harm to the original work, and are sufficiently novel, innovative, and creative in a transformative fashion to stand on their own as original, non-infringing works of art consistent with copyright policy and artistic practices over the years.

WORKS REFERENCED

Patricia Aufderheide, Peter Jaszi, Bryan Bello, and Tijana Milosevic, "Copyright, Permissions, and Fair Use among Visual Artists and the Academic and Museum Visual Arts Communities: An Issues Report," A Report to the College Art Association, February 2014.

Circular 40: "Copyright Registration for Pictorial, Graphic and Sculptural Works," United States Copyright Office, Washington, DC.

Tad Crawford, *Legal Guide for the Visual Artist*, 5th ed., New York: Allworth Press, 2010.

Leonard DuBoff and Christy King, *Art Law*, 3rd ed., St. Paul, MN: Thompson-West, 2000.

Lesley Ellen Harris, "The Selfie Hits Prime Time," http://www.copyrightlaws.com/wp-content/uploads/2014/08/Blog-post-Editorial-Selfie.pdf, 2014.

Dan Hunter, *Intellectual Property*, New York: Oxford University Press, 2012.

Michael E. Jones, Walter Toomey, M. Nancy Aiken, and Michelle Bazin, *Intellectual Property Law Fundamentals*, Durham, NC: Carolina Academic Press, 2014.

Benjamin Kaplan, *An Unhurried View of Copyright*, Clark, NJ: The Lawbook Exchange, Ltd. (Originally published by Columbia University Press, 1967), 2008.

Annette Kur and Vytautas Mizara (eds.), "The Structure of Intellectual Property Law: Can One Size Fit All?," ATRIP Intellectual Property, 2011.

Mary LaFrance, *Copyright Law: In a Nutshell*, St. Paul, MN: West Academic Publishing, 2008.

Robert Lind, Robert Jarvis, and Marilyn Phelan, *Art and Museum Law: Cases and Materials*, Durham, NC: Carolina Academic Press, 2002.

Celia Lerman, "Protecting Artistic Vandalism: Graffiti and Copyright Law," in *NYU Journal of Intellectual Property and Entertainment Law*, 2013.

Richard Stim, *Patent, Copyright & Trademark: An Intellectual Property Desk Reference*, 12th ed., Berkeley, CA: NOLO, 2012.

8

Moral Rights of Artists

"The violation of the artist's moral rights is a copyright infringement, and the artist may recover actual or statutory damages."

—17 U.S.C. Section 504(a)-(c)

The United States (US), Canada, Australia, and the United Kingdom (UK) are all common law countries that traditionally have protected an artist's exclusive economic rights through recognition of a copyright in the physical embodiment in the art. An artist is free to sell, lend, or give away the creation. Additionally, an artist may assign, license, or sell the copyright interest in the art, too. Once a copyright is transferred the new owner—a museum, library, foundation, gallery, or private collector—acquires all the economic rights associated with the copyright that the artist enjoyed. In this case, the artist is divested of all pecuniary privileges and rights associated with the original creation. There is no common law obligation for the new owner to store or care for the art in a particular way or even not deface, crop, or destroy the art. Up until a few decades ago in the US, there was no legal recognition of an artist's right independent of the right of copyright known as "*moral rights*" that would protect an artist's non-economic interests.

In brief, a moral right is a right given to an artist to assert limited authority over a work of art even after the art is sold or transferred. The two limited statutory moral rights recognized in the US concern the right to claim or disclaim authorship, and the right to prevent or claim damages for intentional destruction or mutilation of the artist's work.

In contrast, countries in Latin America and continental Europe view the rights an artist possesses in the art created along the lines of a human or natural right rather than solely an economic right. In its purest form a moral right does not result from a government grant. It arises from the process of creating art. Traditional Roman law countries sought to protect the moral honor and reputation of the artist and the artist's creation by making the right to exert control over the presentation and treatment of the art inalienable or non-transferable. The specific rights associated with moral rights are *personal* to the creator and are in addition to and independent of any copyright nations grant.

The common law countries were late in acknowledging the principles associated with moral rights. The economic and legal system of the US is one that historically and philosophically recognizes and encourages the transfer of property interests and therefore does not blend easily with a set of inalienable personality rights. However, in 1988, the US amended its basic copyright statute (**Copyright Act of 1976**), and joined the **Berne Convention for the Protection of Literary and Artistic Works** (**Berne Convention**). That same year, the UK by an act of Parliament became a signatory nation as well. Upon joining this international Convention both the US and UK committed themselves to a minimal level of moral rights recognition with significant departures from the rights granted European and Latin American artists.

Two years later, Congress implemented a moral rights regime to formally comply with the most minimal Berne Convention obligations. The landmark federal statute enacted, **the Visual Artists Rights Act (VARA)**, effective June 1, 1991, narrowly defines the visual artwork for which an artist ("author") is granted two moral rights: the *right of attribution* and *the right of integrity*.

VISUAL ARTISTS RIGHTS ACT

In general, the special policy based reasons for VARA are threefold. First, the statute recognizes society's interest in encouraging artists to work creatively. Second, the legislation respects the public cultural value in preserving works of art. Post-1990, the public interest in preserving a limited range of visual art trumps what was once a strictly private contract arrangement between an artist and an acquirer of the art. Third, destruction or mutilation of a visual artist's art may be prejudicial to the artist and the artist's ability to exploit the art for personal gain, reputation, and honor. This is a value long cherished in Europe and Latin America, but not previously accepted in the US and the UK.

Moral Rights and Works Covered under VARA

The specific statutory language that revised the **Copyright Act of 1976** is as follows:

17 U.S. Code § 106A. — Rights of certain authors to attribution and integrity

(a) **Rights of Attribution and Integrity.**—Subject to section 107 and independent of the exclusive rights provided in section 106, the author of a work of visual art—

(1) shall have the right—

(A) to claim authorship of that work, and

(B) to prevent the use of his or her name as the author of any work of visual art which he or she did not create;

(2) shall have the right to prevent the use of his or her name as the author of the work of visual art in the event of a distortion, mutilation, or other modification of the work which would be prejudicial to his or her honor or reputation; and

(3) subject to the limitations set forth in section 113(d), shall have the right—

(A) to prevent any intentional distortion, mutilation, or other modification of that work which would be prejudicial to his or her honor or reputation, and any intentional distortion, mutilation, or modification of that work is a violation of that right, and

(B) to prevent any destruction of a work of recognized stature, and any intentional or grossly negligent destruction of that work is a violation of that right.

(b) **Scope and Exercise of Rights.** — Only the author of a work of visual art has the rights conferred by subsection (a) in that work, whether or not the author is the copyright owner. The authors of a joint work of visual art are co-owners of the rights conferred by subsection (a) in that work.

(c) **Exceptions.** —

(1) The modification of a work of visual art which is a result of the passage of time or the inherent nature of the materials is not a distortion, mutilation, or other modification described in subsection (a)(3)(A).

(2) The modification of a work of visual art which is the result of conservation, or of the public presentation, including lighting and placement, of the work is not a destruction, distortion, mutilation, or other modification described in subsection (a)(3) unless the modification is caused by gross negligence.

(3) The rights described in paragraphs (1) and (2) of subsection (a) shall not apply to any reproduction, depiction, portrayal, or other use of a work in, upon, or in any connection with any item described in subparagraph (A) or (B) of the definition of "work of visual art" in section 101, and any such reproduction, depiction, portrayal, or other use of a work is not a destruction, distortion, mutilation, or other modification described in paragraph (3) of subsection (a).

(d) **Duration of Rights. —**

(1) With respect to works of visual art created on or after the effective date set forth in section 610(a) of the Visual Artists Rights Act of 1990, the rights conferred by subsection (a) shall endure for a term consisting of the life of the author.

(2) With respect to works of visual art created before the effective date set forth in section 610(a) of the Visual Artists Rights Act of 1990, but title to which has not, as of such effective date, been transferred from the author, the rights conferred by subsection (a) shall be coextensive with, and shall expire at the same time as, the rights conferred by section 106.

(3) In the case of a joint work prepared by two or more authors, the rights conferred by subsection (a) shall endure for a term consisting of the life of the last surviving author.

(4) All terms of the rights conferred by subsection (a) run to the end of the calendar year in which they would otherwise expire.

(e) **Transfer and Waiver. —**

(1) The rights conferred by subsection (a) may not be transferred, but those rights may be waived if the author expressly agrees to such waiver in a written instrument signed by the author. Such instrument shall specifically identify the work, and uses of that work, to which the waiver applies, and the waiver shall apply only to the work and uses so identified. In the case of a joint work prepared by two or more authors, a waiver of rights under this paragraph made by one such author waives such rights for all such authors.

(2) Ownership of the rights conferred by subsection (a) with respect to a work of visual art is distinct from ownership of any copy of that work, or of a copyright or any exclusive right under a copyright in that work. Transfer of ownership of any copy of a work of visual art, or of a copyright or any exclusive right under a copyright, shall not constitute a waiver of the rights conferred by subsection (a). Except as may otherwise be agreed by the author in a written instrument signed by the author, a waiver of the rights conferred by subsection (a) with respect to a work of visual art shall not constitute a transfer of ownership of any copy of that work, or of ownership of a copyright or of any exclusive right under a copyright in that work.

Another section of the Copyright code, **Section 101**, defines the *visual art works* that qualify for VARA protection. Under the statutory scheme *moral rights* apply only to any work that is "a painting, drawing, print, or sculpture, existing in a single copy, or limited edition of 200 or fewer signed and consecutively numbered." It also includes a still "photograph" only if created for exhibition purposes in signed, numbered editions of no more than 200 copies.

It is for this limited class of protected visual art works that the artist has the right to claim authorship and the right to prevent the use of the artist's name in the event the work has been altered or destroyed in a way that is prejudicial to the artist's reputation. In addition to these rights of attribution, the right of integrity allows a visual artist of "recognized stature" to prohibit the unauthorized modification, distortion, defacement, or destruction of the work of art should it be harmful to the artist's honor and good name. Both the physical and conceptual integrity of a work of art is safeguarded. These moral rights allow an artist to assert control over a work of art even after it has been sold or transferred. Unlike a copyright that may be sold, moral rights may not be assigned to another because they are personal to the creator of the art. They vest in a visual artist only for works created on or after June 1, 1991. The artwork does not have to be formally registered with the US Copyright Office for an affected artist to seek remedies for infringement. Upon the death of the visual artist these personal rights expire, whereas in Europe after death they descend to the artist's heirs.

The range of art that is not covered by VARA is substantial. The law does *not* apply to works for hire, posters, maps, globes, charts, technical drawings, architectural drawings, models, applied art, audio-visual works, motion pictures, electronic publications, advertising items, merchandising items, promotional materials, packaging materials, containers, coverings, books, magazines, newspapers and other publications, databases, electronic information services, and any other work not subject to copyright protection. Mixed media art incorporating any element of an excluded art form may cause the entire work to be excluded from VARA's protection. A policy reason for Congress failing to include works of a literary and digital form specifically under VARA was the sense that various other state and federal laws, such as libel, defamation, unfair competition, and trademarks, were sufficient to satisfy the Berne Convention's minimum level of protection requirements.

Comparing US and European Moral Rights

The concept of moral rights in the US is limited to the aforementioned rights of *attribution* and *integrity*. The term "moral rights" is the English translation of the French name *droit moral*. The nature and duration of these fundamental rights differ from country to country including in Europe. For instance, Germany links the term of an artist's moral rights to the length of copyright or seventy years after the creator's death. On the other hand, France recognizes moral rights in perpetuity even after the works have fallen into the public domain. Much of Europe in some form or other recognizes these basic rights in *droit moral*, which are centered on upholding the reputation and honor of the artist:

The right to create or not create art;

The right to disclose or divulge, which grants the artist the right to determine when a work of art is finished and may be displayed;

The right of attribution or paternity, which lets the creator to be identified as the artist and to disclaim it when authorship is applied to another;

The right of withdrawal, which allows the artist to modify art or withdraw authorship once the work is published;

The right to respect the work or the right of integrity, which permits the artist to object to the display of work in a mutilated, derogatory, or distorted manner.

An example of the differences between the application of moral rights between the US and France occurred in the early 1990s. John Huston was an American screenplay writer who directed the 1950 film, *The Asphalt Jungle*. Shortly after he died in the late 1980s, the Turner Entertainment network, which had acquired the film from MGM, "colorized" it. Huston's daughter, and lawful heir, believed Turner's digital colorization and subsequent French television broadcast distorted and mutilated the original classic black and white film. France, which has a much broader definition of works of art protected by *droit moral* codified in its **Intellectual Property Code**, fined Turner for violating Huston's moral rights after showing the colorized version on television. Motion pictures are not considered works of visual arts in the US so Huston's daughter had no cause of action there to seek relief under VARA. Additionally, John Huston's moral rights would have expired at his death.

France, and many other European nations, recognize a resale right known as *droit de suite*. The right of an artist to collect money when a work of art is resold is limited to sales by auction houses, agents, art galleries, and dealers. It does not apply to private sales between individuals or between an individual and a museum. Art is defined as "any work of graphic or plastic art such as a picture, a collage, a painting, a drawing, an engraving, a print, a lithograph, a sculpture, a tapestry, a ceramic, an item of glassware or a photograph" (**UK Artist's Resale Act**). For an artist to become eligible to receive royalties the artist's work must be registered with an authorized collection agency. In the UK, for instance, the royalty ranges from 4 percent for lower priced resale art to one-quarter percent for works selling for more than about $600,000. Resale royalties are capped at a maximum of around $15,000.

There is no federal resale royalty statute in the US. At the urging of New York Congressman Jerrold Nadler, the **American Royalties Too Act (ART)**, which would give visual artists 5 percent of the resale price for works resold at auction for more than $5,000 with a royalty cap of $35,000, has gained legislative momentum, but is not law. In 2014, California's progressive artist's resale state statute was struck down as unconstitutional for violating the **Commerce Clause** of the **US Constitution**. To date, more than fifty countries have enacted a resale royalty law in the interest of fairness for artists.

LEADING VARA CASES

The first VARA case to reach a federal appeals' court occurred a few years after its passage. The New York decision provided definitional insight on how certain terms within the statute are interpreted. Three sculptor artists were commissioned to create a mural in the lobby of a commercial building. The original owner of the building provided the supplies and oversaw the hiring of assistants. After starting the project, ownership of the building changed hands. The new owner told the artists to stop working on the project, and informed them that the installed work was to be removed. The lower court's original injunction preventing destruction of the mural was overturned because the artists were work for hire, and not independent contractors. The decision was helpful, though, because it judicially acknowledged for the first time the moral right of an artist of recognizable stature to prevent a third party from modifying or destroying the physical work of the art itself (not an image of the art) when it would damage the artist's honor or reputation (*Carter v. Helmsley-Spear*, 861 F.Supp. 303 [S.D.N.Y. 1994], aff'd in part, vacated in part, 71 F.3d 77 [2d Cir. 1995]).

Art incorporated or attached to buildings whether by sculpture, fresco, mural, graffiti, or street art poses unique challenges under VARA. For instance, the same Second Circuit Court of Appeals, two years after *Carter*, once more ruled against a group of artists seeking to exercise moral rights, albeit on different legal grounds. In an attempt to add "life" to a run-down area of the city, a handful of artists created a series of sculptures and murals on publicly owned walls. The artists unsuccessfully sought court protection to prevent the city from destroying the art. The court held that VARA is inapplicable to illegally crafted art on public property (*English v. BFC & R East 11th Street, LLC*, 198 F. 3rd 233 [2d Cir. 1997]).

A strong public policy argument could be made to grant legal status to wall art on public property that over time has earned special community status as cultural property. Street artists such as Banksy, Mr. Brainwash, and Shepard Fairey whose works frequently convey a strong social justice or political message cry out for unique recognition and protection. The few remaining sections of graffiti on the wall that once separated East Berlin from West

Berlin stand out as culturally meaningful monuments worthy of protection. Of course, private real property owners may understandably view unauthorized graffiti as unlawful trespass.

There is no legal duty to conserve art from environmental elements under VARA. An artist whose wall art is destroyed or mutilated by weather elements or the passage of time has no recovery rights against a private or public entity that neglects to preserve the exterior art. A gallery or museum that undertakes best practices to conserve or preserve art, and instead damages or modifies the art, is not subject to damages for violating VARA. The artist is free, however, to disclaim authorship.

The owner of a spray-painted building may remove or confiscate the graffiti-street art. However, the real property owner of the building may not reproduce or create derivative works, such as photograph the image and silk screen it on a coffee mug or T-shirt. These are among the exclusive rights of the copyright owner, the graffiti-street artist. A few years ago, when Amazon tore down its headquarters in Seattle it was within its rights to remove the wall art and reinstall the graffiti art in its new building on the same site.

The British street activist artist Banksy frequently visits foreign cities and spray paints public walls under the protection of darkness. Not long ago, he stencil-painted a series of walls around New York City. Soon after he posted their location to Instagram, local street artists either defaced his work because they didn't appreciate an outsider artist painting on their turf or the building

Figure 8.1.   Unnamed, © Banksy. *Photo image courtesy of Pixaboy.*

owners removed and preserved the art for sale to galleries and private collectors. Figure 8.1 is an example of one of Banksy's visual art public images.

A different occasion of VARA playing a role in a dispute between a museum and an artist demonstrates the pitfalls of a museum commissioning an artist to create a work of installation art without a written contract. The long-running argument between the Hyperrealistic Swiss artist Christoph Buchel and the Massachusetts Museum of Contemporary Art Foundation, better known as Mass MoCA, began years ago. At the outset the museum agreed to buy and transport into the museum all the things Buchel wanted in the assemblage. The items included a movie home, a police car, a bus, a voting booth, and other thought-provoking objects. The list continued to grow and the museum began to run out of funds. The museum became concerned about the length of time the artist was taking to complete the project. Buchel refused to finish the installation after numerous time extensions so the museum used staff members to attempt to bring closure to the project without the artist's permission or instructional oversight. The museum also covered the work in progress to prevent the public from viewing it, which Buchel believed was an act that harmed his reputation.

Ultimately, Mass MoCA filed a civil suit to ascertain its legal rights. The lower federal district court held that unfinished works of art are not covered by VARA. On appeal, the First Circuit Court of Appeals, located in Boston, Massachusetts, reversed the decision. Unfinished works that meet the statutory definition of a "work of art" may be subject to moral rights (*Massachusetts Museum of Contemporary Art Foundation, Inc. v. Buchel*, 593 F.3d 38 [1st Circ. 2010]). There was no finding that the covering of the art by the museum violated the artist's moral right of integrity nor had the museum unlawfully created a derivative art form in violation of his copyright interests. Buchel's installation, titled "Training Ground for Democracy," was never completed or exhibited. Under the parties' out of court agreement Mass MoCA was permitted to sell the removed objects.

The *Mass MoCA* case serves as a lesson for museums, galleries, and installation artists to clearly identify all the parties' material terms and conditions, including time for performance, cost obligations, exhibition schedule, and removal, in writing.

VARA has a provision that does permit the creator of covered works of art to *waive* moral rights. The consent to waive must be in writing, signed, and must specifically identify both the artwork and the intended use of the artwork. When the art is a collaborative effort any one of the creators may bind all the artists by a singular signed waiver.

According to an Executive Summary Report prepared by the Copyright Office for Congress on the impact of the waiver provisions in the statute, many buyers of fine art prefer a sale to include a written agreement that waives all moral rights. The report even cited a Campbell's Soup Art Contest that required all entry submissions to waive moral rights and copyrights in writing ("Waiver of Moral Rights in Visual Artworks: Executive Summary" Copyright Office, Library of Congress, October 24, 1996).

The issue of whether site-specific works or installation art are protected under VARA was not fully addressed by the *Mass MoCA* decision. A 2006 ruling by this same First Circuit Court of Appeals in *Phillips v. Pembroke Real Estate* (459 F.3d 128 [2006]) did address this specific subject. In reversing the lower court's judgment, the appeals' court held that VARA could not both apply to site-specific art and permit its destruction under a statutory exception because then it would amount to a violation of an artist's right of integrity. Therefore, the court held that the twenty-seven site-specific public park sculptures are categorically excluded from protection under VARA. The public presentation exception, which states that a work's presentation does not constitute destruction or modification, applies only to artworks that can be moved without also being destroyed or mutilated.

A Seventh Circuit Court of Appeals (*Kelley v. Chicago Park District*, 635 F.3d 290 [7th. Cir. 2011]), disagreed with the First Circuit's determination in *Phillips* that all site-specific artwork by a recognized artist is always unprotected under VARA. Chapman Kelley is an artist best known for painting flowers and landscapes. The park department in Chicago gave him a permit to install a site-specific wildflower garden, to wit, a display, across the park. As the seasons changed, the blossoming wildflowers changed. After a number of years of express and implied authorized display, the park managers decided to change the shape of the wildflower bed over Kelley's objections. Kelley sued alleging a violation of his right of integrity, and breach of an implied contract. The appeals court never reached the question of whether his reputation was damaged by the changes the park made to his flowerbed. Instead, it ruled under the Copyright Act his work barely qualified as original, but most certainly was altered as much by the whims of nature as his authorship. In conclusion, the court held that "the law must have some limits; not all conceptual art may be copyrighted." The flower gardens of master gardener, Kelley, failed to qualify for copyright protection, therefore, the issue of dishonor to his reputation failed to bloom into a justiciable legal issue.

Controversies concerning the installation, placement, and removal of site-specific art pre-date the passage of VARA. In many cases, these issues illustrate the tension between the artist's First Amendment *rights of free expression* and artistic integrity in juxtaposition against larger government or public interests. This conflict is demonstrated in the well-documented dispute between the sculptor, Richard Serra, and the General Services Administration, a federal government agency, which began in the early 1980s.

Figure 8.2. *Tilted Arc*, Richard Serra. *Photo image courtesy of General Services Administration.*

Serra was commissioned by the federal government to create a steel sculpture in a plaza in Manhattan. The artwork was installed in a location that made it difficult for walkers to pass among the various buildings. The architects who designed the main plaza building were upset because the twelve-foot high and 120-foot long sculpture obstructed the intended viewer sight lines. Four years later, in response to public safety and graffiti concerns, the federal government decided to remove the sculpture. Serra sued, claiming his First Amendment rights were violated. In finding against Serra, the court ruled that "the First Amendment protects the freedom to express one's views, not the freedom to continue speaking forever, the relocation of the sculpture after a lengthy period of initial display does not significantly impair Serra's right to free speech." In 1989, the *Tilted Arc* sculpture as seen in figure 8.2 was removed from the plaza (*Serra v. United States General Services Administration*, 847 F.2d 1045 [2nd Cir. 1988]).

REMEDIES

The remedies under VARA are identical to the remedies for copyright infringement, except there are no criminal law causes of action or penalties.

An artist whose work is modified or damaged may seek *statutory damages* ranging from a few hundred dollars to $30,000 with the amount recoverable at the court's discretion. Works of protected art that are willfully or knowingly distorted or destroyed can lead to statutory damages up to $150,000. In the alternative, for works of art more highly valued by the marketplace actual damages and any profits the offender may have realized may be claimed and captured. A non-monetary *equitable injunctive relief* requesting that the artist's rights of integrity and attribution not be violated is available.

SUMMARY

By joining the Berne Convention, the United States committed itself to ensuring that visual artists receive a minimal level of moral rights protection. Existing federal and state laws regarding copyright, defamation, trademarks, and unfair competition were inadequate to satisfy the minimum requirements of this international treaty. Effective June 1, 1991, Congress amended the Copyright Act and enacted the Visual Artists Rights Act, or VARA, that incorporated two of the rules developed in Europe to protect the moral rights of artists. The right of an artist to claim or disclaim authorship (right of attribution) and the right of an artist to prevent mutilation, destruction, or distortion (right of integrity) are the two European moral rights features the United States accepted. These rights are independent and in addition to the rights granted artists under copyright law. The rights approved under VARA are not transferable, although they may be waived in writing, and last only for the life of the artist. The federal statute tightly defines the "work of visual art" covered. Moral rights protect fine art works that have artistic merit of a "recognized stature." Site-specific installation art presents fascinating gray-area legal challenges regarding the applicability of moral rights.

WORKS REFERENCED

"Artist's Guide to the Visual Artists Rights Act: Understanding Your (Limited) Moral Rights, " St. Louis Volunteer Lawyers and Accountants for the Arts, 2005.

Mary Carpenter, "Drawing a Line in the Sand: Copyright Law and New Museums," in *Vanderbilt Journal of Entertainment and Technology Law*, 13:3, spring 2011.

Tad Crawford, *Legal Guide for the Visual Artist*, 5th ed., New York: Allworth Press, 2010.

Leonard DuBoff and Christy King, *Art Law*, 3rd ed., St. Paul, MN: Thompson-West, 2000.

Erica Esposito, "Commentary: Fixation and Authorship in 'Living Art': A Weakness in Copyright Law," in *Harvard Journal on Sports & Entertainment Law*, 2012.

Daniel Grant, "The Law against Artists: Public Art Often Loses Out in Court," in *Barrons*, August 4, 2014.

Michael E. Jones, Walter Toomey, M. Nancy Aiken, and Michelle Bazin, *Intellectual Property Law Fundamentals*, Durham, NC: Carolina Academic Press, 2014.

Mary LaFrance, *Copyright Law: In a Nutshell*, St. Paul, MN: West Academic Publishing, 2008.

Robert Lind, Robert Jarvis, and Marilyn Phelan, *Art and Museum Law: Cases and Materials,* Durham, NC: Carolina Academic Press, 2002.

Melissa Taitano and Sharon Farb (eds.), "International Moral Rights: Working Document—Moral Rights by Country," InterPARES 2 Project, University of California, Los Angeles, January 2005.

9

Free Expression, Privacy, Publicity, and Other Artists' Rights

"It should be no surprise that expression in the visual arts falls within the intellectual freedom protected by the first amendment to the U.S. Constitution."

—Judge Richard Posner in
Piarowski v. Illinois Community College,
759 F.2d 625 (1985)

Notwithstanding the sweeping language of the **First Amendment** to the **US Constitution** that commands, "Congress shall make no law . . . abridging the freedom of speech or of the press," these guarantees are not absolute. By necessity, even in a democratic society, there is a need for a balancing between individual rights of expression and societal rights of fear from threats to peace, harm to reputation, or violations of copyright and moral rights.

The framers of the Constitution thought of the spoken word when they sought to protect freedom of expression. It took nearly 150 years thereafter for the US Supreme Court to rule that *non-spoken communication*, such as a painting, poster, or comic book or *symbolic speech*, such as burning the American flag or wearing an armband, qualify for constitutional protection. Historically, courts have frowned upon approving regulations that are aimed at suppressing the content of a nonverbal message. In contrast, a regulation that is enacted to protect a recognized societal goal, and is not related to the message's meaning, is more likely to not run afoul of the First Amendment's prohibitions. As discussed further in this chapter, even though the First Amendment does not grant artists an unbridled right to paint or draw whatever they want and wherever they want, it does act as a restraint on government acts of censorship.

Supporting artistic expression as a way to stimulate and challenge the marketplace of ideas or nudge conventional thought is not always popular in democratic societies. Adherence to traditional customs, respect for opposing religious beliefs, following campus edicts banning "hate speech," and countless other factors work to coerce, skewer, and restrict artists whose messages may be deemed gratuitous, insulting, or offensive. The cartoon caricatures mocking the Muslim prophet, Muhammad, by the newspaper *Charlie Hebdo* sparked a worldwide debate on artistic satire as protected free speech against the religious sensitivities of a minority religion in France. The killing of twelve people, including five cartoonists, during an attack on the Paris office of *Charlie Hebdo* by Muslim extremists is indefensible as a civilized response to tasteless and outrageously offensive cartoons. The murders raise grim new fears about the use of physical threats and intimidation as an instrument to subvert the publication of a twisted adult version of *MAD* magazine, while leaving open to discussion whether the crass employment of ink, lines, and imagery to compose the "Nothing Sacred" targeted messages of Charlie Hebdo should be subject to cultural norms of decency, that is, self-imposed or government restrictions.

CENSORSHIP, NUDITY, PROTEST, OBSCENITY, AND ARTISTIC EXPRESSION

Throughout history the works of artists have been subject to restrictions and censorship. In 1505, Pope Julius II first commissioned the great Renaissance artist Michelangelo to create Sistine Chapel fresco paintings that served as metaphors for mankind's search for salvation through Jesus. At that time many Catholic religious leaders viewed his candid depictions of naked figures in the papal chapel as obscene and sacrilegious. In the interest of "decency," the genitals were eventually covered with "fig leafs." It wasn't until 1933 that the paintings were restored to their original condition.

A few years before the turn of the twentieth century Auguste Rodin fashioned a marble sculpture depicting an ill-fated couple embracing from Dante's *Inferno*, known as *The Kiss*. In 1893, a smaller bronze version of the statue was deemed unsuitable for general display because of its nudity at an international exposition in Chicago. Since then, and as recently as the late 1990s, *The Kiss* (figure 9.1) has been subject to censorship concerns at both public and private universities.

Another censorship controversy arose over politics and artistic expression in the early 1930s. The Mexican artist Diego Rivera was commissioned by the industrialist John D. Rockefeller Jr. to create a mural at Rockefeller

Figure 9.1. *The Kiss*, Auguste Rodin. *Photo image courtesy of Wikimedia.org.*

Center in New York City. Contractually, Rivera was retained to depict mankind at a crossroads, while looking ahead to a better future. Under political pressure from friends who thought he sold out to a capitalist, Rivera added the communist revolutionary leader Vladimir Lenin to the mural, that was not part of the original sketch approved by Rockefeller. Rivera refused to paint over Lenin. He was fired, and in a pre-moral rights era, the mural was destroyed.

Even Picasso, considered by many to be the most visionary and influential fine artist of the twentieth century, expressed his personal feelings about external and internal forces on artistic liberty. "Freedom, one must be very careful with that. In painting as in everything else. Whatever you do, you find yourself once more in chains. Freedom not to do one thing requires that you do another, imperatively. And there you have it, chains" (Dore Ashton, *Picasso on Art [Documents of 20th Century Art]* 148 [1977]). Safe to say, the more artists mix and merge explicit political and social themes and messages, the greater the focus on limits to artistic freedom.

GOVERNMENT REGULATION

Symbolic Speech

Around the same time period that Rockefeller was chiseling Rivera's mural off an office wall complex in Manhattan, the US Supreme Court for the first time recognized that nonverbal expression, to wit, symbols, works of visual and written art and performance art, may be "speech" for purposes of **First Amendment** protection. The Court struck down as impermissibly vague a state statute that banned the display of a red flag as a sign or symbol of opposition to organized government (*Stromberg v. California*, 283 U.S. 359 [1931]). In reaching this conclusion, the Court relied upon an earlier holding that recognized the right to free speech is essential to liberty, and is protected by the **First** and **Fourteenth** (due process) **Amendments**. In *Schenck v. United States*, 249 U.S. 47 (1919), Justice Holmes articulated a legal test, since modified, that a person could be prosecuted for speech only upon showing that the "words used are used in such circumstances and are of such a nature as to create a clear and present danger." Fifty years later, in *Brandenburg v. Ohio* (395 U.S. 444 [1969]), the Court struck down a state statute that criminalized the voluntarily assembling of people, a Ku Klux Klansman in this case, to advocate violence or terrorism as a means to accomplish political reform. A new two-prong test was created to analyze whether speech is free or not: is it "directed to incite or produce imminent lawless action" and is it "likely to incite or produce such action." *Brandenburg* remains the current standard for evaluating government attempts to limit inflammatory speech, including incendiary political cartoons, which may incite violence.

While *Brandenburg* recognized the value of "uninhibited, robust, wide-open" political debate as an essential component to democracy, unpatriotic art or artistic acts that defile symbolism of patriotism, such as defacing or desecrating the American flag, remain the subject of censorship controversy. For instance, a student at the Chicago Institute of Art designed a display that asked visitors to comment about his exhibition. The exhibit featured an American flag placed on the floor and a separate assemblage of a photograph of different images of the flag. To record their thoughts visitors had to walk on the displaced flag. Not surprisingly, the exhibition elicited public protests. The city of Chicago, also in response to the exhibition, passed an ordinance making it unlawful to dishonor the American flag. In ruling against the ordinance, a local county judge determined that when the American flag is displayed in a manner to communicate an idea or sentiment the First Amendment protects it.

Three US Supreme Court decisions provide a context for deciding when symbolic speech involving the American flag is protected speech. In the first case, a college student in response to the Kent State shooting tragedy and the United States' military participation in Cambodia hung an American flag upside down from his apartment window. He taped a peace symbol onto both sides of the flag. In striking down his conviction for violating a state statute prohibiting the placement of any words or symbols on an American flag, the Court noted the flag was displayed on private property and did not incite any breach of the peace. In barring the state from prosecuting individuals from using the flag to express a political view, the Court noted, "A person gets from a symbol the meaning he puts into it, and what is one man's comfort and inspiration is another's jest and scorn" (*Spence v. Washington*, 418 U.S. 405 [1974]).

The express goal of preserving the American flag as a revered national symbol arose in a fascinating case where the defendant was an art gallery owner, and not the offending artist. The questionable art, which featured among other creative symbols an American flag in the shape of a phallus jutting from a cross as an expression of protest against the Vietnam War, was displayed publicly. Ultimately, after a series of zigzag opinions that led to conflicting results, a federal court determined that no likelihood of imminent public harm or disorder was demonstrated by the state from the display. Nor did the state demonstrate to the court's satisfaction a strong enough government interest in preserving the flag as a national symbol to justify restricting this form of artistic symbolic speech. Therefore, consistent with the ruling in *Spence*, the regulation criminalizing anyone who casts contempt on the American flag unlawfully served to deprive the gallery owner of his right to express his mind freely (*United States ex rel. Radich v. Criminal Court of New York*, 385 F. Supp. 165 [S.D.N.Y. 1974]).

In 1989, the second major US Supreme Court flag case transpired. In a controversial ruling, the Court overturned the conviction of an alleged communist-leaning person who publicly burned the American flag to protest the policies of President Reagan. A Texas statute, which prevented the desecration of a venerated object including the American flag when such actions were likely to incite violence or anger in others, was deemed unconstitutional. In finding that society's outrage is insufficient on its own to justify prohibiting symbol speech, the Court pointed out a discriminatory aspect to the statute. Texas exempted from prosecution burning and burying a worn-out flag. The majority opinion stated that it is illegal to discriminate in this manner based solely on viewpoint (*Texas v. Johnson*, 491 U.S. 397 [1989]).

The Court in *Johnson* did not validate all forms or types of conduct as sheltered symbolic speech under the First Amendment. To receive consideration for constitutional protection from government regulation or censorship the expressive conduct or acts must be sufficiently imbued with *communicative elements* for others to understand the message that is intended. In Johnson's case, his polarizing act of burning the flag was joined with public anti-American chants that were clearly recognized as protest speech by those who witnessed it. The flag burning conduct did not incite "imminent lawless action" so it met the *Brandenburg* standard despite causing nasty public reaction.

That same year Congress passed a statute making it a federal crime to desecrate the American flag. The identical five-person majority of US Supreme Court justices as in *Johnson* invalidated the **Flag Protection Act** as unconstitutional under the First Amendment (*United States v. Eichman*, 496 U.S. 310 [1990]).

These symbolic speech and protest cases have implications for performance artists including street artists who may engage in visual demonstrations centered on the use of the American flag or other venerable objects to communicate an unpopular sentiment or idea.

Obscenity

Since colonial times, politicians, museums, artists, gallery owners, and the general public have wrestled with the fundamental issue of what is *obscene art*? Starting in the 1880s, statutes directed at regulating lewd and indecent art were enacted authorizing the seizure and destruction of obscene prints, paintings, lithographs, engravings, transparencies, books, and other material. Anyone caught possessing, displaying, or distributing so-called indecent or obscene art was subject to criminal penalties. In a 1942 decision, the US Supreme Court in *Chaplinsky v. New Hampshire* (315 U.S. 568 [1942]) held that there is a narrowly limited class of immoral speech that deserves no constitutional protection because it lacks social value as a step toward truth and is not an essential component to the expression of ideas. Included in this class of speech not protected by the First Amendment is "the lewd and obscene."

The Court in *Chaplinsky* did not define the term "obscene." One of the first semi-successful attempts to give meaning to this confusing term occurred in a decision involving a New York publisher and distributor of books, photographs, and magazines. In violation of a criminal statute prohibiting the mailing of "obscene, lewd, lascivious, or filthy . . . or other publication of an indecent character," the distributor was convicted for sending sexually explicit material to customers. While sustaining the lower court sentence, the Court gave formula guidance to future cases. First, it stated that sex and obscenity are not synonymous words. "Obscene material is material which deals with sex in a manner appealing to prurient interests." The term "prurient interests" refers to material that has a "tendency to excite lustful thoughts." Second, the legal standard for judging whether material is obscene, is "whether, to the average person, applying contemporary community standards, the dominant theme of the material, taken as a whole, appeals to prurient interest" (*Roth v. U.S.* 354 U.S. 476 [1957]).

Lack of legal clarity and increasing litigation in what Justice Harlan referred to as the "intractable obscenity problem" continued to follow after *Roth*. Sixteen years later, in another case implicating the distribution of sexually explicit material or obscene material, the high Court modified the test for obscenity.

In a landmark 5–4 decision penned by Chief Justice Burger, the Court reiterated that obscene materials do not enjoy protection from censorship under the First Amendment. The new guidelines for determining whether books or art or other materials are obscene are:

(a) whether the average person, applying contemporary community standards would find that the work, taken as a whole, appeals to the prurient interest;

(b) whether the work depicts or describes, in a patently offensive way, sexual conduct specifically defined by the applicable state law, and

(c) whether the work, taken as a whole, lacks serious literary, artistic, political, or scientific value.

In addition to these new standards for review, the Court emphasized that both the *content* and *context* of the objectionable material must be considered by the triers of facts (*Miller v. California*, 413 U.S. 15 [1973]).

The *Miller* test is still good law today. The redefined test for obscenity did not resolve all interpretive issues for artists and those who exhibit, display, and sell art. Later cases clarified that the "average person" language means how would a "reasonable person" view the art. Navigating the notion of the contemporary "community" standard, as a perspective for judicial review, is clouded in the ubiquitous world of the Internet. Does "community" mean the collection of viewers who visit a particular art-infused website or does it refer to the actual physical location where the viewer is looking at or downloading the artistic material on a smartphone or laptop? Does not all art, short of child pornography, have "serious artistic" value based on the affirmative testimony of a recognized art expert in the field?

In the absence of a national standard for obscenity, museums, art galleries, and artists must each look to their local communities for leadership and advice in applying the *Miller* standard. The broad-minded community in Provincetown, Massachusetts, which is full of artists and street performers, culturally is significantly different than the principally Mormon community of Provo, Utah. Consequently, an art exhibit imbued with gender identity, sexual references, and images defiling religious figures may constitute obscenity in one locale, but not another.

In a concurring opinion by the ideologically conservative Justice Potter Stewart in between the *Roth* and *Miller* decisions, he famously reached the conclusion that under the First (and Fourteenth) Amendments criminal censorship laws are nearly impossible to constitutionally apply to obscenity cases. His often quoted remark that "hard core pornography" was hard to define, but that "I know it when I see it" intuitively rings true for many art law observers even today (*Jacobellis v. Ohio*, 378 U.S. 184 [1964]).

In contrast to obscenity, the US Supreme Court in 1978 ruled that *indecent* speech in a broadcast medium regulated by the Federal Communications Commission (FCC) is entitled to limited First Amendment protection. In a decision involving the satiric humorist George Carlin, the court determined his "Filthy Word" monologue was not obscene, but indecent. However, the public policy value of protecting children from indecent speech broadcast during certain hours of the day was warranted. The harm of exposing children on radio or television to "patently offensive" material of a "sexual or excretory" nature as measured by "community standards" outweighs any claim to free expression (*FCC v. Pacifica Foundation*, 438 U.S. 726 [1978]).

During the Vietnam protest era, an art professor at the University of Massachusetts Amherst was invited to display his nude paintings on the corridor walls in the school's student union building. After five days, university officials removed the art on the grounds that it was readily observable to the public including children and was deemed offensive in that particular space. Some of the paintings exhibited male and female genitalia in a "clinic" fashion. In denying the artist's assertion that art is fully protected by the First Amendment, the 1st Circuit Court of Appeals determined that although the display was not obscene, it was still subject to reasonable regulation. The finding concluded that the exhibit was inappropriate in the public corridors of a university building. Specifically, the court found the public was a "captive audience" and was entitled to their "privacy" not to be exposed to what administrators considered offensive art (*Close v. Lederle*, 424 F.2d 988 [1st Cir. 1970]).

Fifteen years later, the 7th Circuit Court of Appeals dealt with the now-familiar controversial issue of a college art professor's art not comporting with university standards of decency. The instructor's stained-glass window art was part of a faculty art exhibit. One of the works depicted a naked woman masturbating. Another illustrated a woman engaging in sex with a man. All the works were displayed in a gallery in the main floor of the community college's principal building. Unlike in *Close*, where the art was removed by the school, in this instance, the administration proposed an alternative location to exhibit the nude and semi-nude art. The artist objected on freedom of expression grounds. Writing for the court, Judge Posner found that the art in question had artistic merit, and was not obscene. Nevertheless, in ruling for the school, the court noted that the college space was not a public forum, which otherwise would have limited the administration's authority to regulate the artist's speech. The fact that the art instructor-exhibitor was an employee also increased the ability of the school to control the location of art as speech in the best interests of the school. The sexually explicit nature of the art in the main school building was sufficient grounds for relocating, not banning, the stained-glass art works. *Piarowski v. Illinois Community College*, 759 F.2d 625 [7th Cir. 1985]).

In 1990, the director and the Contemporary Art Center (CAC) of Cincinnati, Ohio, both were indicted for breaching the public peace. The specific criminal charge was the exhibition of two naked children photographs and five photographs depicting sadomasochistic acts all in contravention of the state's obscenity statute. The manner in which the arrests took place shook every art institution in America.

A few hours after the traveling retrospective exhibition *Robert Mapplethorpe: The Perfect Moment* opened, police arrived and demanded that the director, Dennis Barrie, remove the photographs they found offensive. He refused. The police walked around the museum and videotaped the entire exhibition for evidence. Meanwhile, hundreds of visitors were trying to enter the museum, which was now closed per order of the police. After the police left, the director reopened the art center. The museum's board of directors decided to bar anyone under the age of 18 from viewing any of the photographs. Additionally, no one under eighteen years was permitted to open the catalog that accompanied the Mapplethorpe exhibition.

According to a news account of the incident ten years later by reporter John Fox ("Then and Now: Mapplethorpe CAC," *Cincinnati City Beat*, March 30, 2000), "record numbers of Cincinnatians attended the Mapplethorpe show, became CAC members, and marched the street to support Barrie's decision not to back down." Eventually, a jury acquitted Barrie and the museum on the grounds that the state failed to prove all three elements of the *Miller* obscenity test.

In many ways, the Mapplethorpe controversy in Cincinnati reflected the political tug of war on cultural values that was taking place between conservatives and liberals. At the federal level, Senator Jesse Helms of North Carolina, already outraged over public funding for a multimedia exhibit (*Piss Christ* by Andres Serrano) that included a crucifix submerged in a glass of the artist's urine, now had Mapplethorpe's "pornography" to tout in his efforts to shut down the National Endowment for the Arts. Meanwhile, battle-scarred advocates for the arts came together in support of the humanities and a robust art culture.

In a way, to paraphrase Tim Kreider of the *New York Times*, sex in America is our Muhammad, the thing that cannot be portrayed visually without generating controversy ("When Art is Dangerous (or Not)," *New York Times*, January 10, 2015). In the future, museum directors and curators may discover that they have a duty to engage with their audiences in conversations about protected speech, community standards, and the definition of obscene art.

ARTS, PUBLIC FUNDING, AND FREE EXPRESSION

In the aftermath of the Mapplethorpe and Serrano controversies, Congress amended the **National Foundation on the Arts and Humanities Act** by adding a *decency* and *respect* provision to the existing *artistic excellence* and *artistic merit* criteria for federal grant funding of the creative arts. This statutory amendment was a diluted version of the original proposed revision that required a *no-obscenity pledge* from artists. This modification of the law drew vociferous condemnation from established art institutions, academics, and renowned artists. By statute, the director of the National Endowment for the Arts (NEA), who relies upon advisory panels of art experts for grant recommendations, was ordered to consider "general standards of decency and respect for the diverse beliefs and values of the American public before authorizing funding" (20 U.S.C. Section 954[d][1]).

In response to the passage of this controversial Act, four performance artists whose applications for NEA grants were denied funding filed suit alleging the NEA had violated their First Amendment rights. They argued the new standards lead to the rejection of any art that falls outside the mainstream core of American values or offends current standards of decency. The lower court that first heard the case held that limiting grant funding to art that was "decent" was a non-permissive overly broad and vague standard. Upon appeal to the US Supreme Court, Justice Sandra Day O'Connor reversed the lower court ruling. She wrote that Section 954 (d)(1), as amended, was valid, "as it neither inherently interferes with First Amendment rights nor violates constitutional vagueness principles." In a lengthy dissent, Justice David Souter believed the Court's ruling undermines the basic bedrock principle underlying the First Amendment, articulated in *Johnson*, that the government may not prohibit the expression of an idea simply because society disagrees with it or finds it offensive. Souter, in the minority, argued that the decency and respect proviso carries with it "a significant power to chill artistic" speech (*National Endowment for the Arts v. Finley*, 524 U.S. 569 [1998]).

Government support for the arts is not limited to federal funding. The District of Columbia and each state has an agency that promotes and funds the arts. A year after the Court's ruling in *Finley*, the mayor of New York City, Rudolph Giuliani, took offense at an exhibition at the Brooklyn Museum of Art. The exhibition, *Sensation*, was transplanted from the Royal Academy of Art in London, where it drew a record number of visitors. The controversial work of art in the multi-artist exhibition was titled *The Holy Virgin Mary*, painted by Chris Ofili. He used elephant dung and cutouts from sexually explicit magazines in his portrait of the Virgin Mary.

In claiming that the artist's representation of the Virgin Mary was sacrilegious, Giuliani refused to make monthly operating budget payments to the museum that the city had previously authorized. The mayor also began proceedings to evict the museum from its building, which it leased for a dollar a year from the city, and remove the museum's board of trustees from fiduciary oversight responsibilities. In *Brooklyn Institute of Arts and Sciences v. City of New York* (644 F. Supp. 2d 184 [E.D.N.Y. 1999]), the federal court held that the effort by Giuliani to "censor works of expression and to threaten the vitality of a major cultural institution as punishment for failing to abide by government demands for orthodoxy" violates the First Amendment. The parties reached an out-of-court settlement that included continued funding for the museum, while the exhibit drew record crowds in large part due to the publicity surrounding the mayor's actions.

In a parallel time-line decision, the City Council of Miami also lost a court case on First Amendment grounds. It sought to evict the poorly endowed Cuban Museum of Art and Culture from its publicly owned building for holding a fundraising event that included art by Cuban artists that had *not* denounced the Castro regime. The city unsuccessfully cited a county ordinance that barred any public-funded institution from doing business with Cuba.

Shortly before leaving office, Mayor Giuliani and the Brooklyn Museum dueled again. This time it was over an exhibited photograph that showed a nude, black woman portraying Jesus surrounded by his disciples. After describing the work, "Yo Mama's Last Supper," as anti-Catholic, he created an advisory decency commission to establish standards for the city's public funding of the arts. In light of the controversy stirred up by Giuliani's assault on the Brooklyn museum, and following the decision in *Finley* upholding the NEA's decency and respect provision as a consideration for qualifying for federal grant money, other communities have fashioned similar review councils.

In addition to the mandate to direct NEA grants to the arts, at the federal level various agencies have promulgated regulations requiring the incorporation of sculptures, paintings, and other fine arts in the design of new public buildings. The controversy surrounding Richard Serra's "Titled Art" display is an example of a dispute that arose with the General Services Administration based on its art-in-architecture program. Tax incentives are frequently provided that encourage investments to conserve and restore old buildings which indirectly aid the arts community. Charitable tax benefits for individuals and businesses that donate art or supply resources to fund nonprofit museum and art association activities are sources of private funding that benefit the arts.

SATIRE AND DECENCY

Art, religion, and politics dangerously collided in the Paris office of *Charlie Hebdo* when terrorists angry about the magazine's satirical caricatures of their prophet, Muhammad, murderously left twelve dead. The "I am Charlie" ("Je suis Charlie") hashtag was inscribed on T-shirts, displayed on posters, and shared around the world on social media sites, in response.

Despite the occasional protestations by politicians, religious leaders, and patriots condemning degenerate, disparaging, or obscene art, for the most part among modern democracies the system accommodates even the most unpopular art forms. After this tragic event, free speech and press advocates defended the magazine's right to publish crude, ridiculing cartoons that challenged sacred taboos. Yet, many media failed to reprint the rude, anti-religious cartoons on editorial judgment grounds. They expressed a policy of not showcasing images directed toward mocking or inflaming people on the basis of their race, religion, gender, identity, or sexual preference that verged on hate speech. Beyond arts' value as something to be exhibited at the Metro-politan Museum of Art, studied in art school, or a commodity to be auctioned off at Sotheby's, *Charlie Hebdo* demonstrated that art is still relevant today. The attack on the artist-messenger sparked a conversation on free speech and its limits that resonate louder today than ever.

DEFAMATION

The subject of *defamation*, that is, the invasion of a person's interest in his or her reputation, is a state law issue. Each state, as articulated in an earlier chapter, is free to decide the legal standard of proof for written (*libel*) or spo-ken (*slander*) speech communicated to another that has a disparaging impact on reputation. In a prominent US Supreme Court case, Justice William Bren-nan made it clear that the "(d)ebate on public issues should be uninhibited, robust and wide-open" (*New York Times v. Sullivan* 367 US 254 [1964]). The *Sullivan* decision is notable for elevating the requirement of proof in any defamation lawsuit involving a *public official* and now *public figure* to require a showing that the "speech" or "image" was printed, drawn, painted, spoken, or written with "actual malice" or *a reckless disregard for the truth*. In those situations where a prominent person, such as a well-known artist or legendary art dealer, is *not* charged with harming reputation, to create liability for defamation in most states there must be a finding of:

1. a false statement of a purported fact concerning another person or busi-ness;
2. the false statement harmed the reputation of the person or business;
3. the false statement was communicated to a third party who recognized the statement as injuring reputation; and
4. damages occurred.

The most common and *complete defense* to a defamation charge is that the statement was not false, but *true*. In a few isolated instances involving politi-cians, a privilege exists to permit the publication of false statements.

The risks of hastily text messaging or posting on a social media site an art collector's dissatisfaction with an art dealer may have serious legal repercussions. For instance, as reported by the art blogger Daniel Grant (*Communications Art*), an actress sent an email blast that accused an art dealer of selling her fake paintings by well-known artists, as well as overcharging for works by Warhol. Had the dealer actually sold counterfeit works of art and knew or should have known they were forgeries, then her accusations are not subject to a defamation claim. The language used by an irate consumer does matter, however. Claiming the dealer is a "crook" may be defamatory because it implies criminal activity, whereas texting that the dealer is "loathsome" or "disgusting" is mere opinion, not statements of fact, and protected by the First Amendment.

After over 160 years in business, a major New York City art gallery, Knoedler Gallery, closed its doors after "undiscovered" works by Mark Rothko, Barnett Newman, and Robert Motherwell were sold. Forensic testing by the buyers determined that the artworks were all forgeries, painted by a Chinese artist living in New York. After the owner of another gallery was quoted in a magazine as asserting that the head of the gallery "was totally irresponsible" in failing to conduct "due diligence" before selling the paintings to innocent collectors, she was sued for defamation. The Knoedler gallery head apparently was defrauded herself by the cosigner of the forty or so fake works, and had retained experts in the art world to examine the works before selling. Barring an out-of-court resolution, a court must determine whether or not the head of Knoedler qualifies as a public figure, and whether the remarks directed toward her conveyed false statements of actual facts that caused damage or were simply opinion statements under New York's statutory law.

Statements regarding the authenticity of art can be the subjects of defamation analysis. The federal court in *McNally v. Yarnall* (764 F. Supp. 838 [S.D.N.Y. 1991]) determined that comments about the genuineness of certain stained-glass art work attributed to the artist John La Farge were matters of public concern "protected under the First Amendment so long as they do not contain a provably false factual connotation."

PRIVACY AND PUBLICITY RIGHTS

"Privacy is a broad, abstract and ambiguous concept," wrote Justice Hugo Black in *Griswold v. Connecticut* (381 US 479 [1965]), a monumental decision that expanded the right of privacy. The term *privacy*, which does not appear in the Bill of Rights, refers to a variety of ideas and impulses that have proved to be a source of constitutional debate over the type and degree of protection afforded persons. Individual states also uniquely define a person's protected privacy rights in specific areas, such as private affairs in the home, electronic communications, and medical and financial records.

In general, privacy refers to the right to be left alone or free from unsolicited publicity. Photographer Arne Svenson's exhibition at the Chelsea Gallery in New York City, which featured images taken from the artist's apartment of apartment dwellers across the street without their knowledge and permission, brought this issue into perspective. The artist's neighbors were infuriated when they learned Svenson used a telephoto lens to take pictures of them including their children through their floor-to-ceiling glass windows. They sued Svenson alleging a violation of **Section 50** of **New York's Civil Rights Act** that prevents the use of images of children and adults without written permission for commercial and promotional purposes. A New York City judge determined **Section 51** of the statute trumps the prohibition on using photographs for advertising without consent. Specifically, this state law provision permits an artist to communicate his or her thoughts and ideas to the public to promote the enjoyment of art in the form of the displayed exhibition, "The Neighbors," without authorized consent by the subjects. The court also held that New York's privacy statute, in the facts of this particular case where the faces of the neighbors were obscured, yields to First Amendment protection for the photographer (*Foster v. Svenson*, 2013 NY Slip Op 31782 [U], 651826-2013).

In 2007, in *Nussenzweig v. diCorcia* 38 AD3d 339 (2007), as published by the New York State Law Reporting Bureau, a complaint over street photography arose in New York City with a slight religious twist. Philip-Lorca diCorcia, an art instructor at Yale and photographer, is known for taking pictures of random people in urban areas and dramatically highlighting them through strobe lighting. In the 1980s, he was even awarded a grant from the NEA. Nussenzweig was a retired jewelry merchant who alleged diCorcia violated his right to privacy under Section 50 and 51 of New York's privacy act by using his image in a gallery exhibition at Pace/MacGill and commercially selling catalogs that carried this same image, without his written consent. New York's highest court ruled that the works were protected as "artistic expression," under Section 51. Nussenzweig's argument that as an Orthodox Jew the display violated the Commandment in the Torah against publication of graven images fell short under the artist's First Amendment freedom of speech right.

The right of privacy is considered a personal right that arises under statutory tort law. The right of *publicity*, which is a relatively new personal right independent of privacy, is a *property right* related to benefiting from the commercial value of a person's name and likeness.

More than half the states recognize a right of publicity. The state of California in **Cal. Civ. Code Section 3344**, for instance, protects a person's exclusive right for *advertising or commercial purposes* in his or her *name, voice, signature, photograph, and likeness.* The use of the unauthorized publicity right must be directly connected with the advertising or commercial sponsorship to claim financial damages. A major exemption from coverage of the law occurs when the works are used in the public interest or of a political or newsworthy nature, and single and original works of fine art. Publicity rights are not exclusively the province of well-known figures in the sports, entertainment, and art worlds, but celebrities are the source of most of the litigation because they have larger commercial interests to protect.

In 2003, after lengthy court battles, Tiger Woods lost his appeal in a precedent setting right of publicity case. The "sports" artist Rick Rush depicted images of Woods at the 1997 Masters' golf tournament shadowed by images of other prominent golfing champions in limited edition lithographs for sale to the public. In ruling for Rush, and against Woods' claim that he has a right to control the publicity of his name and likeness, that federal court of appeals stated: "A piece of art that portrays a historic sporting event communicates and celebrates the value our culture attaches to such events. It would be ironic indeed if the presence of the image of the victorious athlete would deny the work First Amendment protection" (*ETW Corporation v. Jireh Publishing, Inc.* 332 F.3d 915 [2003]).

In balancing the First Amendment freedom of art speech against a person's right of publicity courts generally rely on one of two tests. The courts in New York examine whether the art primarily has a "public interest" or a "commercial" motivation. Works of art that are important because of their social usefulness are more likely to receive constitutional protection than art whose value rests in commercial sales (*Hoepker v. Kruger*, 200 F. Supp. 2d 340 [S.D.N.Y.2002]). Alternatively, the Supreme Court of California has held that the First Amendment does not protect depictions of celebrities that are attempts to do little more than appropriate the celebrity's economic value. Here the court looks at whether the artist has "transformed" the celebrities' image into something of social or cultural value beyond commercial exploitation (*Comedy III Productions, Inc. v. Saderup*, 25 Cal. 4th 387 [2001]).

Any discussion of an artist's use of celebrity images brings to mind the leading avant-garde figure of the American Pop Art scene, Andy Warhol. His silkscreen portrait prints of glamorous Hollywood stars, politicians, sports figures, and fashion icons, such as Jacqueline Kennedy, Muhammad Ali, Elvis Presley, Chairman Mao, and Marilyn Monroe, were frequently appropriated from copyrighted publicity shots, magazines, and newspapers. Warhol's artistic genius was to document and investigate America's fascination and obsession with celebrities by using common source materials and reproducing them in garish and vivid colors. Both his subject matter and technique revolutionized the notion of what is art, and transformed a generation of new artists, all sufficient grounds for protection under the law.

The right to privacy expires at the death of a person. Around twenty states by statute or common law recognize the right of publicity beyond death. This allows the estates or representatives of famous actors, politicians, artists, sports figures, and other public figures to control their names, likenesses, and images for anywhere from ten years to indefinitely, depending on the jurisdiction.

Privacy and publicity rights, which uniquely protect personal interests of artists or their subjects, are separate from copyright, which protects property interests in the works of artists. A copyrighted photograph of people may have fallen into the public domain. In the event the subjects of the photographs are now deceased movie stars then their estates or representatives may claim a commercial interest in their name and likeness where postmortem publicity rights are recognized. In those instances, anyone who wants to use the photograph for strictly advertising or commercial purpose first may have to seek permission from their heirs.

TRADEMARKS AND ARTISTIC EXPRESSION

A *trademark* is a symbol, name, phrase, shape, or other graphic design that is used to identify and distinguish products and services from one another. A trademark is a limited government recognized monopoly grant governed, in part, by a federal statute known as the **Lanham Act**. One of the thought-provoking arguments asserted by Tiger Woods in his civil suit against Rick Rush was that the lithograph was a violation of the trademark on the image of Woods. The court decided the case on a finding that the painting was more than a mere exact likeness of Woods, and, therefore, protected as free art speech. However, the court went on to say, "as a general rule, a person's image or likeness cannot function as a trademark" (*ETW Corporation v. Jireh Publishing, Inc.* 332 F.3d 915 [2003]).

A federal judge in New York was asked to resolve a different type of trademark dispute between Robert Indiana, a preeminent pioneer of Pop Art best known for his "LOVE" print, and a former business associate who claimed a contract right to call his own works of art as Indiana's. The artist Indiana *disclaimed* authorship in the works, and was sued by the associate. The Lanham Act makes actionable the deceptive and misleading use of trademarks. It also exists to protect parties engaged in commerce against unfair competition. Related to this statutory provision is a federal remedy against a party who uses a trademark in commerce either as a false designation of origin or false representation of any goods or services. In sweeping language the court determined that the Lanham Act *is not available as a means to sue for whether a statement regarding a work of visual art is or is not by a named artist* (*Gilbert v. Indiana*, No. 09-CV-6352 [S.D.N.Y. 2012]). According to an article written by the attorney for Robert Indiana, this holding has a tremendous impact on the potential liability of art experts who are asked for opinions regarding the authenticity of artwork and their opinions are later disputed. No longer may the statute serve as a legal basis for making a financial claim for losses suffered by the purchasers (see Judith Wallace, "Stemming the Tide of Federal Litigation against Art Experts and Authentication Boards for Opinions about the Authenticity of Art," *Mondaq*, December 5, 2012). This decision, though, still leaves in place other legal causes of action against art experts including negligence, fraud, and breach of contract.

Unlike copyrights, which protect original expression, trademarks help perspective buyers identify the source of goods and services. For instance, the artist Thomas Kinkade was known as the "painter of light." This trademarked phrase was Kinkade's brand name that he used to distinguish himself from other fine art painters. Artists occasionally use someone else's trademarks in a work of art. In what is not a new debate, but certainly a novel one, photographers and filmmakers have been sued when they use or incorporate a trademarked slogan or image in their works. For instance, the music Rock and Roll Hall of Fame and Museum located in Cleveland, Ohio, sued photographer Charles Gentile for creating and selling a poster that contained the trademarked words "ROCK 'N ROLL HALL OF FAME" and the distinctly shaped and designed building by the esteemed architect I. M. Pei. Beginning in 1937, courts have allowed for a trademark in the unique design of a building. This lawsuit, however, raised the issue of where to draw the line between a private trademark design right and an image that is freely observable in the public domain. In deciding in the photographer's favor, the court held that for the trademarked words and building's shape to be protected as a valid trademark under the Lanham Act, the artist's poster image must be used in a way that creates a confusing association with the original trademarks. The court noted that while indeed the building's design was "fanciful" under trademark law, it was not fancifully recognized in a manner that consumers associate the building's design with products and services offered by the Hall of Fame. Gentile's image of the building on his poster was similar to the Hall of Fame's pictorial images found on its T-shirts and posters, but not identical (*The Rock and Roll Hall of Fame and Museum, Inc. v. Gentile Productions*, 71 F.Supp.2d 755 [1999]).

The law recognizes the "fair use" by artists of someone else's trademark without prior approval so long as the words, slogans, designs, pictures, and names are not used in a manner that consumers would confuse the artist's poster, sculpture, photograph, or sketch with those of the original trademark owner. Non-commercial informational and editorial uses of trademarks are nearly always permissible.

SUMMARY

In a perfect world artists should be free to practice their art form free of external regulations and constraints. Art is a form of symbolic speech that can reveal themes and ideas that are socially, culturally, and politically contentious. The Supreme Court protects the First Amendment right of artists to use their art as a form of expression to stimulate thought or nudge conventional wisdom. This right, like all speech, is subject to reasonable regulation or even censorship when the idea communicated might incite imminent violent reaction, lacks any redeeming social, political, or artistic value, or harms a person's reputation. Respecting the privacy and publicity rights of subjects of art especially when work composed is of a commercial nature is a way to avoid litigation.

WORKS REFERENCED

"Art on Trial," *The Thomas Jefferson Center*, 2005.

Dore Ashton, *Picasso on Art (The Documents of 20th Century Art)*, New York: Penguin, 1977.

David Barstow, "Giuliani Ordered to Restore Funds for Art Museum," in the *New York Times*, November 2, 1999.

Tad Crawford, *Legal Guide for the Visual Artist*, 5th ed., New York: Allworth Press, 2010.

Leonard DuBoff and Christy King, *Art Law*, 3rd ed., St. Paul, MN: Thompson-West, 2000.

John Fox, "Then and Now: Mapplethorpe CAC," in *CityBeat*, March 30, 2000.

Daniel Grant, "Defamation in the Arts," in *Communication Arts*, 2015.

Tim Kreider, "When Art Is Dangerous (or Not)," in the *New York Times*, January 10, 2015.

"Life of Michelangelo: Most Censored Artist," Censorship in America, censorshipinamerica.wordpress.com/2010/12/03/life-of-michelangelo/, December 3, 2010.

Robert Lind, Robert Jarvis, and Marilyn Phelan, *Art and Museum Law: Cases and Materials,* Durham, NC: Carolina Academic Press, 2002.

Mario Malaro and Ildiko Pogany DeAngelis, *Legal Primer on Managing Museum Collections,* 3rd ed., Washington, DC: Smithsonian Books, 2012.

Christine Schrum, "Art Licensing Hoops & Pitfalls," in *Art Business News*, April 9, 2014.

Judith Wallace, "Stemming the Tide of Federal Litigation against Art Experts and Authentication Boards for Opinions about the Authenticity of Art," in *Mondaq*, December 5, 2012.

Paul Winick and Noel Garcia, "Tiger Woods and the Use of Celebrity Images in Works of Art: Right of Publicity v. First Amendment," in *FindLaw*, March 26, 2008.

Christopher Zara, "Arne Svenson, Photographer Who Spied on Tribeca 'Neighbors,' Wins Legal Battle in Privacy Court Case," in *International Business Times*, August 6, 2013.

10

Grants, Foundations, and Funding of the Arts

"People don't come to America for our airports, people don't come to America for our hotels . . . they come for our culture, real and imagined."

—Garrison Keillor ("Praire Home Companion")

In a free society, the visual fine arts play a fundamental role in the discourse of historical, political, cultural, and social concerns. For instance, the Pop Artist Andy Warhol allowed us to see common familiar mass-marketed products in thought-provoking ways. One of the world's most famous murals, *Guernica* by Pablo Picasso, was completed during intense global political unrest, and eight decades later still offers an emotionally charged visual account of the horrific impact of war. The early nineteenth-century French Barbizon artists who captured the simple lives of ordinary peasants working in the countryside were viewed unfavorably by the aesthetic code of the times. Contemporary spray-painting street artists like Banksy have brought public attention to war, poverty, and the degradation of the environment.

The fine arts also are an integral component of the public's creative and economic capacity. Echoing the above message from radio personality Garrison Keillor, many government entities have come to recognize the importance of a vibrant arts community to the fiscal and cultural well-being of their citizens. This chapter is devoted to detailing various historical and recent innovative approaches to financially supporting the visual fine arts. It also chronicles art foundation disputes that have left a cautionary tale legacy.

FEDERAL GOVERNMENT FUNDING OF THE VISUAL FINE ARTS

Funding for the visual fine arts can take the form of public and private initiatives. One of the first successful legislative efforts by the federal government to support the arts occurred under the administration of President William Howard Taft. In 1910, Congress established a national Commission of Fine Arts as a permanent body to guide the architectural development (parks and buildings) of the nation's capital and advise Congress on matters related to the arts (40 U.S.C. 104, 36 Stat. 371).

Twenty-five years later, when America was in the midst of the Great Depression, Congress established the **Works Progress Administration**, renamed in 1939 to the **Works Projects Administration (WPA)**, to help uplift the economy. The WPA was a part of President Franklin Roosevelt's New Deal. Unlike the Commission of Fine Arts, Congress appropriated money to pay unemployed musicians, writers, actors, and visual fine artists under the WPA's Federal Art Project Number One (FAP) program to teach and produce art for the public. Many of America's most outstanding visual artists found work under this arts funded program. It led to the formation of over 100,000 paintings and murals and 18,000 works of sculpture. The development of community art centers was an integral aspect of the project's outreach goal. The inaugural director of the arts program, Holger Cahill, favored figurative drawings and paintings popular during this Social Realism period. However, a significant group of visual fine artists hired by this federal jobs program, like Jackson Pollock, Willem de Kooning, Mark Rothko, Arshile Gorky, Stuart Davis, Arthur Dove, and Lee Krasner, went on to become the pioneers of the Abstract Expressionist movement.

For example, the Armenian-born artist Arshile Gorky, whose works are on permanent exhibit at the Whistler House Museum in Lowell, Massachusetts, Tate Modern in London, and the Philadelphia Art Museum, is an example of a WPA artist who shaped an enduring legacy. His dazzling abstract murals that portrayed man's aspirations to fly, originally displayed at the Newark (New Jersey) Airport, were a testament to the beginning of the modernism era. Unfortunately, during post–World War II alterations to the airport, all but two of the eight murals were destroyed or lost. The two that survived were restored and are now on exhibit at the Newark Museum of Art. In 1943, the federal government auctioned off thousands of WPA-funded easel paintings, drawings, prints, and illustrations by the pound.

An example of one of the posters created by an unknown WPA artist that announced an art class for children is shown in figure 10.1. It is pulled from the public domain archives of the WPA, now absorbed by the General Services Administration (GSA).

Figure 10.1. Unnamed, unknown artist, WPA poster. *Photo image courtesy of General Services Administration.*

Public funding of WPA artists wasn't without political controversy. For instance, while Lee Krasner eked out a living for herself during the Great Depression as an artist painting murals, she was labeled a Marxist for speaking out at the Artists Union in New York City. Krasner was even arrested for demonstrating on behalf of workers' rights that added to the perception the WPA was inundated with Communists. For a fuller account of her life during this period see Gail Levin's biography, *Lee Krasner* (2011).

It took nearly two decades after the demise of the WPA before the federal government embarked on new legislation to bolster the arts. In 1965, President Lyndon B. Johnson signed into law the **National Foundation for the Arts and the Humanities Act** (20 U.S.C. 951-968). This act established the National Endowment for the Arts (NEA) and the National Endowment for the Humanities (NEH), as two separate agencies. Specifically, the NEA is tasked with the responsibility of funding by *grants* the exemplary work of artists and art scholars via tax-exempt, nonprofit organizations, such as art councils, universities, libraries, archives, and museums, to disseminate arts, culture, and history to the public. The NEA's Art Works category does not specifically fund individual artists. This federal agency is particularly interested in funding artistic efforts that reach traditionally underserved populations through its Challenge America funds.

An example of the type of art project the NEA supports is Art Beyond Sight by a New York–based organization that promotes accessibility to visual art and culture for people with visual impairments. Collaborating with the Art Institute of Chicago, it enabled the museum to enhance its Touch Gallery. This gallery is comprised of works of art from the museum's permanent collection that allows patrons to explore art with their hands.

To celebrate the twenty-fifth anniversary of the milestone **Americans with Disability Act (ADA)**, the NEA supported an initiative by the Matheny Medical and Education Center. The center established a program to enable people with severe disabilities to create their own visual art. A major purpose of the grant was to challenge the public's perception of what it means to be an artist with a disability.

The typical NEA grant is for less than $25,000. No grant is funded below the $10,000 threshold and requests over $100,000 are accepted only under rare national or regional artistic circumstances. The specific grant program legal guidelines for the Arts Works program drawn from www.arts.gov/grants-organizations/art-works/grant-program-description, are as follows:

> The guiding principle of "Art Works" is at the center of everything we do at the NEA. "Art Works" refers to three things: the works of art themselves, the ways art works on audiences, and the fact that art **is** work for the artists and arts professionals who make up the field.
>
> Art works by enhancing the value of individuals and communities, by connecting us to each other and to something greater than ourselves, and by empowering creativity and innovation in our society and economy. The arts exist for beauty itself, but they also are an inexhaustible source of meaning and inspiration.
>
> The NEA recognizes these catalytic effects of excellent art, and the key role that arts and design organizations play in revitalizing them. To deepen and extend the arts' value, including their ability to foster new connections and to exemplify creativity and innovation, we welcome projects that:
>
> - Are likely to prove transformative with the potential for meaningful change, whether in the development or enhancement of new or existing art forms, new approaches to the creation or presentation of art, or new ways of engaging the public with art;
> - Are distinctive, offering fresh insights and new value for their fields and/or the public through unconventional solutions; and

- Have the potential to be shared and/or emulated, or are likely to lead to other advances in the field.

Beyond encouraging projects that demonstrate these characteristics, we want to achieve the following four objectives through the Art Works category:

- Creation: The creation of art that meets the highest standards of excellence,
- Engagement: Public engagement with diverse and excellent art,
- Learning: Lifelong learning in the arts, and
- Livability: The strengthening of communities through the arts.

By federal statute, 40 percent of the NEA's program funding must be allocated to state and regional art councils and organizations. State agencies use these federal dollars to leverage matching funds to benefit local communities. Individual artists apply for funding through these entities consistent with the specific program guidelines.

Not unlike the FAP division of the WPA, the NEA has found itself in the center of political firestorms. As described in an earlier chapter, a legislative attempt to require grant applicants to certify that funds would not be used for "obscene" art was struck down as violating an artist's free speech rights (*Bella Lewitzky Dance Foundation v. John Fronmayer* and *Newport Harbor Art Museum v. National Endowment for the Arts*, 754 F. Supp. 774 [1991]). In response, Congress eliminated the non-obscenity written pledge requirement and replaced it with a new "decency and respect" standard. The nation's highest court in *National Endowment for the Arts v. Finley* (524 U.S. 569 [1998]) ruled 8–1 that this statutory provision did not constitute unlawful viewpoint discrimination. The NEA has suffered periodic budgetary cuts over the years because of political pressure from conservative groups that were unhappy with the allocation of taxpayers' monies for controversial art projects.

STATE FUNDING AND ARTS COUNCILS' SUPPORT

After enactment of the NEA, nearly every state and US territory established an arts council that did not already have one in place to access federal funds. A good example is the state of Maryland, where the State Arts Council supports twenty-four local art councils that work to ensure equitable access to arts across the state. Grants are awarded through a competitive process to nonprofit and tax exempt entities based on three criteria: artistic merit, organizational effectiveness, and service to the community. More than $10 million annually is awarded through this grant program. Individual visual fine artists, such as photographers, painters, illustrators on paper, and sculptors, are eligible for merit-based financial awards of $1,000, $3,000, or $6,000. Maryland's public arts program provides matching money to local efforts to install permanent art accessible to the public. Finally, the state supports professional development study for teachers of art and sponsors Artists in Residence that covers one half the cost of a school's scholar residency program.

The state of New Hampshire through its Council on the Arts sells special motor vehicle license plates to benefit the purchase of art for public buildings. In addition, the legislature authorized a set-aside of half of 1 percent of capital budget appropriations for new buildings or significant renovations to existing buildings to commission visual fine artists to create art for these buildings. This regulation is similar to the federal requirement to incorporate fine arts in the design of new public buildings under the GSA's guidance. Since 1998, New Hampshire's arts council has honored leading artists with an Artists Laureate designation. The nationally recognized master potter and founder of the *Studio Potter*, Gerry Williams, was appointed New Hampshire's first Artist Laureate.

CROWD SOURCING FUNDS

At a recent Aspen Ideas Festival meeting, the founder of Kickstarter (an on-line extension of the old line model of artists seeking support from patrons), surprised the audience when he announced that his crowdfunding website now funds more art projects annually than the NEA. Kickstarter provides a platform and resource for creative artists to seek donations for projects ranging from designing a music album to creating the infamous exploding kittens video game that raised nearly $9 million by attracting over 200,000 donors. Funding on Kickstarter is an all-or-nothing proposition. Artistic creators set a financial goal. Projects must reach their funding goals to receive money. Kickstarter takes a 5 percent cut of successfully funded projects. Nearly 50 percent of all proposals meet their funding goals by tapping into young private donors who desire to give to the arts.

Established arts organizations like the Smithsonian, which is comprised of nineteen different museums and galleries, have taken a cue from individual artists and have begun to tap into crowdfunding appeals to raise money for exhibitions, acquire art, restore works, and renovate or construct buildings with mixed results. A 2015 Kickstarter campaign easily surpassed its goal of raising $500,000 to preserve astronaut Neil Armstrong's Apollo 11 spacesuit. Three years earlier, though, the Smithsonian suffered an embarrassing public relations blow when donors on a website called Causes committed $555 toward its goal of $35,000 to display the art of Chinese dissident Ai Weiwei.

After the Weiwei fundraising disaster, the Smithsonian experimented by offering a range of reward levels, depending on private donors' online financial commitment, with better outcomes.

The use of crowd-source funding websites to connect with the public for preservation and exhibit projects is not limited to the United States. The Philip J. Curie Dinosaur Museum, a Canadian cultural arts institution, tried to raise $1 million on Indiegogo, a crowdfunding online site, to help build a new museum. The social media fund raising effort fell $966,000 short. Dramatic government budget cuts for the arts have encouraged European museums to increase their public solicitations to defray financial gaps with online civic campaigns. The Louvre Museum in Paris raised over $1.5 million from 7,000 online donors to purchase a sixteenth-century painting. A French crowdfunding start-up, My Major Company, has engaged in pilot programs to solicit funds to restore projects at the Pantheon in Paris.

FOUNDATIONS

Crowd-sourcing websites that seek private donations to finance public and private fine arts projects are just one type of tool in the fundraising toolbox. The traditional money-raising channels, such as the aforementioned federal and state grants along with the sale of membership in cultural institutions and renting out space for weddings or corporate outings, remain intact along with support from foundations.

The principal mission of the thousands of private, not-for-profit foundations established by corporations, small businesses, or private donors, is to support innovative art projects or programs that meaningfully impact a community or the growth of an artist's professional career. Private sector foundation funding along with private donations constitute a significant source of income for cultural art institutions, according to a report by the NEA (see www.arts.gov/ sites/default/files/how-the-us-funds-the-arts.pdf). For example, the ten leading foundation organizations account for about 48 percent of all foundation funding for the arts. The Ford Foundation has an endowment exceeding $10 billion that generates $50 million a year in income for the arts and culture. New York's American Art Foundation, Inc. is another leading organization that annually gives more than $100 million to the arts. In 2011, the Walton Family Foundation made the largest cash gift ever to a US art museum when it donated $800 million to the Crystal Bridges Museum of Art in Arkansas. The Rockefeller Foundation's bequests made the Museum of Modern Art possible.

Many of the larger foundations foster mainstream art projects. However, there are plenty of smaller foundations that support "out-of-the-box" visual fine arts projects and artists. In some instances, the foundations work directly with local communities to assist in financing undercapitalized projects or events. In 2015, the John S. and James L. Knight Foundation earmarked $1 million in funding to thirteen Charlotte, North Carolina, arts organizations. Some of the money went directly to support the Knight Artist in Residency program, while additional funds were used to renovate the McColl Center for Visual Arts to enhance the city's reputation as a regional center for artistic excellence. In Detroit, the Kresge Foundation buttresses the professional career growth of local visual fine artists by providing fellowship funding. The Detroit-based College of Creative Services, a nationally recognized institution for art education, administers the annual awards of $25,000 for each artist selected.

The nonprofit Creative Capital foundation offers to fund forty-eight individual artists' projects a year that promise to take an original and imaginative approach to creating art. Part of the open, competitive selection process is a requirement for applicants to discuss how other artists and art movements, as discussed in chapter 2, influence the work of the fine artist applicant. The goal of the award is for it to serve as a catalyst for professional and artistic growth.

In Chicago, the Richard Driehaus Foundation provided financial support to Sing London, a UK-based public-art studio to add monologues to twenty-seven of the Windy City's statues that visitors can activate by scanning codes in posters with their smart phones.

Established in 1925 as a living memorial to the death of their son, Senator and Mrs. Guggenheim formed the John S. Guggenheim Foundation to further the development of scholars and artists without restriction. About 200 fellowship awards across various art professions are issued annually. In 2015, the Finnish-American self-portrait photographer and arts educator, Arno Rafael Minkkinen, joined the likes of respected fine artist photographers like Sally Mann, Diane Arbus, and Robert Frank in earning a fellowship.

The Pollock-Krasner Foundation, Inc. has preserved the legacy of two internationally recognized WPA artists, Jackson Pollock and Lee Krasner. Since the foundation's inception in 1985, it has awarded over 4,000 grants, totaling in excess of $60 million, to individual artists. Criteria for the annual honor are twofold: financial need and to foster professional artist talent. Funds can be used to rent studio space, buy art materials, and even pay for personal living expenses.

One of the artists that was awarded a Pollock-Krasner grant is Nancy Ellen Craig. As a young painter in the 1950s, the *New York Times* referred to her as "the greatest portrait artist since John Singer Sargent." After traveling the world for two decades as a commissioned artist painting nobility, literary giants, and Hollywood screen stars at $50,000 a portrait, she lived in virtual seclusion in Truro, Massachusetts, with her husband. By the mid-2000s, Craig began to paint again after her husband died. The press rediscovered her dramatic paintings when she began to exhibit locally on Cape Cod. During the year that she received financial support from the Foundation, she finished four large paintings. One of those works, measuring 76 inches by 66 inches, was painted like Picasso's *Guernica* in response to the atrocities of war, and is shown in figure 10.2.

Figure 10.2. *The Disaster of War*, 2007. © *The Estate of Nancy Ellen Craig, photo image courtesy of David Perry and Craig Nelson, coexecutors.*

Artists selected for participation in foundation grants or artist-in-residence programs may be asked to donate an original work of art produced during the remunerated period. The question of who owns the copyright to the donated artwork varies. For instance, the Rocky Mountain Artist-in-Residence program supported by the National Park Service requires the written transfer of a copyright for limited non-commercial use upon accession of the art into the park's permanent museum collection. Under this legal framework, the artist retains a royalty free, non-exclusive right to reproduce and license the work. However, the artist must disclose that the reproduced artwork was produced under its Artist-in-Residence program. Non-accessioned art remains the property of the Park for purposes of display and even sale. At a minimum, most artists selected by a foundation or government agency agree to have their names and artwork posted on the grantee's website for publicity and networking purposes. Visual fine artists are advised to read the terms and conditions provision of their grants or awards with precision.

Numerous government and private organizations are dedicated to helping individual visual fine artists and art organizations to identify sources for grants and foundation awards. The Americans for the Arts website at http://www.americansforthearts.org/ explains how the federal government resources funds through art education, block grants, and cultural exchange programs. New York's Foundation for the Arts at www.nyfa.org, is a national information source on grants, fellowships, and other sponsored programs to benefit fine artists. The Foundation Center–San Francisco provides a directory on the names of significant art funders in California and how artists might tap into their resources. Across America there are thousands of arts organizations and initiatives that work to be innovative and imaginative forces to help fine artists financially, enhance a community's culture environment, and expand economic activity.

FOUNDATION DISPUTES

In the first chapter, the subject of estate planning and gift-giving of art by collectors and artists was introduced. It is not uncommon for those who amass collections of fine art to transfer these assets into a foundation for tax and charitable reasons. The leaders or trustees of these charitable institutions are responsible for engaging in philanthropic activities consistent with their charter or by-laws, that is, to exercise their duties in a competent, timely, and faithful manner. There are instances, however, when restrictions placed on the use of an art collection require drastic legal action to preserve the original purpose of the foundation.

In the early 1900s, after amassing a fortune from coinventing a pharmaceutical product that prevented blindness in newborns, Dr. Albert Barnes met Gertrude and Leo Stein, patrons of Picasso and Matisse. They, in turn, assisted Barnes in acquiring art from leading Post-Impressionist and modern artists. Barnes established his foundation to preserve his vision of arts education, while simultaneously displaying his vast holdings to the working class, not for the art connoisseur.

Over time, and after his accidental death, by the 1970s the Barnes Foundation became cash poor and asset rich. However, the governing documents of the foundation limited the ability of its trustees to raise revenue to maintain the cramped residential site where the collection was housed. There were concerns by the governing board over possible theft and unsafe collection conditions. Unlike museums, the foundation could not sell or exchange or even lend its works of art. Also, the bylaws prevented the licensing of reproduction rights on posters or other ephemeral. Any resident of the Commonwealth of Pennsylvania could sue the foundation, at the foundation's expense, were it to host social events, such as public teas or weddings, that were all prohibited under its indenture terms.

In a highly contested series of lawsuits that took years to resolve, a partnership of other foundations led by the Annenberg Foundation and the Pew Charitable Trust pledged financial support to move the Barnes Foundation collection to the arts district of downtown Philadelphia. Newly appointed foundation trustees successfully petitioned a state court to change the terms of its charter documents to permit the move and allow for the monetization of its collection (see *In re Barnes Foundation*, 453 Pa. Super. 243; 683 A.2d 894 [1996]).

A court may amend the original governing terms and conditions of a foundation or trust only when its original intent becomes illegal, impossible, or impracticable to continue to perform. The doctrine that permits this change is known as *cy pres*. The evidence is clear, however, that were Dr. Barnes alive that he would not have ever consented to this dramatic modification of his foundation's guiding principles. In fact, Barnes loathed the very charitable and cultural institutions that spearheaded the move to rewrite his legacy. In 2012, the new Barnes Foundation building adjacent to the Philadelphia Museum of Art opened up its doors to the paying public.

The nature of the litigation that engulfed the Barnes Foundation is unusual. More often, disputes arise regarding trustee fees and expenses, and breach of fiduciary duties. For instance, in 2014, a Florida court awarded three trustees of the Estate of Robert Rauschenberg the sum of nearly $25 million. The trustees' job was to operate the Rauschenberg estate's trust for the benefit of the Rauschenberg Foundation. The late Robert Rauschenberg was a painter and graphic artist who bridged the area between Abstract Expressionism and Pop Art. Christopher Rauschenberg was his son, and chairperson of the Rauschenberg Foundation. He challenged the bills the three trustees submitted for payment as "unconscionably" excessive. The foundation's charitable purpose was to make grants to arts organizations and provide residencies to artists in Captiva, Florida.

In finding a middle ground to the value of the services rendered by the trustees, all of whom were long-time friends and business associates of the artist, the court relied upon a prior case, *West Coast Hospital Association v. Fl. National Bank of Jacksonville* (100 So. 2d 807 [1958]). In that case, judges were instructed to examine several factors to determine whether compensation is reasonable. The factors consider the trustees' skill, loyalty, time, nature of the work, success of their efforts, experience, customary payment for those that perform similar work, and size of the estate. In this instance, the Rauschenberg trustees were praised for their extraordinarily diligent handling of complex copyright and tax issues. In addition, the court noted their allegiance to the artist's legacy by managing several exhibitions and preventing a decline in the value of the $600 million trust by not flooding the commercial market by overselling his works.

Nearly twenty years earlier, in another estate-foundation lawsuit, the decision was not favorable for those charged with managing an artist's estate. Mark Rothko was an Abstract Expressionist who was gifted at expressing human emotions in color. He died tragically by suicide. In his will he essentially bypassed his children and left nearly all of his 2,000 artworks to the Rothko Foundation. His three executors also served on the foundation's board. These foundation board members contracted with a leading New York art dealer, the Marlborough Gallery, at allegedly favorable and highly profitable terms to buy and sell Rothko's art. Two of these board members had professional relationships with the gallery that led to charges of self-dealing, and failing to act in the best interests of the foundation and estate of Rothko.

In a decision that the *New York Times* referred to as "the biggest, most publicized legal wrangle in art-world history," a New York court rescinded the gallery contracts, issued fines and damages against three executors/foundation board members of over $9 million, reconstituted the foundation, and awarded half of the paintings to the Foundation and the other half to Rothko's two adult children (see *Matter of Estate of Rothko*, 84 Misc. 2d 830, 379 N.Y.S. 2d 923 [Surr. Ct. 1975]).

The attorney general of the state also oversees not-for-profit art foundations, such as those established by Mark Rothko and Robert Rauschenberg. The state's concern is to ensure that the foundation is operated for the benefit of the public it is authorized to serve. New York, for instance, has a statute on charitable institutions that limits the maximum amount a foundation may give away to 50 percent of the value of the estate. The children or heirs of the Rothko estate successfully demonstrated that their father's foundation exceeded this philanthropic amount. It is not unusual for the state to join the heirs of the decedent who established the art foundation in petitioning the appropriate court to rescind business transactions or dealings that were entered into improperly by the trustees charged with controlling the foundation.

SUMMARY

There are a variety of contact sources for visual fine artists and arts organizations that seek financial aid. The federal government first took an active role to help unemployed artists during the Depression through President Roosevelt's WPA program. Thirty-five years later, President Johnson supported the arts by signing into law a federal statute that established the NEA. Despite up and down budgetary backing for the arts by Congress for political reasons, this agency continues to provide grants to arts organizations and state art councils.

Innovative fine artists have learned to pitch their creative art-making ideas on crowdfunding websites like Kickstarter. Arts organizations including museums around the world have followed suit by seeking online contributions for specific arts-related projects with varied success. Private foundations are now significant donors to enhancing the professional lives of artists by offering art in residency programs, in addition to awarding grant money that enhances the lives of artists and helps stimulate local economies.

Barring extraordinary circumstances, trustees of foundations are duty-bound to operate consistent with the expressed charitable intent of its governing documents and state philanthropic gift giving laws. Any failure to comply with its bylaws or charter or not to act in the best interests of the foundation might lead to litigation from the estate's decedents or the state attorney general acting on behalf of the public. The civil law suits surrounding the art foundations established by Mark Rothko and Robert Rauschenberg are two high-profile cases which demonstrate the nature of the disputes that can arise when interested parties attack the motives and labor of trustees.

This chapter illustrates the remarkable interplay between artists, arts organizations, ethics, and law that is a constant theme throughout this book. The broad subject of visual fine art law incorporates a cluster of legal concerns and disciplines that seek to both regulate and facilitate the practice of making, collecting, preserving, exhibiting, licensing, selling, and investing in objects of art.

WORKS REFERENCED

"About Us," *New Hampshire State Council on the Arts*, www.nh.gov/nharts, 2016.

"Artist-In-Residence Program," *Rocky Mountain-National Park Service*, www.nps.gov, 2016.

Paulette Beete, "Touch and See," in *NEA Arts Magazine*, Issue 2015, Number 1.

Katherine Boyle, "Yes, Kickstarter Raises More Money for Artists Than the NEA. Here's Why That's Not Really Surprising," in the *Washington Post*, July 7, 2013.

Doreen Carvajal, "In Need, French Museums Turn to Masses, Chapeaux in Hand," in the *New York Times*, December 23, 2012.

"Challenging Notions: Accessibility and the Arts," in *NEA Arts Magazine*, Issue 2015, Number 1.

Jessica Curley, "Rauschenberg Estate Sage of Trust and Fees Explained," Center for Art Law, October 29, 2014.

Lisa Dent, "The Creative Capital Award: What Is the Application Process Like?," blog.creative-capital.org/2014, January 27, 2014.

"Detroit Arts and Culture," *The Kresge Foundation*, www.kresge.org, 2014.

Leonard DuBoff and Christy King, *Art Law*, St. Paul, MN: West Publishing, 2010.

"Federal Art Project of the Works Progress Administration WPA," in *The Art Story*, www.theartstory.org, 2010.

Grace Glueck, "Rothko Art Dispute Ends Quietly after 15 Years," in the *New York Times*, August 20, 1986.

"Government in the Arts," On Stage, www.pbs.org, 2015.

"Grants for Organizations," *National Endowment for the Arts*, www.arts.gov/grants, 2015.

Michelle Hackman, "Chicago Statues Find a Voice," in the *Wall Street Journal*, August 7, 2015.

"Introduction to Crowdfunding," *Women Arts*, www.womenarts.org/skills/crowdfunding, 2015.

"Knight Artist in Residence and Renovation McColl Center for Visual Art," www.knightfoundation.org, August 2014.

"Knowledge Base," *Grant Space*, www.grantspace.org, 2015.

Gail Levin, *Lee Krasner: A Biography*, New York: William Morrow, 2011.

"MSCA Programs," Maryland State Arts Council, www.msac.org/programs/grants-organizations, 2016.

"NYFA Source," New York Foundation for the Arts, www.source.nyfa.org, 2016.

Elizabeth Olson, "Soliciting Funds from the Crowd? Results Will Vary," in the *New York Times*, March 19, 2014.

James Panero, "Outsmarting Albert Barnes," in *Philanthropy Magazine*, summer 2011.

"The Pollock-Krasner Foundation, Inc.," www.pkf.org, Jan. 2015.

"The Smithsonian Is Finally Getting Crowdfunding Right," www.crowdfundinginternet.com, July 24, 2015.

"Tools and Resources for Philanthropy," Foundation Center, www.foundationcenter.org, 2016.

"Why Should Government Support the Arts," National Assembly of State Art Agencies, www.nasaa-arts/.org, 2015.

Index

About the Author

Michael E. Jones's first exposure to the visual fine arts occurred at a young age under the tutelage of his mother, Marlen Naumann Jones, a professional artist. From her, he learned to observe and sketch. Later in life, after years of education in the fields of economics, business, and law, he continued his passion for critical inquiry and exploration in the fields of painting and drawing at the Art Students League and the Cape Cod School of Art.

For over thirty years Jones has taught sports, entertainment, and art law at the University of Massachusetts Lowell. Drawing upon his experience as a noted professor of law, trial court judge, and professional artist he developed an international reputation as one of the foremost authorities on the interplay between copyright law and the rights of artists. Professor Jones has lectured at leading universities and museums throughout the world on copyright and moral right issues facing visual artists. Numerous museums and visual rights societies have sought his counsel on topics ranging from how to craft an ethical acquisition and provenance policy regarding Nazi-era art to who owns the rights to reproduce Alberta Korda's famous photograph of Che Guevara. Besides serving as an advisor to curators, visual fine artists, art students, university professors, and museum directors, he spent ten years as a member of the board of trustees for the New Hampshire Institute of Art.

Jones has penned dozens of academic journals related to art law. His most recent texts include *Rules of the Game: Sports Law* (2016), *Intellectual Property Law Fundamentals* (2015), and *Timeless: The Photography of Rowland Scherman* (coedited with his wife Christine Jones) (2014). In addition, he has excelled as an artist. For the last four summer Olympic Games, including the 2016 Rio Olympics, he created the official USOC poster for the sport of triathlon. After the Beijing Olympics he painted Michael Phelps's portrait.

His posters, paintings, and sketches have been exhibited at the US Embassy in China, Hong Kong Museum of Art, International Olympic Committee Museum, Sports Museum of Boston, Barcelona Olympic Museum, the Whistler House Museum, University of Baltimore Museum, Denison University's Art Museum, and the Cape Cod Museum of Art.